Borgo Cataloging Guides
Number Two

I0273664

MYSTERY AND DETECTIVE FICTION
in the Library of Congress Classification Scheme

Michael Burgess

R. REGINALD
The Borgo Press
San Bernardino, California □ MCMLXXXVII

For Art Nelson and Marty Bloomberg:
"Seri[n]t arbores quae alteri seculo prosint"
—Caecilius Statius

CONTENTS

Introduction		3
I.	Subject Headings	5
II.	Classification Numbers	18
	Index to Classification Numbers	27
III.	Author Main Entries and Literature Numbers	31
	LC Literature Tables	179
IV.	Motion Picture Main Entries and Numbers	182
V.	Television Program Main Entries and Numbers	183
VI.	Comic Strip Main Entries and Numbers	184

Library of Congress Cataloging-in-Publication Data:

Burgess, Michael, 1948-
 Mystery and detective fiction in the Library of Congress classification scheme.

 (Borgo cataloging guides, ISSN 0891-9615 ; no. 2)
 Includes index.
 1. Classification—Books—Detective and mystery stories. 2. Classification, Library of Congress. I. Title. II. Series.
Z697.D48B87 1987   025.4'33   84-12344
ISBN 0-89370-818-6 (cloth, $22.95)
ISBN 0-89370-918-2 (paper, $12.95)

Copyright © 1987 by Michael Burgess.
All rights reserved. No part of this book may be reproduced in any form without the expressed written consent of the author. Printed in the United States of America by Van Volumes Ltd., Wilbraham, MA.

Produced, designed, and published by Robert Reginald and Mary Burgess, The Borgo Press, P.O. Box 2845, San Bernardino, CA 92406, USA. Cover design by Highpoint Type & Graphics, Pomona, CA.

First Edition——December, 1987

INTRODUCTION

This cataloging manual, which has been prepared in tandem with similar books on science fiction and westerns, provides a guide to the cataloging of criminous literature (*i.e.*, mystery and detective fiction, spy stories, and suspense novels, with peripheral coverage of horror, gothic, and macabre literature) in the Library of Congress classification scheme, including subject headings, classification numbers, author main entries and literature numbers, and the main entries and class numbers of artists, motion pictures, TV programs, and comics associated with the field.

The list of authors has been derived in large part from *Crime Fiction, 1749-1980: A Comprehensive Bibliography*, by Allen J. Hubin; *Mystery Index*, by Steven Olderr; the mystery collection of the Pfau Library, California State University, San Bernardino; Ruth Winfeldt's Scene of the Crime bookstore; plus my own research. I have concentrated on those authors apt to be found in the modern collection of mystery literature, most of them active in the last two decades; fewer writers of horror fiction are included than those working exclusively in detective fiction. Also listed are mainstream authors who have written one or two books in the genre. Those authors not included are generally obscure even within the field; most also lack literature numbers.

I presume here some general familiarity on the reader's part with cataloging theory and practice, and with the LC classification scheme in particular, although I have made an effort to explain general principles and specific applications more fully for the neophyte or fan. The science of cataloging may be compared to the practice of law, in that it uses a set of logical rules, plus a series of precedents interpreting those rules, to determine how specific books may be classed. As with the law, cataloging has many quirks, inconsistencies, and exceptions, and may be applied differently by different practitioners; nonetheless, behind these rules and practices there is an established, logical body of thought that is intended to work in a certain fashion and to do certain things. I have tried to provide here some basis for understanding how LC classifies literature, so that even the beginner may gain some insight into what those little numbers on the spine of a book actually mean.

The release in 1978 of the Second Edition of the *Anglo-American Cataloging Rules* (popularly known as AACR2) caused an uproar among librarians, who immediately began taking sides over the question of whether the massive changes proposed in the rules should be adopted. This question was largely settled when the Library of Congress agreed to accept AACR2 in 1980, since LC generates the cataloging records which most large American libraries (particularly in academe) follow.   It was only later that the library world discovered, much to its collective dismay, that LC's adoption of AACR2 was somewhat conditional, in that, under long-established LC policy, books were not recataloged retroactively, and main entries which should have been changed under AACR2 were not—and have not—been altered (as they should have been). Thus, while the rules themselves are fairly explicit, their interpretation remains in many cases obscure; furthermore, the nature of both cataloging and literature is such that many of the proposed changes have yet to be applied by LC to specific authors—*and may never be!*   In addition, the practices of individual catalogers, even at LC, vary slightly; such variations have increased under the pressure of AACR2. Finally, the influence of OCLC (On-Line Computer Library Center, Inc.), the largest cataloging service and database in North America (with some 7500 member libraries and 17,000,000+ bibliographical records in 1987), continues to grow, and is beginning to serve as a counterbalance to both AACR2 and LC; where OCLC practice differs from AACR2, I have always accepted the former.

    I could not have completed this book without the cooperation of two former Tech Services librarians, Arthur E. Nelson, now Library Director at California State University, San Bernardino, and Marty Bloomberg, Associate Library Director, who supported my requests for release time, graciously allowed me the use of the facilities, and were always interested in "talking shop."   To both of these gentlemen, my heartfelt thanks. Thanks also to Johnnie Ralph, former Head of Material Services at CSUSB, and Ruth Winfeldt, at the Scene of the Crime. Whatever cataloging wisdom I've acquired I owe to my instructor at USC, Vivian Prince, and to Mike Brown, Head of Tech Services at Cal State when I joined the staff there in 1970. I also wish to thank my friend and colleague at Cal State, Buckley Barrett, currently Head of Material Services, and a Class-A cataloger in his own right, who was with me when we copped the ten millionth record in OCLC. Finally, a tip of the hat to my long-suffering wife, Mary, who allowed me to work on these manuals—when I should have been doing something else!

Michael Burgess,
Chief Cataloger,
Pfau Library,
California State University,
San Bernardino

I
SUBJECT HEADINGS

INTRODUCTION

This section includes Library of Congress subject headings in use through mid-1987, plus any major headings which have been cancelled as of that date (so indicated below). Also listed are the standard subdivisions which have actually been used by LC; these may seem repetitious to the casual observer, but I have included them anyway to provide the researcher with some indication where the major scholarly activity in the field is taking place.

Most of the entries require little explanation. Anthologies of stories by more than one author are usually classed under the main subject of the anthology (*e.g.*, "Detective and mystery stories") without further subdivision. Such headings may also be applied to nonfiction books. Books about fictitious characters customarily receive two headings: the first includes the name of the character plus description appellation [*e.g.*, "Tarzan (Fictitious character)"]; the second reflects the name of the writer (*e.g.*, "Burroughs, Edgar Rice, 1875-1950—Characters—Tarzan"). Such books are classed under the author's literature number as criticism.

Books about the work of a specific writer use the main entry of the writer as established under AACR2, plus the standard subdivision, "Criticism and interpretation." A biography or autobiography generally has as its subject the name of the author, without further subdivision. There are, of course, many other standard subdivisions which may be applied to authors, some of which may be found below under the sample entries for Agatha Christie and Sir Arthur Conan Doyle.

I have used pre-AACR2 filing rules in this section only because the breakdowns of subdivisions are easier to follow with this arrangement. Completists should note that current rules actually require filing these headings on a strict, word-by-word basis, thus intermingling national subheadings (*e.g.*, "Detective and mystery stories, American") with the subdivisions under the heading, "Detective and mystery stories."

It is also worth noting that the number of subject headings in the mystery field is less than that in my manual on science fiction, indicating less scholarly and fan interest (although the number of authors is far greater), and that the number of corresponding classification numbers is similarly less compared to science fiction and fantasy.

MYSTERY SUBJECT HEADINGS

Adventure and adventurers in literature.
Adventure films.
"   —History and criticism.
Adventure stories.
"   —Bibliography.
"   —History and criticism.
"   —Juvenile literature.
"   —Translations into German.
"   —Translations into Russian.
"   —Translations into Russian—Bibliography.
Adventure stories, Afrikaans.
Adventure stories, American.
"   —History and criticism.
Adventure stories, Australian.
Adventure stories, Canadian.
"   —Bibliography..
Adventure stories, English.
"   —History and criticism.
"   —Translations from French.
Adventure stories, French.
"   —History and criticism.
"   —History and criticism—Congresses.
"   —Translations into English.
Adventure stories, German.
"   —History and criticism.
"   —Translations from foreign languages.
Adventure stories, Japanese.
"   —History and criticism—Addresses, essays, lectures.
Adventure stories, Russian.
"   —Translations from foreign languages.
"   —Translations from foreign languages—Bibliography.
Adventure stories, Scottish.
Adventure story comics.
Black mask.
"   —Addresses, essays, lectures.
"   —Indexes.
Bond, James (Fictitious character)
Brigands and robbers in literature.
Charlie Chan films.

Christie, Agatha, 1890-1976.
" —Addresses, essays, lectures.
" —Biography.
" —Biography—Marriage.
" —Characters.
" —Characters—Jane Marple.
" —Criticism and interpretation.
" —Dictionaries, indexes, etc.
" —Dramatic works.
" —In fiction, drama, poetry, etc.
" —Journeys—Syria.
" —Language.
" —Miscellanea.
" —Plots.
Classification—Books—Detective and mystery stories.
Code and cipher stories.
Crime and criminals—Fiction.
Crime and criminals—Korea—Fiction.
Crime and criminals in literature.
" —Addresses, essays, lectures.
" —Congresses.
Crime and criminals in mass media.
" —Europe—Congresses.
" —Great Britain—Congresses.
" —Netherlands.
" —United States.
Crime in television.
" —United States.
Dast magazine—Indexes.
Detective and mystery films.
" —Catalogs.
" —Dictionaries.
" —France—History and criticism.
" —History and criticism.
" —History and criticism—Addresses, essays, lectures.
" —History and criticism—Indexes.
" —Miscellanea.
" —United States—History and criticism.
" —United States—Plots, themes, etc.
Detective and mystery plays.
" —Bibliography.
" —Dictionaries.
Detective and mystery plays, American.
" —History and criticism.
Detective and mystery plays, English.

" —History and criticism.
DETECTIVE AND MYSTERY STORIES.
" —Authorship.
" —Bibliography.
" —Bibliography—Catalogs.
" —Bibliography—First editions.
" —Bio-bibliography.
" —Book reviews.
" —Collectors and collecting—Periodicals—Indexes.
" —Congresses.
" —Dictionaries.
" —Dictionaries—German.
" —History and criticism.
" —History and criticism—Addresses, essays, lectures.
" —History and criticism—Bibliography.
" —History and criticism—Bibliography—Catalogs.
" —History and criticism—Indexes.
" —History and criticism—Periodicals.
" —Illustrations.
" —Juvenile literature.
" —Miscellanea.
" —Periodicals.
" —Periodicals—History.
" —Periodicals—Indexes.
" —Stories, plots, etc.
" —Technique.
" —Technique—Addresses, essays, lectures.
" —Technique—Bibliography.
" —Translations into Chinese.
" —Translations into Danish.
" —Translations into German.
" —Translations into Swedish.
" —Women authors—Bio-bibliography.
Detective and mystery stories, Afrikaans.
" —Bibliography.
Detective and mystery stories, American.
" —Bibliography.
" —Bibliography—Addresses, essays, lectures.
" —Bio-bibliography.
" —Bio-bibliography—Periodicals.
" —Book reviews.
" —Chronology.
" —History and criticism.
" —History and criticism—Addresses, essays, lectures.

     " —History and criticism—Bibliography.
     " —History and criticism—Periodicals.
     " —History and criticism—Periodicals—Indexes.
     " —Indexes.
     " —Miscellanea.
     " —Periodicals—Indexes.
     " —Translations into German.
     " —Translations into Norwegian.
     " —Translations into Spanish.
     " —Translations into Swedish.
     " —Women authors—History and criticism.
Detective and mystery stories, Argentine.
Detective and mystery stories, Australian.
   " —Bibliography—First editions.
Detective and mystery stories, Bengali.
Detective and mystery stories, Brazilian.
Detective and mystery stories, Burmese.
Detective and mystery stories, Canadian.
Detective and mystery stories, Chilean.
Detective and mystery stories, Chinese.
   " —Translations from foreign languages.
Detective and mystery stories, Croatian.
Detective and mystery stories, Cuban.
   " —History and criticism.
Detective and mystery stories, Czech.
Detective and mystery stories, Danish.
   " —Bibliography.
   " —History and criticism.
   " —Translations from foreign literature.
   " —Translations from Norwegian.
Detective and mystery stories, Dutch.
Detective and mystery stories, English.
   " —Appreciation.
   " —Bibliography.
   " —Bibliography—Addresses, essays, lectures.
   " —Bibliography—First editions.
   " —Bio-bibliography.
   " —Bio-bibliography—Periodicals.
   " —Book reviews.
   " —Chronology.
   " —Dictionaries.
   " —History and criticism.
   " —History and criticism—Addresses, essays, lectures.
   " —History and criticism—Bibliography.
   " —History and criticism—Bibliography—Indexes.

" —History and criticism—Periodicals.
" —History and criticism—Periodicals—Indexes.
" —Indexes.
" —Miscellanea.
" —Periodicals.
" —Stories, plots, etc.
" —Translations from French.
" —Translations from German.
" —Translations from Japanese.
" —Translations from Spanish.
" —Translations into German.
" —Translations into Italian.
" —Translations into Norwegian.
" —Translations into Swedish.
" —Women authors.
" —Women authors—History and criticism.
Detective and mystery stories, Finnish.
" —History and criticism.
Detective and mystery stories, French.
" —Bibliography—Exhibitions.
" —History and criticism.
" —Translations from English.
" —Translations into English.
Detective and mystery stories, French-Canadian.
Detective and mystery stories, German.
" —History and criticism.
" —Translations from English.
" —Translations from foreign literature.
" —Translations from Russian.
" —Translations into English.
Detective and mystery stories, Greek (Modern)
Detective and mystery stories, Hindi.
" —History and criticism.
Detective and mystery stories, Hungarian.
Detective and mystery stories, Italian.
" —History and criticism.
" —Translations from English.
Detective and mystery stories, Japanese.
" —Addresses, essays, lectures.
" —Collected works.
" —History and criticism.
" —History and criticism—Addresses, essays, lectures.
" —Periodicals.
" —Translations into English.
" —Yearbooks.

Detective and mystery stories, Korean.
" —Translations from foreign literature.
Detective and mystery stories, Lithuanian.
Detective and mystery stories, Mexican.
Detective and mystery stories, New Zealand.
Detective and mystery stories, Norwegian.
" —History and criticism.
" —Translations into Danish.
Detective and mystery stories, Polish.
" —Translations into Ukrainian.
Detective and mystery stories, Romanian.
" —History and criticism.
Detective and mystery stories, Russian.
" —Translations into German.
Detective and mystery stories, Slovak.
Detective and mystery stories, South African (English)
" —Bibliography.
Detective and mystery stories, Spanish.
" —Translations from English.
Detective and mystery stories, Spanish American.
" —History and criticism.
" —Translations into English.
Detective and mystery stories, Swedish.
" —Bibliography.
" —History and criticism.
" —Translations from English.
Detective and mystery stories, Thai.
Detective and mystery stories, Ukrainian.
" —Translations from Polish.
Detective and mystery stories, Venezuelan.
Detective and mystery television programs.
" —History and criticism.
Detective Book Club.
Detectives in literature.
" —Addresses, essays, lectures.
" —Pictorial works.
Detectives in mass media.
" —Dictionaries.
" —History.
" —Miscellanea.
" —United States.
Doyle, Arthur Conan, Sir, 1859-1930.
" —Allusions.
" —Bibliography.
" —Bibliography—Catalogs.
" —Bibliography—First editions.

" —Bibliography—Indexes.
" —Biography.
" —Characters.
" —Characters—Dr. Watson.
" —Characters—Dr. Watson—Addresses, essays, lectures.
" —Characters—Sherlock Holmes.
" —Characters—Sherlock Holmes—Addresses, essays, lectures.
" —Characters—Sherlock Holmes—Bibliography.
" —Characters—Sherlock Holmes—Pictorial works.
" —Correspondence.
" —Criticism and interpretation.
" —Criticism and interpretation—Addresses, essays, lectures.
" —Dictionaries, indexes, etc.
" —Film adaptations.
" —Friends and associates.
" —Illustrations.
" —In fiction, drama, poetry, etc.
" —Indexes.
" —Influence—Bibliography.
" —Influence—Jack London.
" —Journeys—United States.
" —Juvenile literature.
" —Knowledge—Medicine.
" —Parodies, imitations, etc.
" —Parodies, travesties, etc.
" —Quotations.
" —Settings.
" —Societies, etc.
" —Societies, periodicals, etc.
" —Sources.
" —Style.
Doyle, Arthur Conan, Sir, 1859-1930. Adventures of Sherlock Holmes.
" —Bibliography.
Doyle, Arthur Conan, Sir, 1859-1930. Return of Sherlock Holmes.
" —Bibliography.
Doyle, Arthur Conan, Sir, 1859-1930. Sign of the four.
" —Bibliography.
Dracula, Count (Fictitious character)
" —Juvenile literature.
" —Name.
" —Poetry.
Fanzines.
" —Indexes.

Fleming, Ian, 1908-1964.
" —Bibliography—Catalogs.
" —Characters—James Bond.
" —Correspondence.
" —Criticism and interpretation.
" —Film adaptations.
" —Library.
G-8 (Fictitious character)
Gangster films.
" —Addresses, essays, lectures.
" —France—History and criticism.
" —History and criticism.
" —Miscellanea.
" —United States—History and criticism.
" —United States—Plots, themes, etc.
Gibson, Walter Brown, 1897- —Characters—Shadow.
Gothic literature.
Gothic revival (Literature)
" —Addresses, essays, lectures.
" —Bibliography.
" —England.
" —Germany.
" —History and criticism.
" —Italy—History and criticism—Addresses, essays, lectures.
" —Portugal.
" —Portugal—Bibliography.
Hand-to-hand fighting, Oriental, in motion pictures.
Heroes in art.
Heroes in literature.
" —Addresses, essays, lectures.
Heroes in mass media.
" —Dictionaries.
Heroes in motion pictures.
" —Addresses, essays, lectures.
Hogan, Robert J.—Characters—G-8.
Holmes, Sherlock (Fictitious character)
" —Addresses, essays, lectures.
" —Bibliography.
" —Bibliography—First editions.
" —Bibliography—Indexes.
" —Dictionaries.
" —Drama.
" —Fiction.
" —Juvenile fiction.
" —Library.

      " —Pictorial works.
      " —Societies, etc.
Horror—Literary collections.
Horror—Periodicals.
Horror comics.
Horror films.
      " —Addresses, essays, lectures.
      " —Biography.
      " —Catalogs.
      " —Dictionaries.
      " —Dictionaries—German.
      " —Great Britain—Plots, themes, etc.
      " —History and criticism.
      " —History and criticism—Addresses, essays, lectures.
      " —History and criticism—Juvenile literature.
      " —History and criticism—Periodicals.
      " —Hungary.
      " —Juvenile literature.
      " —Plots, themes, etc.
      " —Poetry.
      " —Production and direction—Juvenile literature.
      " —Psychological aspects.
      " —Quizzes.
      " —United States—History and criticism.
Horror in art.
      " —Exhibitions.
Horror in literature.
Horror in mass media.
      " —Addresses, essays, lectures.
      " —Bibliography.
Horror plays.
Horror plays, American.
Horror radio programs.
      " —Dictionaries.
HORROR TALES.
      " —Addresses, essays, lectures.
      " —Authorship.
      " —Bibliography.
      " —Bibliography—Catalogs.
      " —Bio-bibliography.
      " —Dictionaries.
      " —History and criticism.
      " —Illustrations.
      " —Periodicals.
      " —Stories, plots, etc.

| | —Translations from English.
| " | —Translations from foreign literature.
| " | —Translations from French.
| " | —Translations from Spanish.
| " | —Translations into Czech.
| " | —Translations into English.
| " | —Translations into German.
| " | —Translations into Hungarian.
| " | —Translations into Italian.
| " | —Translations into Spanish.
| " | —Translations into Swedish.
| " | —Women authors.

Horror tales, American.
    " —Bibliography.
    " —Hawaii.
    " —History and criticism.
    " —History and criticism—Addresses, essays, lectures.
    " —History and criticism—Bibliographv.
    " —Women authors.
    " —20th century.

Horror tales, Australian.
Horror tales, British.
Horror tales, Czech.
Horror tales, Dutch.
Horror tales, English.
    " —Bibliography.
    " —Bibliography—First editions.
    " —History and criticism.
    " —History and criticism—Addresses, essays, lectures.
    " —History and criticism—Bibliography.
    " —Translations from French.
    " —Women authors.

Horror tales, Finnish.
Horror tales, French.
    " —Translations into English.
Horror tales, German.
Horror tales, Hungarian.
Horror tales, Italian.
Horror tales, Japanese.
    " —Japan—Tohoku region.
Horror tales, Korean.
Horror tales, Mauritian (English)
Horror tales, Philippine (English)
Horror tales, Spanish.

Horror tales, Swedish.
Horror television programs.
" —Spain—Andalusia.
" —Dictionaries.
James Bond films.
" —History and criticism.
" —History and criticism—Pictorial works.
" —Miscellanea.
Law in art.
" —Exhibitions.
" —History.
" —United States—Exhibitions.
Law in literature.
" —Addresses, essays, lectures.
" —Bibliography.
" —Juvenile literature—Abstracts.
Legal novels.
" —Bibliography.
Mafia—Fiction.
Mafia in literature.
Marple, Jane (Fictitious character)
Murder—Fiction.
Murder in art.
" —Exhibitions.
Murder in literature.
Operator 5 (Fictitious character)
Penny dreadfuls.
" —Bibliography—Exhibitions.
Police—Fiction.
Police in literature.
Prisoners as authors.
Prisons in literature.
Shadow (Fictitious character)
Sherlock Holmes films.
Spy films.
" —Catalogs.
" —History and criticism.
" —History and criticism—Indexes.
Spy stories.
" —Bibliography.
" —Bio-bibliography.
" —History and criticism.
" —History and criticism—Addresses, essays, lectures.
" —History and criticism—Indexes.
" —Periodicals.

    "   —Periodicals—History.
    "   —Periodicals—Indexes.
    "   —Stories, plots, etc.
Spy stories, American.
    "   —Bibliography.
    "   —Bio-bibliography.
    "   —History and criticism.
    "   —20th century—Bibliography.
Spy stories, Chinese.
Spy stories, English.
    "   —Bibliography.
    "   —Bio-bibliography.
    "   —Handbooks, manuals, etc.
    "   —History and criticism.
    "   —20th century—Bibliography.
Spy stories, French.
    "   —History and criticism.
Spy stories, French-Canadian.
Spy stories, Japanese.
Spy stories, Korean.
Spy stories, Romanian.
Spy stories, Russian.
Spy television programs.
Steele, Curtis—Characters—Operator 5.
Stout, Rex, 1886-1975—Characters—Nero Wolfe.
Terrorism in literature.
Terrorism in mass media.
    "   —Italy.
    "   —United States—Addresses, essays, lectures.
Terrorism in television.
Trials—Drama.
Violence in art.
    "   —Exhibitions.
Violence in literature.
    "   —Addresses, essays, lectures.
    "   —Congresses.
Violence in mass media.
    "   —Bibliography.
    "   —United States.
    "   —United States—Addresses, essays, lectures.
    "   —Venezuela.
Violence in motion pictures.
    "   —Addresses, essays, lectures.
Violence in television.
    "   —Congresses.
Wolfe, Nero (Fictitious character)

II
CLASSIFICATION NUMBERS

INTRODUCTION

This section is arranged by classification number, with an index of subjects at the end. The Library of Congress classes criticism and anthologies into their respective national literatures, or, if none predominates, into PN (general literature). Most of the numbers listed herein consist of two parts, general classification plus subject cutter (which is immutable); to these must be added a first or second cutter (for main entry), and a publication date. Note that anthologies are established under title main entries, with added entries for their editors. Thus, a 1987 anthology of American mystery stories entitled *Deadly Games* might be classed in PS648.D4D43 1987.

General criticism of mystery and detective literature is classed in PN3448.D4, specific criticism of national literatures being classed into their respective tables (PS374.D4 for American detective fiction, PR830.D4 for British, etc.). Anthologies are similarly classed into PN6071.D45/PN6120.95.D45, PS648.D4, and PR1309.D4/PR1111.C7, respectively. Most mystery anthologies with even half of their stories by American writers are actually classed into PS648.D4. Collections of stories by one author are classed with that author's literature number, as is criticism on a specific writer. Criticism on two writers is classed under the first author's literature number; criticism on three or more authors is considered general or national criticism. There is no consistency in the assignment of subject cutters in the various national literatures—for mystery fiction, for example, one can find any range from D4-D7. Similarly, there is no consistency in the development of appropriate subject headings, which LC generates as needed.

CLASS GV (RECREATION. LEISURE)

Games and amusements. Puzzles. Other, A-Z

    GV1507   .D4   Detective and mystery puzzles

CLASS N (ART)

Drawing. Design. Illustration.
Drawing for reproduction. Illustration. Special subjects, A-Z

NC961.7 .D46 Detective and mystery fiction

Periodical illustration. Special subjects, A-Z

NC968.5 .H6 Horror tales

CLASS P (LANGUAGES AND LITERATURE)

Communication. Mass Media. Special aspects. Other, A-Z

P96	.C74	Crime and criminals
	.D4	Detective and mystery fiction
	.H46	Heroes
	.H65	Horror
	.T472	Terrorism
	.V5	Violence

CLASS PE (ENGLISH PHILOLOGY & LANGUAGES)

Modern English. Grammar. Readers. Special subjects, A-Z

PE1127 .V5 Violence

CLASS PL (ORIENTAL LANGUAGES AND LITERATURE)

JAPANESE LITERATURE

History. Prose. Fiction. By period, 1945- . Special topics, A-Z

PL747.82 .D45 Detective and mystery fiction

CHINESE LITERATURE

History. Special aspects and topics. Treatment of special subjects, A-Z

PL2275 .D48 Detective and mystery stories

Collections. Fiction. Special topics, A-Z

    PL2629   .D4   Detective and mystery fiction

CLASS PN (GENERAL LITERATURE)

Theory. Philosophy. Esthetics.
  General Special. Relation to and treatment of special elements and subjects. Other special topics, A-Z. Class here works that are not limited to one form, nor to one national literature.

    PN56   .C7   Crime
                .G7   Grotesque
                .H6   Horror
                .L338 Law and lawyers

Literary history. Juvenile literature. History and criticism. Special topics, A-Z

    PN1009.5   .V54   Violence

Broadcasting. Television broadcasting
  Special Topics. Other special topics, A-Z

    PN1992.8   .D48   Detective and mystery TV programs

Motion Pictures. Special topics, A-Z

    PN1995.9   .A3   Adventure films
                  .C37   Charlie Chan films
                  .D4   Detective and mystery films
                  .G3   Gangster films
                  .H3   Hand-to-hand fighting [in films]
                  .H6   Horror films
                  .J3   James Bond Films
                  .J8   Justice. Law [in films]
                  .J87   Juvenile delinquency [in films]
                  .O84   Outlaws [in films]
                  .S5   Sherlock Holmes films
                  .S68   Spy films
                  .V47   Villains [in films]
                  .V5   Violence [in films]

PROSE. PROSE FICTION.

Technique. Authorship. Special forms, subjects, etc. Other, A-Z

    PN3377.5   .D4   Detective and mystery

Prose. Prose fiction. Special topics. Special races, classes, types, etc., in fiction. Other, A-Z

    PN3426   .L37   Lawyers

Special kinds of fiction. [criticism]

PN3448	.A3	Adventure stories
	.D4	Detective and mystery stories
	.S66	Spy stories

Collections of general literature. By subject, A-Z. [anthologies]

PN6071	.A38	Adventure stories
	.B76	Brigands and robbers
	.D4	Death
	.D45	Detective and mystery stories
	.G24	Gambling
	.H4	Heroes
	.H727	Horror
	.M14	Mafia
	.P68	Prisons
	.R42	Revenge
	.R55	Rogues and vagabonds
	.S64	Spy stories. Spies
	.S78	Substance abuse
	.V5	Violence

Poetry. Special. By subject or form, A-Z

PN6110	.C88	Crime and criminals
	.P8	Prisons and prisoners
	.T5	Terror and wonder

Drama. Special. By subject or form, A-Z

    PN6120   .M9   Mystery plays (Modern)

Fiction. Special. By subject or form, A-Z. [anthologies]

    PN6120.95   .D45   Detective and mystery stories
    [other subdivisions for PN6120.95 same as for PN6071]

Wit and humor. Special topics, A-Z. [anthologies]

    PN6231   .C73   Crime and criminals
                    .P59   Police
                    .R45   Revenge

CLASS PQ (ROMANCE LITERATURE)

FRENCH LITERATURE

History. Special subjects, classes, etc. [criticism]

    PQ145.1   .D33   Death
    PQ145.4   .P7   Prisons and prisoners

History. By period. 20th century. Special topics, A-Z

    PQ307   .H4   Heroes
                  .P68   Prisons

Prose and prose fiction. Special. Prose fiction. Special topics, A-Z. [criticism]

    PQ637   .D4   Detective and mystery stories

MEXICAN LITERATURE

Collections. Prose. Fiction. Special. By form or subject, A-Z. [anthologies]

    PQ7276.5   .D48   Detective and mystery stories, Mexican

ARGENTINIAN LITERATURE

Collections. Prose. Fiction. Special. By form or subject, A-Z. [anthologies]

    PQ7776.5   .D48   Detective and mystery stories, Argentinian

CLASS PR (ENGLISH LITERATURE)

HISTORY OF ENGLISH LITERATURE [criticism]

History. Special topics. Treatment of special classes, A-Z

    PR151   .L37   Law

History. By period. Modern. Special topics, A-Z

    PR408   .G68   Gothic literature

    Treatment of special subjects, A-Z

    PR409   .H45   Heroes

History. By period. 17th century. Treatment of special subjects, A-Z

    PR439   .C73   Crime and criminals

    By period. 18th century. Treatment of special subjects, A-Z

    PR448   .G6   Gothic literature

    By period. 19th century. Special topics, A-Z

    PR468   .M85   Murder

Drama. By period. Medieval. 16th century. Special topics, A-Z

    PR658   .H42   Heroes

Prose. By form. Prose fiction. The novel. Special topics. Other topics, A-Z. [criticism]

    PR830   .A38   Adventure stories
                     .C68   Courtroom fiction
                     .C74   Crime and criminals
                     .D37   Death
                     .D4   Detective and mystery stories
                     .P7   Prisons
                     .S65   Spy stories
                     .T3   Tales of terror. Gothic tales. Horror tales
                     .T47   Terrorism

By period. 18th century. Other topics, A-Z

    PR858   .H4   Heroes and heroines

By period. Victorian period. Special topics, A-Z

    PR878   .D4   Detective and mystery stories.

By period. 20th century. Special topics, A-Z

    PR888   .D4   Crime writing
                .S65   Spies

COLLECTIONS OF ENGLISH LITERATURE [anthologies]

General collections. Special topics (prose and verse), A-Z

    PR1111   .C7   Crime
                 .G67   Gothic revival
                 .G7   Grotesque

Drama. Special forms, A-Z

    PR1259   .D4   Detective and mystery plays

Prose (General). Special subjects and forms, A-Z

    PR1309   .D4   Detective and mystery stories
                 .D55   Dime novels
                 .H55   Holmes, Sherlock
                 .H6   Horror tales
                 .P45   Penny dreadfuls

AUSTRALIAN LITERATURE

History and criticism. History. Treatment of special subjects, A-Z

    PR9605.6   .P75   Prisoners

CLASS PS (AMERICAN LITERATURE)

HISTORY OF AMERICAN LITERATURE [criticism]

History. Other classes of authors, A-Z

    PS153   .P74   Prisoners

History. Treatment of special subjects. Other, A-Z

    PS169   .L37   Law

By period. 19th century. Special topics, A-Z

    PS217   .L37   Law

Prose. Special topics, A-Z

    PS366   .S95   Swindlers and swindling

History. Special forms. Prose. Prose fiction.
Special forms and topics, A-Z. [criticism]

    PS374   .A35   Adventure stories
                    .D4   Detective and mystery stories
                    .D5   Dime novels
                    .G68   Gothic revival
                    .H67   Horror tales
                    .L34   Law
                    .P57   Police
                    .V53   Victims

COLLECTIONS OF AMERICAN LITERATURE [anthologies]

Special topics (Prose and verse), A-Z

    PS509   .A3   Adventure stories
                    .C7   Crime
                    .D4   Death
                    .P6   Poe, Edgar Allan

Prose (General). Special forms and topics, A-Z

    PS648   .C7   Crime stories
                    .D4   Detective and mystery stories

.H6   Horror tales
.R48 Revenge
.S85 Spy stories

CLASS PT (GERMANIC LITERATURES)

GERMAN LITERATURE

History. Prose. Prose fiction. Special kinds, A-Z. [criticism]

PT747   .A38   Adventure stories
        .D4   Detective and mystery stories

Collections. Prose fiction. Special forms, A-Z. [anthologies]

PT1340 .D4   Detective and mystery stories
        .H6   Horror tales

DANISH LITERATURE

History. Prose. Special forms. Other, A-Z. [criticism]

PT7855 .D46   Detective and mystery stories

NORWEGIAN LITERATURE

Collections. Prose. Fiction. Special, A-Z. [anthologies]

PT8723 .D4   Detective and mystery stories

SWEDISH LITERATURE

History. Prose. Prose fiction. Special subjects. Other, A-Z. [criticism]

PT9487 .D4   Detective and mystery stories

P-PZ TABLES

History and criticism. Prose. Fiction. History. Special topics, A-Z
  Table XX—107   Table XXI—12.6
            .P74   Prisoners

.V56 Violence

Collections. Prose. Fiction. Special. By form or subject, A-Z
Table XX—176.5   Table XXI—17.35
                          .D48   Detective and mystery stories

CLASS Z (LIBRARY SCIENCE AND BIBLIOGRAPHY)

Libraries. Library science. Classification and notation. By subject or form, A-Z

Z697   .D48   Detective and mystery stories

National Bibliography. United States. American literature. Special topics, A-Z

Z1231   .D4   Detective and mystery stories
               .D55   Dime novels

Subject bibliography. Fiction. Special topics, A-Z

Z5917   .D5   Detective and mystery stories
               .L3   Legal novels
               .S69   Spy stories

Tables. Table I, p. 272-273

(14)   .H67   Horror tales

INDEX TO CLASSIFICATION NUMBERS

Adventure films: PN1995.9.A3.
Adventure stories. Collections: PN6071.A38; American prose and verse: PS509.A3. Criticism: PN3448.A3; American prose fiction: PS374.A35; English prose fiction: PR830.A38; German prose fiction: PT747.A38.
Brigands and robbers in literature. Collections: PN6071.B76.
Charlie Chan films: PN1995.9.C37.
Courtroom fiction. Criticism: English prose fiction: PR830.C68.
Crime and criminals.
    Collections: American literature: PS509.C7. American prose (general): PS648.C7. English literature: PR1111.C7.
    Criticism: English 17th century literature: PR439.C73; English prose fiction: PR830.C74; English 20th century prose fiction: PR888.D4.
    Mass media: P96.C74.
    Poetry. Collections (general): PN6110.C88.
    Theory, philosophy: PN56.C7.
    Wit and humor collections (general): PN6231.C73.
Death in literature. Collections: PN6071.D4; American prose and verse: PS509.D4. Criticism: English prose ficiton: PR830.D37.
Detective and mystery films: PN1995.9.D4.
Detective and mystery plays. Collections: PN6120.M9. English drama collections: PR1259.D4.
Detective and mystery puzzles: GV1507.D4.
Detective and mystery stories.
    Bibliography. American literature: Z1231.D4. Subject bibliography: Z5917.D5.
    Classification and notation: Z697.D48.
    Collections [anthologies]. General: PN6071.D45/PN6120.95.D45. American prose (general): PS648.D4. Argentinian prose fiction: PQ7776.5.D48. Chinese fiction: PL2629.D4. English prose and verse: PR1111.C7. English prose (general): PR1309.D4. German prose fiction: PT1340.D4. Mexican prose fiction: PQ7276.5.D48. Norwegian prose fiction: PT8723.D4. P-PZ general literature tables: 17.35/176.5.D48.

Criticism. General: PN3448.D4. American prose fiction: PS374.D4. Chinese literature: PL2274.D48. Danish prose: PT7855.D46. English prose fiction: PR830.D4; Victorian period: PR878.D4; 20th century: PR888.D4. French prose and prose fiction: PQ637.D4. German prose fiction: PT747.D4. Japanese prose fiction: PL747.82.D45. Swedish prose fiction: PT9487.D4. Drawing. Design. Illustration: NC961.7.D46.
Mass media: P96.D4.
Technique. Authorship: PN3377.5.D4.
Detective and mystery television programs: PN1992.8.D48.
Dime novels. Bibliography: American literature: Z1231.D55. Collections: English prose: PR1309.D55. Criticism: American prose fiction: PS374.D5.
Gambling in literature. Collections: PN6071.G24.
Gangster films: PN1995.9.G3.
Gothic literature, Gothic revival. Collections: English prose and verse: PR1111.G67. Criticism: American prose fiction: PS374.G68; English literature: PR408.G68; English 18th century literature: PR448.G6.
Grotesque in literature. Collections: English prose and verse: PR1111.G7. Theory, philosophy: PN56.G7.
Hand-to-hand fighting in films: PN1995.9.H3.
Heroes. Collections: PN6071.H4. Criticism: English 16th century drama: PR658.H42. English literature: PR409.H45. French 20th century literature: PQ307.H4. Mass media: P96.H46.
Holmes, Sherlock. Collections: English prose: PR1309.H55.
Holmes, Sherlock films: PN1995.9.S5.
Horror films: PN1995.9.H6.
Horror tales.
Bibliography: Z schedule, Table I: (14).H67.
Collections [anthologies]. General: PN6071.H727. American prose (general): PS648.H6. English prose (general): PR1309.H6. German prose fiction: PT1340.H6.
Criticism. American prose fiction: PS374.H67. English prose fiction: PR830.T3.
Mass media: P96.H46.
Periodical illustration: NC968.5.H6.
Theory, philosophy: PN56.H6.
James Bond films: PN1995.9.J3.
Justice and law in films: PN1995.9.J8.
Juvenile deliquency in films: PN1995.9.J87.
Law and lawyers in literature. Bibliography: Z5917.L3. Criticism: PN3426.L37; American literature: PS169.L37; American prose fiction: PS374.L34; American 19th century literature: PS217.L37; English literature: PR151.L37. Theory, philosophy: PN56.L338.
Mafia in literature. Collections: PN6071.M14.

Murder in literature. Criticism: English 19th century literature: PR468.M85.
Outlaws in films: PN1995.9.O84.
Penny dreadfuls. Collections: English prose: PR1309.P45.
Poe, Edgar Allan. Collections: American prose and verse: PS509.P6.
Police in literature. Criticism: American prose fiction: PS374.P57. Wit and humor: PN6231.P59.
Prisons and prisoners in literature. Collections: PN6071.P68. Criticism: American literature: PS153.P74 [prisoners as authors]; Australian literature: PR9605.6.P75; English prose fiction: PR830.P7; French 20th century literature: PQ307.P68; P-PZ literature tables: 12.6/107.P74. Poetry collections: PN6110.P8.
Revenge in literature. Collections: American prose: PS648.R48. Wit and humor: PN6231.R45.
Rogues and vagabonds in literature. Collections: PN6071.R55.
Spy films: PN1995.9.S68.
Spy stories. Collections: PN6071.S64; American prose: PS648.S85. Criticism: PN3448.S66; English prose fiction: PR830.S65; English 20th century literature: PR888.S65.
Swindlers and swindling in literature. Criticism: American literature: PS366.S95
Tales of terror—see: Horror tales.
Terror and wonder in poetry: PN6110.T5.
Terrorism in literature. Criticism: English prose fiction: PR830.T47.
Terrorism in mass media: P96.T472.
Victims in literature. Criticism: American prose fiction: PS374.V53.
Villains in films: PN1995.9.V47.
Violence in films: PN1995.9.V5.
Violence in literature. Collections: PN6071.V5. Criticism: English juvenile literature: PN1009.5.V54; P-PZ literature tables: 12.6/107.V56. English readers: PE1127.V5. Mass media: P96.V5.

III
AUTHOR MAIN ENTRIES
AND LITERATURE NUMBERS

INTRODUCTION

Publication in 1978 of the second edition of the *Anglo-American Cataloging Rules*, and the subsequent adoption of these rules by the Library of Congress in 1980, has resulted in many changes in author main entries. In simplified form, AACR2 requires that catalogers use the writer's name as it actually appears on most of his or her books; authors using more than one name may either have their works centralized under the preeminent name, or split among several or all of his pseudonyms, if none truly predominates. Prior to AACR2, LC sometimes used common forms of names, but just as frequently adopted convoluted variations which bore little resemblance to the originals.

On the surface, AACR2 seems a logical simplification of previously abstruse cataloging rules, but problems have arisen in practice. The first changes were made in 1980, with a massive retrospective "sweep" through MARC (LC's giant data base), OCLC, and the other library data bases; a second large "sweep" was conducted in the summer of 1987 in OCLC, and such automated comparisons with LC's Name-Authority File will apparently be necessary for the indefinite future. Since LC does not normally recatalog books without reason, a great many authors who are dead or inactive, and whose status does not give them high literary visibility, continue to be listed in the *National Union Catalog* (and OCLC) under forms which are obsolete under AACR2; these names will be changed (if ever) only when a book by or about that author is newly cataloged by LC. Some libraries have arbitrarily assigned AACR2 forms to such writers when cataloging their books in OCLC; these names may differ slightly or radically from those already used by LC through 1980, from forms adopted after 1980, by LC or others, or from those which LC may ultimately choose, at some vague future date. Compounding the problem is the recent addition to OCLC of the national data bases of the British Library and the National Library of Canada, which often use forms of names which differ from those employed elsewhere. Thus, what began with the best of intentions as a "great simplification" has actually spawned greater inconsistencies than the system it replaced.

The Library of Congress must share some of the blame for the haphazard way in which the rules have been applied. On occasion, it will choose forms which clearly contradict AACR2 rules, or (more commonly) it will continue to use forms not precisely correct. For example, Douglas Menville, a film editor and critic, is cataloged by LC as Douglas Alver Menville, despite the fact that he never uses a middle name or initial; this form derives from his first published book, which was an exact reproduction of his thesis, middle name included. Although clearly erroneous under AACR2, it has not been changed by the Library of Congress. One can only presume that LC has made a conscious choice with certain middle-level writers to leave their entries as they existed prior to AACR2, on the theory that few users will care or even notice. This is unfortunate, since no one outside of the Library of Congress reviews these changes or is even aware of them until after they occur.

AACR2 also provides for the addition of dates to main entries to distinguish writers with the same names from each other; when dates cannot be determined, no further effort is made to separate them. The Library of Congress, however, sometimes adds such dates to previously-established main entries years after the original authority was first created, to resolve conflicts posed by newer main entries about which it has less information. Similarly, LC will occasionally split or merge main entries of authors with more than one pseudonym after doing precisely the opposite for extended periods of time. For example, Dean Koontz's main entry was split after the assumption of AACR2 into his component pseudonyms, his literature number being maintained under his real name (which he continued to use on some of his books). In the summer of 1987, after Koontz began to reissue his old books under his real name, LC changed its authority record, centralizing all of his names under "Koontz, Dean R. (Dean Ray), 1945- ". Thus, a library which had cataloged a book by "K.R. Dwyer" in the spring of 1987 would have used the main entry "Dwyer, K. R., 1945- ", with appropriate see also references; six months later, a different library cataloging the same book would have used "Koontz," with appropriate see references. In all likelihood, the original library will never notice the change.

Such wholesale retrospective alterations to LC's data base are unsettling and largely invisible, since few libraries in the 1980s (if any) are capable of catching such changes after the fact. OCLC does not include internal see references other than those generated (sometimes falsely) by its occasional "sweeps"; one must search LC's Name-Authority File to find them. Another example of this disturbing trend can be seen with "M.E. Chaber," a pseudonym of Kendell Foster Crossen. Crossen's books had been centralized under his real name prior to AACR2, but were split by LC in 1980 among his various pseudonyms. The effects of such splits are insidious; the 1987 OCLC data base "sweep," for example, did not affect books cataloged under "Crossen" which under the new rules should have been recataloged under his pennames, since "Crossen" itself remains a valid AACR2 heading—the system is too unsophisticated to identify errors of this type. Such discrepancies increase with each passing day; the 1987 OCLC "sweep" also erroneously matched several authors with see references generated for other writers in LC's Name-Authority File, and moved their records to inappropriate main entries.

These changes, although hidden from most librarians and patrons, have and will become more visible, with serious, long-term implications for data integrity, both at local and national levels. Searching OCLC well has become difficult even for the most sophisticated user, requiring considerable training and experience just to understand the vagaries of the system; this can only increase as the size of OCLC mushrooms (now increasing at the rate of 2.2 million records annually). Automated "sweeps," while useful in catching gross errors, are clearly only a stopgap. The Library of Congress must take the lead in reestablishing some commonsense standard for determining main entries, and must assist the library world in dealing with the tens of thousands of older author names that have yet to be "converted" to forms compatible with AACR2.

The main entries listed below have been checked in LC's Name-Authority File through the summer of 1987, and are correct as given; some will undoubtedly change before the second edition of this manual is published. Note that the Library of Congress, while it may add a date of birth (or even a *day* of birth, if necessary) to resolve name conflicts, does not normally add dates of death to an entry unless the author is long dead and his dates are well known, or unless his entire body of work is being reevaluated, as happened several years ago with Charles Beaumont; occasionally, such changes will occur serendipitously, often when an author dies just before his first or last book is published. More complete forms of an author's name are sometimes added in parentheses to differentiate similar names (*e.g.*, Compton, D. G. (David Guy), 1930-); the parenthesis or hyphen is considered terminating punctuation in such entries, no period being added. OCLC differs from AACR2 in placing titles such as "Sir" or "Mrs." after the author's given name, and I have followed such practice here.

In a previous cataloging manual, I tried to anticipate the adoption of AACR2 forms, with mixed results. Shortly after that book went to press, in 1984, LC's Name-Authority File was made available to OCLC users, and I have relied on it heavily in this book, despite the fact that it lacks many authors cataloged before 1980. I have dropped any forms which cannot be confirmed by LC's actual usage, reverting to pre-AACR2 forms where new versions are as yet unavailable.

AACR2 also issued new filing rules in 1978, changing to a system which closely resembles computer filing practices. Thus, blank spaces and most punctuations file ahead of anything else, numbers and symbols ahead of letters, each word being treated as a separate entity for filing purposes. This in turn has changed the way in which cutter numbers are assigned to both authors and titles in the literature schedules. Authors whose names were affected by the filing changes, and whose books were cataloged for the first time after 1980, have received literature numbers which put their names in proper alphabetical order under the new rules; but previously-established authors who had already received permanent literature numbers were not moved, and under LC's policy of leaving well enough alone, will not be. This has resulted in many discrepancies in the tables, most obviously with authors whose names begin with "Mc"; under the old rules, such names were filed as if spelled "Mac," subject cutters being assigned appropriately. Under AACR2, these names are now filed in strict order, and the subject cutters have changed to "C" for those authors who have been assigned numbers for the first time post-1980.

LC also decided that only one literature number would be assigned to each author, even if his main entries were split under more than one name; this may sometimes result in an author's literature number being out of sequence under the new rules, even when his entries *are* centralized (see, for example, the Authority record for Dennis Lynds, all of whose records are now centralized under his pseudonym, William Arden, but whose literature number continues to be generated from his real name; such anomalies are common under AACR2). Note that the alternate literature numbers assigned by LC between 1969-1980 to PZ3 and PZ4 classifications are not regarded by LC as permanent unless confirmed by later assignments. For a fuller explanation of LC's policies regarding the assignment of literature numbers for authors with split entries, see its *Cataloging Service Bulletin* No. 20 (Spring, 1983): 47-49.

In theory, the Library of Congress assigns literature numbers by language, nationality, and period, in that order. Under each period, authors are given numbers which put their names in strict alphabetical order (note again, however, that the change in filing rules in 1978 may affect the sequence of these names—and their classification numbers). American literature, for example, has two spans of numbers for the twentieth century, PS3500-3549 for authors active between 1900-1960, and PS3550-3576 for those active after 1960. The demarcations between these boundaries are often vague and ill-defined. PS3500 and PS3550 are reserved for anonymous works and for authors whose names consist only of punctuation or initialisms. PS3551-3576 corresponds, on a letter by number basis, to each letter of the alphabet, PS3551, for example, standing for all American writers active in the latter half of the twentieth century whose last names begin with "A."

Cutter numbers (from tables originally designed by Charles Cutter) complete the classification, providing a unique and unchangeable identification for each literary author (prior to 1900, authors may sometimes be given a span of numbers, particularly those with large bodies of work). The initial letter of the cutter corresponds to the second letter of the author's surname (or, in some foreign classifications, to the first changing element of the author's name). The number part of the classification is derived from the third letter of the author's name, and is expanded to whatever length may be necessary to create a unique number while maintaining proper alphabetical sequence. Very generally, the number "3" corresponds to the letter "a," "4" to "e," "5" to "i," "6" to "o," "7" to "r," "8" to "u," and "9" to "y"; these are not fixed, and may be adjusted to fit particular circumstances. For example, Edmund Cooper has the number PR6053.O5469; this falls between O53 (for Michael Cooney) and O55 (for Giles Cooper). Each digit of the number represents a further *sub*division, not some greater amount. This becomes more obvious when one looks closely at the tables. A more detailed explanation of the literature tables can be found at the end of this section.

The author's literature number is immutable once assigned; a second cutter is used to create a similar number for each of the writer's literary works. Hence, Robert A. Heinlein's novel, *Friday*, could be classed in PS3515.E288F7 1987, for a printing issued in 1987. All of an author's fiction, drama, poetry, and other literary productions are assigned numbers which place them in strict alphabetical sequence, with some exceptions (explained at the end of this section); books on other subjects, including literary subjects, receive classification numbers appropriate to those subjects, and are not classed as literature.

The literature numbers provided below are those actually developed by LC, as permanent or alternate numbers, through mid-1987, unless the latter are clearly erroneous (perhaps a half dozen); the alternate numbers may eventually change (when confirmed) if the author's main entry has changed, or if some other conflict has since developed, but most will remain the same. Where no literature number exists, or where only juvenile numbers (PZ7+) have been assigned, I use the word "none." LC does not normally catalog mass market paperback fiction; thus, only writers with cloth or trade paperback editions to their credit usually have classification numbers. I also include here (in brackets) bibliography numbers from the "Z" schedule, for the few authors who have them. The "Z" schedule was the first to be developed at LC, in the late 1890s, and it remains the most primitive, in both style and function. Essentially, it puts authors in alphabetical order by main entry, assigning whole and subdivided numbers in a span from Z8000-8999. Many libraries have abandoned these numbers, preferring to class bibliographies with other nonfiction books about the author. Note that writers may have more than one valid literature number, if they have written original books in more than one language (Vladimir Nabokov wrote in Russian, French, and English, and thus has three numbers). There are also several authors who have accidentally been assigned more than one number by LC, without priority; I list both numbers until the conflict is resolved.

MYSTERY AUTHORS AND LITERATURE NUMBERS

Aalben, Patrick.	none
Aaron, Chester.	none
Aaron, David.	PS3551.A6
Aarons, Edward S. (Edward Sidney), 1916-1975.	none
Aarons, Will B.	none
Aasheim, Ashley.	none
Abbey, Edward, 1927-	PS3551.B2
Abbey, Kieran—see: Reilly, Helen Kieran.	
Abbey, Ruth.	none
Abbot, Anthony—see: Oursler, Fulton, 1893-1952.	
Abbott, Alice.	none
Abbott, Bruce.	none
Abbott, Keith, 1944-	PS3551.B26
Abbott, Sandra.	none
Abdullah, Achmed, 1881-1945.	PS3501.B3
Abe, Kobo, 1924-	PL845.B4
Abel, Joel S.	none
Abercrombie, Barbara.	PS3551.B345
Ableman, Paul.	PR6051.B5
Abrahams, Peter.	PR9199.3.A17
Abshire, Richard K.	none
Ackroyd, Peter.	PR6051.C64
Acre, Stephen—see Gruber, Frank, 1904-1969.	
Adam, Nicholas.	none
Adams, Cleve Franklin, 1895-	none
Adams, Clifton.	PS3551.D34
Adams, Harold, 1923-	PS3551.D367
Adams, Herbert, 1874-	PR6001.D284
Adams, Ian.	PR9199.3.A25
Adams, Joey, 1911-	none
Adams, John Festus, 1930-	PR6051.D337
Adams, Morley.	none
Adams, Nathan M.	none
Adams, Samuel Hopkins, 1871-1958.	PS3501.D317
Adamson, M. J.	none
Addeo, Edmond G., 1936-	none
Addison, Gwen.	none
Addleman, D. R.	none
Adkins, Bill.	none
Adleman, Robert H., 1919-	PS3551.D57
Adler, Warren.	PS3551.D64
Adrian, Jack.	none
Aeby, Jacquelyn.	none
Agel, Jerome.	PS3551.G43

Agnew, Spiro T., 1918-	PS3551.G58
Agniel, Lucien D.	none
Ahern, Jerry.	none
Aickman, Robert.	PR6051.I3
Aiken, Joan, 1924-	PR6051.I35
Aiken, John, 1913-	PR6051.I36
Ainsworth, Harriet—see: Cadell, Elizabeth.	
Ainsworth, William Harrison, 1805-1882.	PR4002-4003 [Z8020.2]
Aird, Catherine.	PR6051.I65
Airth, Rennie, 1935-	PR6051.I67
Alan, Ray.	PR6051.L2
Albano, Peter.	none
Alben, Alex.	PS3551.L256
Albert, Marvin H.	PS3551.L26
Albrand, Martha.	PS3551.L28
Alcott, Louisa May, 1832-1888.	PS1015-1018
Aldanov, Mark Aleksandrovich, 1886-1957.	PG3476.A327
Alding, Peter.	PR6060.E43
Aldridge, James.	PR9619.3.A5
Aldyne, Nathan.	PS3551.L346
Alexander, David.	none
Alexander, David M.	PS3551.L349
Alexander, Jan.	none
Alexander, Joan.	PR6051.L36
Alexander, Karl.	PS3551.L3569
Alexander, Lawrence.	PS3551.L35696
Alexander, Marsha.	none
Alexander, Martin.	none
Alexander, Patrick, 1926-	PR6051.L37
Alexander, Sue, 1933-	PS3551.L3576
Alibrandi, Tom.	none
Alington, Adrian, 1895-1958.	PR6001.L48
Allain, Marcel, 1885-1969.	PQ2601.L57
Allan, Dina.	none
Allan, Francis K.	PS3501.L4775
Allan, Joan.	none
Allan, Stella.	PR6051.L475
Allardyce, Paula—see: Blackstock, Charity.	
Allbeury, Ted.	PR6051.L52
Allegretto, Michael.	PS3551.L385
Allen, Anita.	PS3551.L387
Allen, E. C.—see: Ward, Elizabeth C.	
Allen, Elisabeth Offutt.	none
Allen, Grant, 1848-1899.	PR4004.A2
Allen, Henry.	PS3551.L3928

Allen, Jan.	none
Allen, John—see: Perry, Ritchie, 1942-	
Allen, Michael Derek, 1939-	PR6051.L5395
Allen, Steve, 1921-	PS3501.L5553
Allen, Thomas B.	PS3551.L43
Allingham, Margery, 1904-1966.	PR6001.L678
Allington, Maynard.	none
Allis, Sarah.	PS3551.L45
Allison, Clyde.	none
Allison, E. M. A. (Eric Mary Ann)	PS3551.L454
Allyson, Alan.	PR6051.L59
Almquist, Gregg.	none
Alpert, Hollis, 1916-	PS3551.L7
Alter, Robert Edmond.	PS3551.L767
Altman, Thomas—see: Black, Campbell.	
Alvarez, A. (Alfred), 1929-	PR6051.L9
Alverson, Charles E.	PS3551.L86
Amare, Rothayne—see: Byrne, Stuart J.	
Amberley, Richard.	PR6051.M3
Ambler, Eric, 1909-	PR6001.M48
Ames, Edna.	none
Ames, Delano, 1906-	PR6001.M54
Ames, J. Edward.	none
Ames, Jennifer, 1902-	PS3513.R5772
Ames, Leslie—see: Ross, W. E. D. (William Edward Daniel), 1912-	
Ames, Norma.	none
Amiel, Joseph.	PS3551.M53
Amis, Kingsley.	PR6001.M6 [Z8032.52]
Amis, Martin.	PR6051.M5
Andersen, Ian.	PS3551.N346
Anderson, Frances.	none
Anderson, J. R. L. (John Richard Lane), 1911-	PR6051.N3934
Anderson, Jack, 1922-	PS3551.N365
Anderson, James, 1936-	PR6051.N393
Anderson, Jessica.	PR9619.3.A57
Anderson, Mary Désirée, 1902-	PR6001.N46
Anderson, Patrick, 1936-	PS3551.N377
Anderson, Poul, 1926-	PS3551.N378
Anderson, Rex.	PS3551.N379
Anderson, Sue Lynn.	none
Anderson, William C.	PS3551.N4
Andersson, C. Dean.	none
Andrau, Marianne, 1905-	PQ2601.N258
André, Alix.	PQ2601.N27
Andress, Lesley.	PS3569.A5125

Andrews, Charlton, 1874-1939.	PS3501.N5615
Andrews, Mark.	none
Andrews, Michael.	PR6051.N466
Andrews, Phillip.	none
Andrews, V.	none
Andrews, V. C. (Virginia C.)	PS3551.N454
Angus, Sylvia.	PS3551.N5
Annandale, Barbara, 1925-	PR6051.N62
Anne, David.	PR6051.N63
Anne-Mariel—see: Mariel, Anne, 1907-	
Ansle, Dorothy Phoebe.	PR6001.N75
Anson, Barbara.	none
Anthony, David, 1929-	PS3551.N72
Anthony, Elizabeth.	none
Anthony, Evelyn.	PR6069.T428
Anthony, Piers.	PS3551.N73
Anthony, Robert.	none
Antonio, San—see: San Antonio.	
Appel, Benjamin, 1907-	none
Appel, William.	PS3551.P556
Applin, Arthur, 1883-	PR6001.P65
Arbor, John H., 1939-	PS3551.R25
Arch, E. L.—see: Payes, Rachel Cosgrove.	
Archer, Frank—see: O'Connor, Richard, 1915-1975.	
Archer, Jeffrey, 1940-	PR6051.R285
Ard, William.	none
Arden, Andrew.	none
Arden, William, 1924-	PS3562.Y44
Ardies, Tom.	PS3551.R39
Ardman, Harvey.	none
Arent, Arthur.	PS3551.R4
Aricha, Amos, 1933-	PS3551.R435
Arkwright, Richard.	PR4007.A68
Arlen, Michael, 1895-1956.	PR6001.R7
Arleo, Joseph.	PS3551.R45
Arley, Catherine.	PQ2661.R58
Arliss, Joen.	none
Armour, John—see: Paine, Lauran.	
Armour, Toby.	none
Armstrong, Anthony—see: Willis, Anthony Armstrong, 1897-	
Armstrong, Charlotte, 1905-1969.	PS3501.R566
Armstrong, F. W.	none
Armstrong, Victor.	none
Arnaldi, Jean.	PS3551.R485
Arnold, Elliott, 1912-	PS3501.R5933
Arnold, Margot.	PS3551.R536

Arnold, Jean—see: Arnaldi, Jean.
Arnothy, Christine, 1930-   PQ2661.R684
Arnston, Harrison.   none
Aronson, Harvey.   PS3551.R6
Arrighi, Mel.   PS3551.R7
Arrigio, Frank.   none
Arroyo, Santana.   none
Arthur, Frank, 1906-   PR6001.R79
Arthur, Robert.   none
Arvay, Harry.   PR6051.R66
Arvonen, Helen.   none
Asbury, Herbert, 1891-1963.   none
Ash, William, 1917-   PR6051.S4
Ashbaugh, Nancy.   PS3551.S36
Ashby, Kay.   none
Ashdown, Clifford.   PR6001.S42
Ashe, B. D.   none
Ashe, Gordon—see: Creasey, John.
Ashe, Rosalind.   PR6051.S47
Asher, Miriam.   none
Ashford, F. U.   none
Ashford, Jeffrey.   PR6060.E43
Ashforth, Albert.   PS3551.S376
Ashley, Martin.   none
Ashley, Michael.   none
Ashley, Steven—see: McCaig, Donald.
Ashman, Howard.   none
Ashton, Ann, 1929-   PS3561.I417
Ashton, Mark.   none
Ashton, Sharon—see: Van Slyke, Helen, 1919-
Asimov, Isaac, 1920-   PS3551.S5
Asinof, Eliot, 1919-   PS3551.S54
Askew, Alice.   none
Askew, Claude.   none
Aspinall, Ruth.   none
Aspler, Tony, 1939-   PR6051.S7
Asprey, Robert B.   PS3551.S59
Astley, Juliet—see: Lofts, Norah, 1904-
Aswad, Betsy.   PS3551.S9
Atcheson, George, 1923-   PS3551.T35
Atkey, Bertram.   none
Atkins, Meg Elizabeth.   PR6051.T5
Atkins, Thomas R., 1939-   PS3551.T56
Atkinson, Hugh.   PR9619.3.A8
Atlee, Philip.   none
Atwater, James D., 1928-   PS3551.T77

Aubrey, Edmund—see: Ions, Edmund S.
Aubrey, Frank. PR6001.U27
Audemars, Pierre. PR6051.U3
Audrenn, Joël. PQ2661.U33
August, Leo. none
Auster, Paul, 1947- PS3551.U77
Austin, Alex. PS3551.U78
Austin, Marilyn. none
Austin, Max. none
Austin, Richard. PR6051.U84
Austin, Frederick Britten, 1885-1941. PR6001.U8
Auswaks, Alex, 1934- none
Avallone, Michael. PS3551.V3
Aveline, Claude, 1901- PQ2601.V45
Avery, Ira. PS3551.V4
Awin, Margery. none
Axler, James. none
Axton, David—see: Koontz, Dean R. (Dean Ray), 1945-
Ayers, Paul—see: Aarons, Edward S. (Edward Sidney), 1916-1975.
Ayers, Ronald. none
Ayling, Keith Oliver, 1898- none
Babbin, Jacqueline. none
Babcock, Dwight Vincent, 1909- none
Babcock, Nicholas—see: Lewis, Tom, 1940-
Babson, Marian. PS3552.A25
Bacheller, Irving, 1859-1950. PS1054.B3
Bachman, Richard. PS3561.I483
Bachmann, Lawrence Paul, 1912- PS3503.A159
Badgley, Anne V. PS3552.A315
Bagby, George, 1906- PS3537.T3184
Bagley, Desmond, 1923- PR6052.A315
Bahadur, Krishna Prasad, 1924- none
Bahr, Edith-Jane. PS3552.A36
Bahr, Jerome. PS3503.A413
Bailey, F. Lee (Francis Lee), 1933- PS3552.A366
Bailey, Henry Christopher, 1878-1961. PR6003.A374
Bailey, Hilary. PR6052.A3186
Bainbridge, Beryl, 1933- PR6052.A3195
Bainbridge, Chuck. none
Bair, Patrick. PR6052.A32
Baird, Thomas, 1923- PS3552.A39
Baker, Carlos Heard, 1909- PS3552.A4
Baker, Elliott. PS3552.A424
Baker, Ivon, 1928- PR6052.A334
Baker, Lucinda, 1916- PS3552.A4315
Baker, Nicholas. none

Baker, Peter, 1921-	PR6003.A484
Baker, Will, 1935-	PS3573.E199
Baker, William Howard.	PR6052.A37
Balchin, Nigel, 1908-1970.	PR6003.A52
Baldwin, Michael.	PR6052.A39
Balfour, James.	none
Balham, Joe.	none
Ball, Brian N.	PR6052.A42
Ball, John Dudley, 1911-	PS3552.A455
Ballard, K. G.—see: Holly, Roth.	
Ballard, P. D.—see: Ballard, Todhunter, 1903-	
Ballard, Todhunter, 1903-	PS3503.A5575
Ballem, John Bishop.	PR9199.3.B36
Ballenger, Dean W.	none
Balling, L. Christian.	PS3552.A468
Ballinger, Bill S. (Bill Sanborn), 1912-	PS3552.A47
Ballinger, W. A.	none
Balmer, Edwin, 1883-	none
Balnave, James.	none
Balneaves, Elizabeth.	none
Bandy, Franklin.	PS3552.A4754
Bangs, John Kendrick, 1862-1922.	PS1064.B3
Banko, Daniel.	PS3552.A479
Banks, Barbara.	PR6052.A484
Banks, Carolyn.	PS3552.A485
Banks, Iain.	PR6052.A485
Banks, Oliver T.	PS3552.A488
Banks, Russell, 1940-	PS3552.A49
Banning, John.	none
Bannister, Jo.	PR6052.A497
Bannon, Don.	none
Banville, John.	PR6052.A57
Barak, Michael—see: Bar-Zohar, Michael, 1938-	
Barber, Nöel.	PR6052.A623
Barcelo, E. C.	none
Barclay, Ben.	none
Barclay, Ian.	none
Bardsley, Michael.	PS3552.A616
Bark, Conrad Voss—see: Voss Bark, Conrad.	
Barker, Albert, 1900-	none
Barker, Clive, 1952-	PR6052.A6475
Barker, Dudley.	PR6003.A679
Barker, Joseph, 1929-	PR6052.A6487
Barker, Pat.	PR6052.A6488
Barker, Wade.	none
Barkley, Deanne.	PS3552.A6714

Barlay, Bennett, 1910-	PS3505.R89224
Barlay, Stephen.	PR6052.A654
Barling, Charles.	none
Barling, Tom.	none
Barlow, James, 1921-	PR6052.A66
Barnaby, Peter.	none
Barnao, Jack.	PR9199.3.B3717
Barnard, Robert.	PR6052.A665
Barnes, Dallas L., 1941-	PS3552.A6738
Barnes, Joanna.	PS3552.A674
Barnes, Linda.	PS3552.A682
Barnes, Robert C.	none
Barnett, James, 1920-	PR6052.A69
Barns, Glenn M.	none
Barone, Mike.	none
Barr, Elisabeth.	PR6052.A714
Barr, Justin.	none
Barr, Robert.	PR6052.A715
Barr, Robert, 1850-1912.	PR4069.B38
Barratt, Robert.	none
Barrett, Frank, 1848-1926.	PR4069.B55
Barrett, Geoffrey John.	PR6052.A717
Barrett, Max.	PR9619.3.B34
Barrett, Michael.	none
Barrett, Susan, 1938-	PR6052.A723
Barrett, William Edmund, 1900-	PS3503.A62873
Barrie, James Matthew, Sir, Bart., 1860-1937.	PR4074
Barrington, Pamela.	none
Barroll, Clare.	PS3552.A7369
Barron, Ann.	none
Barron, Donald Gabriel.	PR6052.A725
Barron, Hugh.	none
Barry, Charles—see: Bryson, Charles, 1877-	
Barry, Iris, 1895-	PS3503.A643
Barry, Jerome.	none
Barry, John James, 1933-	PS3552.A7417
Barry, Loretta.	none
Barry, Mike—see: Malzberg, Barry N.	
Barry, Nora.	PS3552.A7425
Barth, Lois.	PS3552.A754
Barth, Richard, 1943-	PS3552.A755
Barthelme, Peter.	PS3552.A7633
Bartholomew, Cecilia.	PS3552.A764
Bartlett, Jean Anne.	none
Bartram, George, 1931-	PS3553.A4335
Barwick, James—see: Barwick, Tony, 1934-	

Barwick, Tony, 1934-	none
Bar-Zohar, Michael, 1938-	PR9510.9.B3
Base, Ron.	PR9199.3.B3757
Basile, Gloria Vitanza.	none
Bass, Milton R.	PS3552.A82
Bass, Ronald.	PS3552.A8215
Batchelor, Reg—see: Paine, Lauran.	
Battin, B. W.	none
Bavin, Bill.	none
Bawden, Nina, 1925-	PR6052.A84
Bax, Roger—see: Garve, Andrew, 1908-	
Baxt, George.	PS3552.A8478
Baxter, John, 1939-	PR9619.3.B36
Bay, Austin.	PS3552.A8586
Bay, Roger.	none
Bayer, William.	PS3552.A8588
Baylus, Robert F.	none
Bayne, Neil.	none
Bazal, Jean.	PQ2662.A9
Beach, Edward Latimer, 1918-	PS3552.E12
Beal, Mary F.	PS3552.E134
Bear, David.	PS3552.E155
Beardwood, Roger, 1932-	PR6052.E186
Beare, George.	PR9619.3.B38
Bearshaw, Brian, 1932-	none
Beaton, M. C.	PR6052.E196
Beattie, Tasman.	none
Beaty, David.	PR6003.E264
Beaumont, Charles, 1929-1967.	PS3552.E2316
Beck, K. K.	PS3552.E248
Beck, Robert, 1918-	PS3552.E25
Becker, Stephen D., 1927-	PS3552.E26
Beckett, Jenifer.	PR6052.E28
Bedford, John, 1935-	none
Bedford-Jones, Henry, 1887-1949.	none
Beeby, Otto.	PR9619.3.B4
Beechcroft, William.	PS3552.E32
Beeching, Jack.	PR6003.E295
Beeding, Francis, pseud.	PR6003.E3
Beedle, John.	none
Beekman, E. M., 1939-	PS3552.E34
Beer, Olivier.	PQ2662.E334
Beevor, Antony, 1946-	PR6052.E323
Begg, Ken.	none
Behm, Marc.	PS3552.E38
Behn, Noel.	PS3552.E4

Behr, Edward, 1926-	PR6052.E327
Behrend, Arthur.	none
Beinhart, Larry.	PS3552.E425
Belanger, Chuck.	none
Belfort, Sophie.	PR6052.E39
Bell, Gerard.	PR6052.E44
Bell, Josephine, 1897-	PR6003.A525
Bell, Madison Smartt.	PS3552.E517
Bell, Neil, 1887-1964.	PR6037.O843
Bellah, James.	none
Bellairs, George, 1902-	PR6003.E4465
Bellem, Robert Leslie, 1902-1968.	PS3503.E4438
Belloc, Hilaire, 1870-1953.	PR6003.E45
Belsky, Dick.	PS3552.E5338
Benassi, Mark.	none
Benchley, Nathaniel, 1915-	PS3503.E487
Benchley, Peter.	PS3552.E537
Benedict, Lynn.	none
Benedictus, David.	PR6052.E45
Benjoya, Mitchell.	PS3552.E5454
Bennet, Robert Ames, 1870-	PS3503.E54547
Bennett, Arnold, 1867-1931.	PR6003.E6
Bennett, Barbara Curry.	none
Bennett, Charles.	none
Bennett, Dorothea.	PR6052.E52
Bennett, Dorothy.	none
Bennett, Emerson, 1822-1905.	PS1094.B45
Bennett, Gregory Mantin.	none
Bennett, Hal, 1930-	PS3552.E546
Bennett, Jack, 1934-	PR9619.3.B476
Bennett, Janice.	none
Bennett, Jay.	PS3552.E5464
Bennett, John McGrew.	PS3552.E54735
Bennett, Margot, 1903-	PR6003.E646
Bennett, Robert D.	none
Bennett, W. R.	none
Bennetts, Pamela.	PR6052.E533
Benoît, Pierre, 1886-1962.	PQ2603.E583
Bensen, D. R. (Donald R.), 1927-	PS3552.E54765
Benson, Ben.	none
Benson, Daniel—see: Cooper, Colin.	
Benson, Edward Frederic, 1867-1940.	PR6003.E66
Benson, Eugene P.	none
Benson, O. G.	PS3552.E547663
Bentinck, Henry.	none
Bentley, E. C. (Edmund Clerihew), 1875-1956.	PR6003.E7247

Bentley, John.	none
Bentley, Joyce.	none
Bentley, Nicolas, 1907-	PR6003.E7248
Bentley, Robert.	PS3552.E56
Benton, John, 1933-	PS3552.E57
Benton, Kenneth, 1909-	PR6052.E545
Berckman, Evelyn.	PS3552.E68
Bercovici, Eric.	PS3552.E6897
Beres, Michael.	none
Beresford, John Davys, 1873-1947.	PR6003.E73
Berg, Adam W.	none
Berger, Thomas, 1924-	PS3552.E719
Bergman, Andrew.	PS3552.E7193
Berkeley, Anthony, 1893-1971.	PR6005.O855
Berliner, Ross.	PS3552.E7249
Bernanos, Georges, 1888-1948.	PQ2603.E5675
Bernard, George.	none
Bernard, Jay—see: Sawkins, Raymond H., 1923-	
Bernard, Joel.	none
Bernard, Judd.	none
Bernard, Robert.	PS3563.A728
Bernard, Trevor.	none
Berne, Karin.	none
Bernhard, Robert.	PS3552.E7314
Bernier, John M.	none
Bernstein, Ken.	PS3552.E734
Berrow, Norman.	PR6052.E643
Beste, R. Vernon.	PR6052.E75
Bester, Alfred.	PS3552.E796
Betteridge, Don—see: Newman, Bernard, 1897-1968.	
Betz, Ingrid.	none
Bickers, Richard Leslie Townshend, 1917-	none
Bickham, Jack M.	PS3552.I3
Biederman, Marcia, 1949-	PS3552.I344
Biggers, Earl Derr, 1884-1933.	PS3503.I54
Biggle, Lloyd, 1923-	PS3552.I43
Billing, Graham.	PR9639.3.B5
Bindloss, Harold, 1866-1945.	none
Bingham, Carson—see: Cassiday, Bruce.	
Bingham, John, 1908-	PR6053.L283
Bingham, Roger.	none
Bingham, Stella.	PR6052.I777
Bingley, Margaret.	none
Binnie, Stewart.	PR6052.I778
Binns, Ottwell, 1872-	PR6003.I736
Binyon, T. J.	PS3552.I58

Bioy Casares, Adolfo.	PQ7797.B535
Bird, Al.	PS3552.I69
Bird, Kenneth.	none
Bird, Michael J., 1928-	PR6052.I7914
Birkin, Charles.	none
Birmingham, Maisie.	PR6052.I7955
Bishop, George, 1924-	PS3552.I7598
Bishop, Mary.	none
Bishop, Sheila.	none
Bissell, Elaine.	PS3552.I7728
Bjorgum, Kenneth.	PS3552.J56
Black, Betty.	PS3552.L29
Black, Campbell.	PR6052.L25
Black, David, 1945-	PS3552.L32
Black, Gavin—see: Wynd, Oswald, 1913-	
Black, Hermina.	none
Black, Ian Stuart, 1915-	PR6052.L3
Black, Jonathan—see: Von Block, B. W.	
Black, Laura.	PR6052.L32
Black, Ladbroke Lionel Day, 1877-	none
Black, Lionel—see: Barker, Dudley.	
Black, Mansell—see: Trevor, Elleston.	
Black, Veronica.	PR6052.L335
Blackburn, John, 1924-	PR6052.L34
Blacker, Irwin R.	PS3552.L3423
Blackledge, Ethel H.	none
Blackmore, Jane.	PR6052.L3415
Blackstock, Charity.	PR6052.L3417
Blackwood, Algernon, 1869-1951.	PR6003.L3
Blagowidow, George.	PS3552.L344
Blair, Alan—see: Bayfield, William John, 1871-1958.	
Blair, Iain.	none
Blair, Jennifer.	none
Blair, Marcia.	none
Blais, Marie Claire.	PQ3919.B6
Blaisdell, Anne—see: Shannon, Dell, 1921-	
Blake, Christina—see: Stead, Christina, 1902-	
Blake, Katherine, fl. 1965-	PS3552.L3485
Blake, Ken—see: Bulmer, Kenneth, 1921-	
Blake, Nicholas—see: Day Lewis, C. (Cecil), 1904-1972.	
Blake, Patrick—see: Egleton, Clive.	
Blake, Vanessa.	none
Blake, William Dorsey.	none
Blakeston, Oswell.	PR6052.L35
Blanc, Suzanne.	PS3552.L365
Bland, Jennifer—see: Annandale, Barbara, 1925-	

Blankenship, William D.	PS3552.L366
Blankfort, Michael, 1907-	PS3503.L477
Blayn, Hugo—see: Fearn, John Russell, 1908-1960.	
Blazer, J. S.—see: Scott, Justin.	
Bleeck, Oliver, 1926-	PS3570.H58
Blickle, Katrinka.	PS3552.L48
Bloch, Donald, 1943-	PS3552.L55
Bloch, Robert, 1917-	PS3503.L718
Blochman, Lawrence Goldtree, 1900-	none
Block, Lawrence.	PS3552.L63
Blodgett, Michael.	PS3552.L6355
Blom, K. Arne, 1946-	PT9876.12.L545
Bloodworth, Dennis.	PR6052.L59
Bloom, Murray Teigh, 1916-	PS3552.L6394
Bloomfield, Anthony, 1922-	PR6052.L64
Bloomfield, Robert—see: Edgley, Leslie, 1912-	
Bloxham, Peter.	PR6052.L67
Blum, Ralph, 1932-	PS3552.L84
Blum, Richard H.	PS3552.L842
Blumberg, Gary.	none
Blumenthal, John.	PS3552.L8485
Boast, Philip.	none
Bobker, Lee R.	PS3552.O256
Bobkins, Denk.	none
Bocca, Geoffrey.	PR6052.O2
Bodeen, DeWitt.	PS3552.O267
Bodelsen, Anders, 1937-	PT8176.12.O34
Boggis, David.	none
Bogner, Norman, 1935-	PS3552.O45
Bohle, Edgar Henry, 1909-	PS3552.O497
Boileau, Pierre, 1906-	PQ2603.O27
Boileau-Narcejac.	PQ2603.O27
Boland, John, 1913-	PR6052.O36
Boldrewood, Rolf, 1826-1915.	PR9619.2.B76
Boles, Paul Darcy, 1916-	PS3552.O584
Bolt, Ben—see: Binns, Ottwell, 1872-	
Bolt, Carol.	PR9199.3.B58
Bolton, Carole.	PS3552.O5876
Bond, Evelyn—see: Hershman, Morris, 1926-	
Bond, Michael.	PR6052.O52
Bond, Ruskin.	PR6052.O57
Bond, Walter.	none
Bonett, Emery—see: Bonett, John, 1906-	
Bonett, John, 1906-	PR6005.O79
Bonfiglioli, Kyril.	PR6052.O574
Bonham, Frank.	PS3503.O4315

Bonnamy, Francis—see: Walz, Audrey.	
Bonnecarrère, Paul.	PQ2662.O5975
Bontly, Thomas J.	PS3552.O643
Booth, Martin.	PR6052.O63
Boothby, Guy Newell, 1867-1905.	PR4149.B957
Booton, Kage.	PS3552.O68
Borgen, Johan, 1902-	PT8950.B713
Borgenicht, Miriam.	PS3552.O75
Borland, Kathryn Kilby.	PS3552.O754
Borlik, Linda Stahl.	none
Borneman, Ernest, 1915-	PR6003.O613
Bornemark, Kjell-Olof, 1924-	PT9876.12.O76
Borniche, Roger.	PQ2662.O6855
Borthwick, J. S.	PS3552.O756
Bosak, Steven.	PS3552.O7568
Bosse, M. J. (Malcolm Joseph), 1926-	PS3552.O77
Bosworth, Frank—see: Paine, Lauran.	
Boucher, Anthony, 1911-1968.	PS3545.H6172
Boucher, Bernard.	PR6052.O795
Boulle, Pierre, 1912-	PQ2603.O754
Bourgeau, Art.	none
Bourjaily, Vance Nye.	PS3503.O77
Bourne, Hester.	none
Bova, Ben, 1932-	PS3552.O84
Bowden, Jean.	none
Bowen, John, 1924-	PR6052.O85
Bowen, Marjorie, pseud.	PR6003.O676
Bowen, Robert Sidney, 1900-	none
Bowering, George, 1935-	PR9199.3.B63
Bowick, Dorothy Müller.	PS3552.O8736
Bowker, Richard.	PS3552.O8739
Bowman, Robert.	PS3552.O8758
Bowser, Jim.	none
Bowyer, John.	none
Box, Edgar—see: Vidal, Gore, 1925-	
Boyd, Edward.	PR6052.O918
Boyd, John, 1919-	PS3571.P35
Boyer, Bruce Hatton, 1946-	PS3552.O888
Boyer, Richard L.—see: Boyer, Rick.	
Boyer, Rick.	PS3552.O895
Boyle, Ann.	none
Boyle, Kay, 1902-	PS3503.O9357
Boyle, Robert.	PR6052.O95
Boyle, Thomas, 1939-	PS3552.O933
Brace, Timothy—see: Pratt, Theodore, 1901-	
Brackett, Leigh.	PS3503.R154

Bradbury, Ray, 1920-	PS3503.R167
Bradbury, Wilbur.	PS3552.R213
Braddon, M. E. (Mary Elizabeth), 1837-1915.	PR4989.M4
Braddon, Russell.	PR6052.R25
Bradford, Michael.	none
Bradley, David, 1950-	PS3552.R226
Bradley, Marion Zimmer.	PS3552.R228
Bradley, Michael—see: Blumberg, Gary.	
Bradley, Michael Anderson, 1944-	PR9199.3.B67
Brady, Charles.	PS3552.R238
Brady, James, 1928-	PS3552.R243
Brady, Leo, 1917-	PS3503.R233
Brady, Michael.	PS3552.R2436
Brady, Nicholas.	none
Brady, Ryder.	PS3552.R245
Brahms, Caryl, 1901-	PR6001.B6
Brain, Leonard—see: Peck, Leonard, 1906-	
Brain, Robert.	PR9619.3.B65
Braly, Malcolm, 1925-	PS3552.R28
Bramah, Ernest, 1869?-1942.	PR6037.M425
Bramble, Forbes, 1939-	PR6052.R2687
Bramwell, Charlotte, 1929-	PS3561.I417
Brand, Christianna, 1907-	PR6023.E96
Brand, Max, 1892-1944.	PS3511.A87
Brand, Susan.	PS3552.R293
Brandel, Marc, 1919-	PS3503.R25784
Brandner, Gary.	PS3552.R313
Brandon, Beatrice—see: Krepps, Robert W., 1919-	
Brandon, Jay.	none
Brandon, Ruth.	PS3552.R316
Brandt, Roger.	none
Brandt, Tom—see: Dewey, Thomas Blanchard, 1915-	
Branston, Frank, 1939-	PR6052.R278
Braudy, Susan.	PS3552.R343
Braun, Lilian Jackson.	PS3552.R354
Braun, Matthew.	PS3552.R355
Brautigan, Richard.	PS3503.R2736
Braxton, Henry.	none
Brean, Herbert.	none
Brebner, Percy James, 1864-	none
Brechin, David.	PR6052.R35
Breem, Wallace.	PR6052.R36
Breen, Jon L., 1943-	PS3552.R3644
Breen, Richard, 1936-	PS3552.R3646
Brennan, Alice.	none
Brennan, Dan.	none

Brennan, J. H.	PR6052.R412
Brennan, Jan—see: Brennan, J. H.	
Brennan, Joseph Payne, 1918-	PS3503.R455
Brennan, Peter.	PS3552.R382
Brent, Loring—see: Worts, George Frank, 1892-	
Brent, Madeleine.	PR6052.R419
Brent, Peter Ludwig.	PR6052.R42
Brent, R. L.	none
Breslin, Catherine.	PS3552.R388
Breslin, Jimmy.	PS3552.R39
Bretnor, Reginald.	PS3552.R395
Breton, Thierry.	PQ2662.R4832
Bretonne, Anne-Marie.	none
Brett, Barbara.	none
Brett, David.	PR6052.R429
Brett, Hy.	PS3552.R398
Brett, John Michael—see: Brett, Michael, 1921-	
Brett, Michael, 1921-	PS3552.R413
Brett, Mike.	none
Brett, Simon.	PR6052.R4296
Brett, Stephen.	none
Brewer, Gil.	none
Brewer, Mark.	PS3552.R4213
Brez, E. M.	PS3552.R44
Bridge, Ann—see: O'Malley, Mary Dolling Saunders, Lady, 1889-1974.	
Bridges, Roy, 1885-	none
Bridges, Victor.	PR6003.R3754
Brieno, Linda.	none
Brierley, David.	PR6052.R4432
Brin, David.	PS3552.R4825
Bringle, Mary.	PS3552.R485
Brink, Caroline.	none
Brinton, Henry, 1901-	none
Brisco, Pat.	none
Bristow, Gwen, 1903-	PS3503.R576
Britton, Christopher.	PS3552.R4975
Brock, Lynn—see: McAllister, Alister, 1877-	
Brock, Rose—see: Hansen, Joseph, 1923-	
Brock, Stuart—see: Trimble, Louis, 1917-	
Brodeur, Paul.	PS3552.R62
Brodie, Gordon.	none
Brody, Marc—see: Wilkes-Hunter, R.	
Broinowski, Alison.	PR9619.3.B7
Brome, Vincent, 1910-	PR6052.R573
Bromley, Gordon.	none
Bronte, Louisa—see: Roberts, Janet Louise, 1925-1982.	

Brookes, Owen.	PR6052.R5815
Brookhouse, Christopher, 1938-	PS3552.R658
Brooks, Edwy Searles, 1889-	none
Brooks, Kate.	none
Brosnan, Kate.	none
Brothers, Jay.	PS3552.R675
Brown, Antony.	PR6052.R589
Brown, Carter, 1923-	PR6052.R5893
Brown, Charles Brockden, 1771-1810.	PS1134.
Brown, Christy, 1932-	PR6052.R5894
Brown, Dale, 1956-	PS3552.R68543
Brown, Elizabeth.	PS3552.R68546
Brown, Fredric, 1906-1972.	PS3503.R8135
Brown, George Douglas, 1869-1902.	PR4174.B6
Brown, James Ambrose, 1919-	PR9369.3.B72
Brown, James Cooke, 1921-	PS3552.R68565
Brown, John, 1924-	PR6052.R6134
Brown, John Edward, 1920-	PS3552.R6857
Brown, L. Virginia.	none
Brown, Mary Monroe.	none
Brown, R. D.	none
Brown, Rae.	none
Brown, Rosel George.	PS3503.R828437
Brown, Wenzell, 1912-	none
Brown, Zenith Jones, 1898-	none
Browne, Douglas G. (Douglas Gordon), 1884-	PR6003.R49
Browne, Gerald A.	PS3552.R746
Browne, Howard, 1908-	PS3503.R8436
Browner, John.	none
Browning, John.	PR6052.R619
Broyles, R. L.	none
Bruce, Jean, 1921-	PQ2603.R914
Bruce, Leo, 1903-1980.	PR6005.R673
Brunner, John, 1934-	PR6052.R8
Bruton, Eric.	none
Bryan, Sofi O.	none
Bryant, Dorothy, 1930-	PS3552.R878
Bryant, Peter.	PR6057.E54
Bryant, Will.	PS3552.R898
Bryce, Robert.	none
Bryers, Paul.	PR6052.R94
Brykczynski, Terry.	PS3552.R98
Bryson, Charles, 1877-	none
Buchan, John, 1875-1940.	PR6003.U13
Buchan, Sinclair.	PR9619.3.B78
Buchan, Stuart.	PS3552.U317

Buchanan, Patrick.	PS3552.U33
Buchanan, William J., 1926-	PS3552.U332
Buchard, Robert, 1931-	PQ2662.U25
Buck, Paul, 1946-	PR6052.U25
Buck, Pearl Sydenstricker, 1892-1973.	PS3503.U198
Buckingham, Nancy.	PR6052.U26
Buckley, William F. (William Frank), 1925-	PS3552.U344
Buckman, Peter.	PR6052.U267
Buckmaster, Henrietta.	PS3503.U227
Bude, John.	none
Budrys, Algis, 1931-	PS3552.U349
Buell, John.	PR9199.3.B766
Buffer, Joe.	none
Bulliet, Richard W.	PS3552.U44
Bullivant, Cecil Henry.	none
Bullock, Lotte.	none
Bulmer, Kenneth, 1921-	none
Bulwer-Lytton, Edward—see: Lytton, Edward Bulwer-Lytton, Baron, 1803-1873.	
Bunker, Edward, 1933-	PS3552.U47
Bunn, Thomas, 1944-	PS3552.U472
Buntline, Ned, 1822 or 3-1886.	PS2156.J2
Burge, Milward Rodon Kennedy, 1894-	none
Burger, Neal R.	none
Burgess, Anthony, 1917-	PR6052.U638 [Z8976.72]
Burgess, Eric, 1912-	PR6052.U639
Burgess, Gelett, 1866-1951.	PS3503.U6
Burgoyne, Victoria.	none
Burke, Alan Dennis.	PS3552.U7213
Burke, J. F., 1915-	PS3503.U6126
Burke, John Frederick, 1922-	PR6003.U54
Burke, Jonathan—see: Burke, John Frederick, 1922-	
Burke, Lee John.	none
Burke, Stewart.	PR6052.U64435
Burke, Thomas, 1886-1945.	PR6003.U55
Burkey, Dave.	none
Burkholz, Herbert, 1932-	PS3552.U725
Burleson, Clyde W., 1934-	none
Burley, W. J. (William John), 1914-	PR6052.U647
Burmeister, Jon.	PR9369.3.B8
Burnett, W. R. (William Riley), 1899-	PS3503.U6258
Burns, Alma.	none
Burns, Rex.	PS3552.U7325
Burrage, Alfred McLelland.	PR6003.U566
Burrows, Julie.	PR6052.U669

Burton, Anne—see: Woods, Sara, pseud.	
Burton, Anthony.	PR6052.U69
Burton, Miles, 1884-1964.	PR6037.T778
Busby, Roger.	PR6052.U76
Busch, Niven, 1903-	PS3503.U746
Bush, Christopher, 1885-	PR6003.U63
Butler, Gerald.	none
Butler, Gwendoline.	PR6052.U813
Butler, K. R.	PR6052.U816
Butler, Michael.	none
Butler, Ragan.	PR6052.U825
Butler, Richard, 1925-	PR6052.U85
Butler, William, 1929-	PS3552.U83
Butler, William Vivian, 1927-	PR6052.U875
Butterworth, Michael, 1924-	PR6052.U9
Byers, Bruce.	none
Byfield, Barbara Ninde.	PS3552.Y65
Byrd, Elizabeth.	PS3552.Y67
Byrd, Max.	PS3552.Y675
Byrne, Beverly.	PS3552.Y69
Byrne, Robert, 1930-	PS3552.Y73
Byrne, Stuart J.	none
Byrom, James, 1911-	PR6003.R243
Byron, Christopher.	PS3552.Y78
Cade, Alexander.	PR6053.A33
Cade, Robin, 1930-	PR9320.9.N5
Cadell, Elizabeth.	PR6005.A225
Cafferty, Jake.	none
Caidin, Martin, 1927-	PS3553.A38
Caillou, Alan, 1914-	PR6053.A347
Cain, James M. (James Mallahan), 1892-1977.	PS3505.A3113
Caine, Hamilton T.—see: Smoke, Stephen L., 1949-	
Caine, Jeffrey, 1944-	PR6053.A35
Caird, Janet.	PR6053.A36
Cairns, Alison.	PR6053.A373
Cairns, Colleen.	PS3553.A394
Cake, Patrick.	PS3553.A3944
Calde, Mark A., 1945-	PS3553.A3946
Calder, Robert.	PS3553.A3949
Caldwell, Celeste.	none
Caldwell, George S.	PS3553.A395
Caldwell, Taylor, 1900-	PS3505.A364
Calef, Noël, 1907-	PQ2605.A317
Callahan, James.	none
Callahan, Jay.	none
Callan, Michael Feeney.	none

Calland, Mary. none
Callison, Brian. PR6053.A39
Calmer, Ned. PS3553.A425
Calnan, T. D., 1914- none
Calvin, Henry—see: Hanley, Clifford.
Camacho, George. none
Cambards, Michelle. PQ2605.A327
Cameron, Eleanor Elford. none
Cameron, Ian, 1924- PR9619.3.P3
Cameron, Kate—see: DuBreuil, Linda.
Cameron, Kenneth M., 1931- PS3553.A4335
Cameron, Lou, 1924- PS3553.A434
Camp, William, 1928- PS3553.A439
Campbell, Alice. none
Campbell, Jeffrey. PR6053.A4857
Campbell, Karen. PR6053.A487
Campbell, R. T.—see: Todd, Ruthven, 1914-
Campbell, R. Wright. PS3553.A4867
Campbell, Ramsey, 1946- PR6053.A4855
Campbell, Robert—see: Campbell, R. Wright.
Campbell, Scott. none'
Canaday, John, 1907- PS3505.A53196
Canary, Glen. none
Canby, Vincent. PS3553.A4894
Candy, Edward. PR6064.E83
Cannell, Charles—see: Vivian, Evelyn Charles H.
Cannell, Dorothy. PS3553.A499
Canning, Victor. PR6005.A486
Cannon, Curt—see: Hunter, Evan, 1926-
Cannon, Elliott. none
Cannon, P. H. (Peter H.) PS3553.A529
Canon, Jack. none
Cantrell, Lisa W. none
Capes, Bernard Edward Joseph, d. 1918. PR6005.A53 [sic]
Capon, Paul, 1912- PR6005.A4868
Capote, Truman, 1924- PS3505.A59
Caputi, Anthony Francis, 1924- PS3553.A62
Carco, Francis, 1886-1958. PQ2605.A55
Cardiff, Sara. PS3553.A663
Carew, Henry. PR6005.A4896
Carey, Bernice. none
Carey, Constance. none
Carey, Webster. none
Carfax, Catherine—see: Fairburn, Eleanor M.
Carkeet, David. PS3553.A688
Carleson, Donald V. none

Carleton, Marjorie Chalmers.	PS3505.A724
Carlino, Lewis John.	PS3553.A7
Carlisle, D. M.	PR6053.A6838
Carlisle, Henry, 1926-	PS3553.A72
Carlon, Patricia.	none
Carlson, P. M.	none
Carlton, Mitchell.	none
Carmichael, Harry—see: Ognall, Leopold Horace.	
Carnac, Carol—see: Rivett, Edith Caroline, 1894-	
Carnac, Nicholas.	PR6053.A6856
Carney, Daniel, 1944-	PR6053.A687
Carney, William, 1922-	PS3553.A758
Carol, Robin.	none
Carothers, A. J.	none
Carpenter, Carleton.	none
Carpentier, Charles.	PS3553.A7624
Carpozi, George.	none
Carr, Albert H. Z.	PS3553.A7627
Carr, Glyn—see: Styles, Showell, 1908-	
Carr, Jess.	PS3553.A763
Carr, John Dickson, 1906-1977.	PS3505.A763
Carr, Kirby.	PS3553.A7632
Carr, Margaret—see: Carroll, Martin.	
Carr, Philippa—see: Plaidy, Jean, 1906-	
Carrel, Mark—see: Paine, Lauran.	
Carrick, John.	none
Carrington, Glenda.	none
Carroll, Charles.	none
Carroll, James, 1943-	PS3553.A764
Carroll, Jock.	none
Carroll, Joy.	none
Carroll, Martin.	PR6053.A697
Carroll, Robert—see: Alpert, Hollis, 1916-	
Carson, Robert, 1909-	PS3505.A77825
Carter, Alberta Simpson.	none
Carter, Amanda.	none
Carter, Angela, 1940-	PR6053.A73
Carter, Diana.	PR6053.A735
Carter, John.	none
Carter, John Franklin, 1897-1967.	PS3505.A7922
Carter, Nicholas.	none
Carter, Nick.	none
Carter, Noël Vreeland.	none
Carter, Youngman, 1904-1969.	PR6005.A7643
Cartwright, Justin.	PR6053.A746
Carvic, Heron.	PR6053.A75

Casberg, Melvin A., 1909-	PS3553.A78975
Case, David, 1937-	PS3553.A79
Case, Jim.	none
Case, Peg.	none
Casey, Kevin.	PR6053.A814
Casey, Mervin.	none
Casey, Robert.	PS3553.A7936
Cashman, John.	PR6053.A822
Casler, Ronald.	none
Caspary, Vera, 1904-	PS3505.A842
Cass, Zoë.	PR6053.A824
Cassells, John—see: Duncan, William Murdoch, 1909-	
Cassels, Louis.	none
Cassiday, Bruce.	none
Cassidy, John, 1922-	PS3553.A7956
Cassilis, Robert.	PR6053.A82413
Cassill, R. V. (Ronald Verlin), 1919-	PS3553.A796
Castang, Viola.	none
Castle, Frank.	none
Castle, Jayne—see: Krentz, Jayne Ann.	
Castle, Mort.	none
Castoire, Marie.	PS3553.A8148
Caswell, Helen Rayburn.	PS3505.A8565
Catto, Max, 1909-	PR6005.A83
Caudwell, Sarah.	PR6053.A855
Caulfield, Max.	none
Caunitz, William J.	PS3553.A945
Cave, Emma.	PR6053.A859
Cave, Hugh B. (Hugh Barnett), 1910-	PS3505.A912
Cave, Peter L.	none
Caveney, Philip.	PR6053.A87
Cawley, Robert.	none
Cecil, Henry, pseud.	PR6053.E3
Cederberg, Fred.	none
Chaber, M. E., 1910-	PS3505.R89224
Chabrey, François.	none
Chacko, David.	PS3553.H2
Chadwick, Jocelyn—see: Chadwick, Joseph L.	
Chadwick, Joseph L.	none
Chais, Pamela, 1930-	PS3553.H243
Chalker, Jack L.	PS3553.H247
Challis, Mary—see: Woods, Sara, pseud.	
Chaloner, John, 1924-	PR6053.H283
Chamberlain, Anne.	PS3505.H232
Chambers, Dana—see: Leffingwell, Albert, 1895-1946.	
Chambers, Elwyn Whitman, 1896-	none

Chambers, Peter, 1924-	PR6066.H463
Chambers, Robert, 1933-	PS3553.H26
Chambers, Robert W. (Robert William), 1865-1933.	PS1280-1288
Chambers, Whitman—see: Chambers, Elwyn Whitman, 1896-	
Chambers, William E.	none
Champion de Crespigny, Rose Key.	none
Chance, John Newton.	PR6005.H28
Chance, Lisbeth, 1946-	PS3553.H266
Chance, Stephen.	PR6053.H3178
Chancellor, John.	PR6053.H318
Chandler, Bryn.	none
Chandler, David.	PS3553.H27
Chandler, Peter.	none
Chandler, Raymond, 1888-1959.	PS3505.H3224 [Z8159.15]
Chang, Lee—see: Rosenberger, Joseph.	
Chantler, David Thomas.	PS3553.H275
Chaplin, Patrice.	PR6053.H348
Chapman, Hester W., 1899-1976.	PR6005.H317
Chapman, John.	none
Chapman, Raymond.	PR6005.H323
Charbonneau, Louis, 1924-	PS3575.O7
Charles, Iona.	none
Charles, Robert.	PR6069.M53
Charles, Theresa.	PR6005.H3436
Charles, Will—see: Willeford, Charles Ray, 1919-	
Charleston, Wally.	none
Charlton, John—see: Woodhouse, Martin, 1932-	
Charteris, Leslie, 1907-	PR6005.H348 [Z8161.8]
Charyn, Jerome.	PS3553.H33
Chase, Elaine Raco.	none
Chase, James Hadley, 1906-	PR6035.A92
Chase, Philip.	none
Chastain, Thomas.	PS3553.H3416
Chaze, Elliott.	PS3505.H633
Cheatham, Lillian.	PS3553.H348
Chernenok, Mikhail.	PG3479.5.H3715
Chernyonok, Mikhail—see: Chernenok, Mikhail.	
Chesbro, George C.	PS3553.H359
Chesney, Weatherby—see: Hyne, Charles John Cutcliffe Wright, 1864-1944.	
Chester, Alfred.	none
Chester, George Randolph, 1869-1924.	PS3505.H684
Chester, Roy.	none
Chester, Samuel Beach.	none

Chesterton, G. K. (Gilbert Keith), 1874-1936.	PR4453.C4
Chetwynd-Hayes, Ronald.	PR6053.H47
Chevalier, Paul, 1925-	PR6053.H473
Chevigny, Paul, 1935-	PS3553.H44
Cheyney, Jeanne.	none
Cheyney, Peter, 1896-1951.	PR6005.H48
Child, Roderick.	none
Childers, Erskine, 1870-1922.	PR6005.H52
Childs, Marquis William, 1903-	none
Childs, Timothy, 1941-	PS3553.H488
Chimenti, Francesca.	PS3553.H489
Chiodo, Daniel J.	none
Chittenden, Margaret.	none
Chiu, Tony.	PS3553.H54
Christian, John, 1930 Jan.6-	PR6054.I95
Christian, Nick—see: Pollitz, Edward A., 1937-	
Christie, Agatha, 1890-1976.	PR6005.H66
Christner, D. W.	none
Christopher, Jay.	none
Christopher, John.	PR6053.H75
Chronister, Alan B.	none
Chubin, Barry.	PR9105.9.C55
Chudley, Ron, 1937-	none
Churchill, Luanna.	PS3553.H855
Churchward, John.	none
Citro, Joseph A.	none
Clair, William R.	none
Clancy, Ambrose, 1948-	PS3553.L237
Clancy, Leo.	PR6053.L282
Clancy, Tom, 1947-	PS3553.L245
Clapperton, Richard.	none
Clare, Marguerite.	none
Claremon, Neil.	PS3553.L25
Clarins, Dana.	none
Clark, Al C.—see: Goines, Donald, 1937-1974.	
Clark, Cecily.	none
Clark, Douglas.	PR6053.L294
Clark, Eric, 1937-	PR6053.L295
Clark, Ernest.	none
Clark, Evert.	none
Clark, Gail.	PR6053.L298
Clark, Lydia Benson.	none
Clark, Mary Higgins.	PS3553.L287
Clark, Philip, fl. 1948-1949.	PS3505.L3666
Clark, William, 1916-	PR6053.L324
Clarke, Anna, 1919-	PR6053.L3248

Clarke, Colin.	none
Clarke, Edward.	PR6053.L3258
Clarke, Robert—see: Paine, Lauran.	
Clarke, Thomas Ernest Bennett, 1907-	PR6005.L453
Clason, Clyde B.	none
Claudia, Susan—see: Johnston, William, 1924-	
Clausse, Suzanne.	none
Clay, Patrick.	none
Clayton, Donald D.	PS3553.L3874
Clayton, Richard—see: Haggard, William.	
Cleary, Denis J.	none
Cleary, Jon, 1917-	PR9619.3.C54
Cleaver, Anastasia.	none
Cleeve, Brian Talbot, 1921-	PR6053.L43
Cleife, Kenneth Philip Hubert.	PR6053.L47
Clemeau, Carol.	PS3553.L392
Clemens, Brian.	PR6053.L474
Clement, Charles Baxter.	PS3552.L393
Clement, Dick.	none
Clement, Henry.	none
Clements, Abigail.	none
Clerc, Michel.	PQ2663.L4166
Clerk, Ernie.	none
Clevely, Hugh.	none
Clifford, Eth, 1915-	none
Clifford, Francis.	PR6070.H66
Cline, C. Terry.	PS3553.L53
Clinton-Baddeley, V. C. (Victor Clinton), 1900-1970.	PR6053.L5
Clive, John.	PR6053.L53
Close, Robin.	PR6053.L56
Clothier, Peter, 1936-	PR6053.L57
Clouston, J. Storer (Joseph Storer), 1870-1944.	PR6005.L845
Coates, Robert M. (Robert Myron), 1897-1973.	PS3505.O1336
Cobb, Belton, 1892-	PR6053.O15
Cobb, Sylvanus, 1823-1887.	PS1356.C57
Cobb, Thomas, 1854-1932.	none
Cobban, J. Maclaren (James Maclaren), 1849-1903.	none
Coburn, Andrew.	PS3553.O23
Cochran, Alan.	PS3553.O247
Cockburn, Alexander.	PR6053.O219
Cockain, Frank.	none
Cody, James P.	none
Cody, Liza.	PR6053.O247
Coe, Tucker—see: Westlake, Donald E.	
Coen, Franklin.	PS3505.O236
Coffey, Brian—see: Koontz, Dean R. (Dean Ray), 1945-	

Coffey, Frank.	PS3553.O35
Coffman, Virginia.	PS3553.O415
Coggins, Paul.	none
Cogswell, Georgia.	none
Cohane, M. E.	none
Cohen, Anthea.	PR6053.O34
Cohen, Barney.	none
Cohen, Octavus Roy, 1891-1959.	PS3505.O2455
Cohen, Stanley, 1928-	PS3553.O43
Cohen, William S.	PS3553.O434
Cohler, David Keith.	PS3553.O4347
Coker, Carolyn.	PS3553.O4367
Colburn, Laura.	none
Colby, Lydia.	none
Colby, Robert.	none
Cole, Allison.	PS3553.O449
Cole, Barry.	PR6053.O4
Cole, Burt, 1930-	PS3553.O45
Cole, G. D. H. (George Douglas Howard), 1889-1959.	PR6005.O226
Cole, Margaret, 1893-1980.	none
Coleman, Francis X. J.	none
Coles, Manning, pseud.	PS3505.O285
Collee, John.	PR6053.O423
Collett, Dorothy.	none
Colley, I. B.	none
Collier, Jane.	none
Collier, Peter.	PS3553.O47465
Collin, Richard.	PS3553.O474694
Collingwood, Charles.	PS3553.O4747
Collins, Cornelius J.	none
Collins, Eliza G. C.	PS3553.O474784
Collins, Gilbert, 1890-	none
Collins, Jackson, 1939-	PS3553.O474795
Collins, Larry.	PS3553.O47487
Collins, Max Allan.	PS3553.O4753
Collins, Michael—see Arden, William, 1924-	
Collins, Michelle.	none
Collins, Norman, 1907-	PR6005.O36534
Collins, Randall, 1941-	PS3553.O476
Collins, Thomas.	none
Collins, Wilkie, 1824-1889.	PR4490-4498 [Z8184.6]
Colter, Frank.	none
Coltrane, James.	PS3553.O4775
Combes, Sharon.	none
Comfort, Iris Tracy.	PS3553.O4834

Comport, Brian.	none
Compton, D. G. (David Guy), 1930-	PR6053.O45
Conaway, James.	PS3553.O486
Conaway, Jim C.	none
Condé, Nicholas.	PS3553.O4867
Condon, Richard.	PS3553.O487
Conger, Donald.	none
Connable, Alfred.	PS3553.O496
Connell, Candace.	PS3553.O498
Conner, K. Patrick.	PS3553.O5117
Conners, Bernard F.	PS3553.O512
Connington, J. J.—see: Stewart, Alfred W. (Alfred Walter), 1880-	
Connolly, Colm.	PR6053.O486
Connolly, Ray, 1940-	PR6053.O487
Connolly, Vivian.	none
Connor, Ralph, 1860-1937.	PR9199.2.G6
Conot, Robert E.	none
Conrad, Barnaby, 1922-	PS3553.O515
Conrad, Joseph, 1857-1924.	PR6005.O4
Conroy, Al.	none
Constable, Lawrence.	PR9639.3.C6
Constantine, Eddie, 1917-	PQ2663.O593
Constantine, K. C.	PS3553.O524
Conte, Charles.	none
Conty, J. P.	none
Conway, Joan Ditzel.	none
Conway, Keith.	none
Conway, Laura—see: Ansle, Dorothy Phoebe.	
Conway, Norman.	none
Conway, Peter.	none
Cook, Bruce, 1932-	PS3553.O55314
Cook, Eugenia.	none
Cook, John Lennox, 1923-	PR6053.O5195
Cook, Judith.	PR6053.O5196
Cook, Kenneth, 1929-	PR9619.3.C57
Cook, Robin, 1940-	PS3553.O5545
Cook, Sy.	PS3553.O5546
Cook, Thomas H.	PS3553.O55465
Cook, William Wallace, 1869-1933.	PS3505.O5593
Cooke, David C. (David Coxe), 1917-	PS3553.O555
Cooke, M. E.—see: Creasey, John.	
Cooke, William.	none
Cookson, Catherine.	PR6053.O525
Cooney, Caroline B.	PS3553.O578
Cooney, Michael.	PR6053.O53
Cooper, Brian, 1919-	PR6053.O546 [sic]

Cooper, Bryan.	PR6053.O543
Cooper, Colin.	PR6053.O5464
Cooper, Craig.	PS3553.O58
Cooper, Dominic, 1944-	PR6053.O5467
Cooper, Evelyn Barbara.	PR6053.O547
Cooper, Hugh Homfray.	PR6053.O555
Cooper, Jamie Lee.	PS3553.O588
Cooper, Jeffrey, 1950-	none
Cooper, Lettice Ulpha, 1897-	PR6005.O4977
Cooper, Louise Field, 1905-	PS3505.O62516
Cooper, Lynna.	PS3553.O5954
Cooper, M. K. (Mae Klein)	PS3553.O5955
Cooper, Matthew.	PR6053.O574
Cooper, Morton, 1925-	PS3553.O62
Cooper, Parley J.	PS3553.O622
Cooper, Roderick.	PR6053.O594
Cooper, Tom.	none
Cooper, Will.	PS3553.O627
Copeland, Richard—see: McLeave, Hugh.	
Copeland, William.	PS3553.O634
Coppel, Alfred.	PS3553.O64
Copper, Basil.	PR6053.O658
Coram, Christopher—see: Walker, Peter Norman.	
Corbett, James.	none
Corby, Jane Irenita, 1899-	none
Cordell, Alexander.	PR6053.O67
Cordell, Melissa.	none
Corder, Eric, 1941-	PS3553.O645
Coriola.	none
Corlett, William.	PR6053.O7
Corley, Edwin.	PS3553.O648
Cormier, Robert.	none
Cornwell, Bernard.	PR6053.O75
Cornwell, John.	none
Corradi, Lou.	none
Corren, Grace—see: Hoskins, Robert, 1933-	
Corrington, John William.	PS3553.O7
Corrington, Joyce H.	none
Corris, Peter.	PR9619.3.C595
Cory, Desmond, 1928-	PR6053.O774
Cosgrave, Patrick.	PR6053.O775
Costello, Matthew J.	none
Cotelo, C. S.	none
Cotter, John.	none
Coughlin, T. Glen.	PS3553.O775
Coughlin, William Jeremiah, 1929-	PS3553.O78

Coulson, Juanita.	PS3553.O83
Coulson, Robert.	PS3553.O84
Coulter, Stephen, 1913-	PR6053.O8
Court, Katherine, 1918-	PS3553.O8617
Courter, Gay.	PS3553.O86185
Courtier, Sidney Hobson.	PR6005.O817
Courtis, Gerald.	none
Cousin, Michel.	PQ2663.O84
Cousins, Edmund George, 1893-	none
Covert, Paul.	none
Coville, Bruce.	none
Cowen, Frances.	none
Cowen, Ron.	PS3553.O9
Cox, Anne-Marie.	none
Cox, Richard Hubert Francis, 1931-	PR6053.O969
Coxe, George Harmon, 1901-	PS3505.O9636
Coyle, John B.	none
Coyne, John.	PS3553.O96
Coyne, P. J.	PS3563.A82
Crabb, Ned.	PS3553.R18
Craig, Alisa—see: MacLeod, Charlotte.	
Craig, Bill, 1930-	PR6053.R25
Craig, David, 1929-	PR6070.U23
Craig, John, 1921-	PR9199.3.C68
Craig, Jonathan—see: Smith, Frank E., 1919-	
Craig, M. S.—see: Shura, Mary Francis.	
Craig, Mary—see: Shura, Mary Francis.	
Craig, Philip, 1933-	PS3553.R23
Craig, William, 1929-	PS3553.R25
Crais, Robert.	none
Crane, Caroline.	PS3553.R2695
Crane, Frances Kirkwood.	PS3505.R267
Crane, Robert.	PS3513.L646
Crawford, Link.	none
Crawford, Max, 1938-	PS3553.R293
Crawford, Oliver.	PS3553.R294
Crawford, Petrina.	none
Crawford, Robert—see: Rae, Hugh C.	
Crawford, Stanley G., 1937-	PS3553.R295
Crawford, William.	none
Creasey, John.	PR6005.R517
Crecy, Jeanne—see: Williams, Jeanne, 1930-	
Creed, David.	PR6053.R435
Creekmore, Donna.	none
Creighton, Jo Anne.	none
Creighton, John—see: Chadwick, Joseph L.	

Crichton, Michael, 1942-	PS3553.R48
Crichton, William.	none
Crider, Bill, 1941-	PS3553.R497
Crisp, N. J.	PR6053.R497
Crisp, Quentin, 1908-	PR6005.R65
Crisp, William, 1942-	PS3553.R518
Crispin, Edmund, 1921-1978.	PR6025.O46
Crockett, S. R. (Samuel Rutherford), 1860-1914.	PR4518.C3
Croft-Cooke, Rupert, 1903-	PR6005.R673
Crofts, Andrew.	none
Crofts, Freeman Wills, 1879-1957.	PR6005.R675
Cromie, Alice.	PS3553.R538
Cromie, Robert, 1856-1907.	PR4518.C554
Cronin, A. J. (Archibald Joseph), 1896-1981.	PR6005.R68
Cronin, Brendan Leo.	PR6053.R57
Cronin, George P.	none
Cronin, Michael—see: Cronin, Brendan Leo.	
Crosby, John, 1912-	PS3553.R55
Cross, Amanda, 1926-	PS3558.E4526
Cross, Beverley, 1931-	PR6005.R694
Cross, David—see: Chesbro, George C.	
Cross, E. B.	none
Cross, Gilbert B.	none
Cross, Gillian.	none
Cross, Ralph D.	none
Crossen, Kendell Foster, 1910-	PS3505.R89224
Croudace, Glynn.	PR6053.R64
Crow, C. P.	PS3553.R587
Crowcraft, Peter.	none
Crowe, Cecily.	PS3553.R59
Crowe, John—see: Arden, William, 1924-	
Crowley, Duane.	none
Crowther, Bruce, 1933-	PR6053.R657
Crowther, John, 1939-	PS3553.R67
Cruickshank, Charles Greig.	none
Crumley, James, 1939-	PS3553.R78
Cruz, Mark.	none
Cudahy, Sheila.	PS3553.U27
Cudlip, David R.	PS3553.U275
Cullen, Anthony D., 1920-	none
Cullinan, Thomas.	PS3553.U33
Cullingford, Guy.	none
Cullum, Ridgwell, 1867-1943.	PR6005.U4
Culpan, Maurice.	PR6053.U415
Culver, Timothy J.—see: Westlake, Donald E.	
Cumberland, Marten.	PR6005.U45

Cummings, Jack, 1925-	PS3553.U444
Cummings, Jack, 1940-	PS3553.U4443
Cunningham, Albert Benjamin, 1888-	none
Cunningham, Chet.	none
Cunningham, E. V.—see: Fast, Howard, 1914-	
Cunningham, Jere.	PS3553.U475
Cunningham, Scott.	none
Cuomo, George.	PS3553.U6
Curran, Terrie.	PS3553.U666
Currington, O. J., 1924-	PR6053.U74
Curry, Avon—see: Annandale, Barbara, 1925-	
Curtis, Marjorie.	PR6005.U762
Curtis, Mike, 1943-	none
Curtis, Peter—see: Lofts, Norah, 1904-	
Curtis, Richard.	none
Curtis, Spencer.	none
Curtis, Susannah.	none
Curtis, Sydney Albert.	none
Curtis, Wade—see: Pournelle, Jerry, 1933-	
Curtiss, Ursula Reilly.	PS3505.U915
Curzon, Clare.	none
Cushman, Dan.	PS3553.U738
Cussler, Clive.	PS3553.U75
Cutler, Roland.	PS3553.U835
Cutter, Leela.	PS3553.U86
Da Cruz, Daniel, 1921-	PS3554.A24
D'Agneau, Marcel.	none
Dahl, Roald.	PR6054.A35
Dale, Adrian.	none
Dale, Celia.	PR6054.A38
Dale, Jo Anne.	none
Daley, Joseph A.	PS3554.A42
Daley, Robert.	PS3554.A43
Dalheath, David.	none
Dallas, John—see: Duncan, William Murdoch, 1909-	
Dalton, John J.	PS3554.A443 [sic]
D'Alton, Martina.	PS3554.A438
Dalton, Moray.	PR6007.A494
Dalton, Pat.	PS3554.A444
Daly, Carroll John, 1889-1958.	PS3507.A4673
Daly, Elizabeth, 1878-	PS3507.A4674
Daly, Treve.	none
D'Amato, Barbara.	none
Damien, Christine.	none
Damore, Leo.	PS3554.A495
Dan, Uri.	none

Dana, Richard—see: Paine, Lauran.
Dana, Rose—see: Ross, W. E. D. (William Edward Daniel), 1912-
Dane, Clemence. PR6001.S5
Dane, Eva. none
Daniel, David, 1945- PS3554.A5383
Daniel, Roland. none
Daniels, A. Frederick. none
Daniels, Dorothy, 1915- PS3554.A563
Daniels, Jeffrey R. PR6054.A52
Daniels, Les, 1943- PS3554.A5637
Daniels, Philip. PR6054.A522
Daniels, Jan—see: Ross, W. E. D. (William Edward Daniel), 1912-
Daniels, Norman A. none
Danton, Rebecca—see: Roberts, Janet Louise, 1925-1982.
Darbon, Leslie. PR6054.A64
Darby, Catherine. none
Darby, Emma. PS3554.A65
Dard, Frédéric. PQ2607.A558
Dark, James. none
Dartey, Léo. none
Date, John H. none
Datesh, John Nicholas. none
Davenport, Diana. PS3554.A8598
Davey, Jocelyn. PR6035.A64
David-Neel, Alexandra, 1868-1969. PQ2607.A927
Davidov, Len. none
Davidson, Avram. PS3554.A924
Davidson, David Albert, 1908- PS3507.A66596
Davidson, Lionel. PR6054.A87
Davidson, Muriel. PS3554.A9258
Davie-Martin, Hugh—see: McCutcheon, Hugh.
Davies, Frederick. PR6054.A879
Davies, Gwynneth. none
Davies, Jack, 1913- PR6054.A884
Davies, L. P. (Leslie Purnell) PR6054.A886
Davies, Martin. none
Davies, Melissa. none
Davies, Rhys, 1903- PR6007.A78
Davis, Bart, 1950- PS3554.A9319
Davis, Berrie. PS3554.A932
Davis, Dorothy Salisbury. PS3554.A9335
Davis, Elizabeth—see: Davis, Lou Ellen, 1936-
Davis, Frederick C. (Frederick Clyde), 1902- PS3507.A728
Davis, George. PR6054.A8917
Davis, Gordon—see: Hunt, E. Howard (Everette Howard), 1918-
Davis, Gordon A. none

Davis, Gwen.	PS3554.A9346
Davis, Howard Charles.	none
Davis, J. R.	none
Davis, John Gordon.	PR6054.A8924
Davis, Kenn.	none
Davis, L. V.	none
Davis, Lou Ellen, 1936-	PS3554.A9355
Davis, Mildred B.	PS3507.A7424
Davis, Phil.	none
Davis-Goff, Annabel.	PS3554.A9385
Davison, Geoffrey.	PR6054.A895
Davison, Gilderoy, 1892-	none
Davison, Jean.	PS3554.A939
Davison, Norma.	none
Dawe, Carlton, 1865-1935.	none
Dawson, Clare.	none
Dawson, Janis.	none
Day, Chet.	none
Day Lewis, C. (Cecil), 1904-1972.	PR6007.A95
De Bilio, Beth.	PS3554.E176
De Blasis, Celeste.	PS3554.E11144
De Borchgrave, Arnaud.	PR6054.E27
De Crespigny, Philip Champion, Mrs.—see: Champion de Crespigny, Rose Key.	
De Felitta, Frank.	PS3554.E35
De Filippo, Eduardo, 1900-	PQ4815.I48
De Ford, Miriam Allen, 1888-	PS3507.E338
De Fraga, Geoff, 1913-	PR6054.E34
De Gramont, Sanche—see: Morgan, Ted, 1932-	
De Larrabeiti, Michael.	PR6054.E134
De La Torre, Lillian, 1902-	PS3507.E1695
De Lauer, Marjel Jean.	PS3554.E4414
De Lillo, Don.	PS3554.E4425
De Maria, Robert.	none
De Marne, Denis.	none
De Mille, James, 1837-1880.	PS1534.D3
De Polnay, Peter, 1906-	PR6007.E635
De Pre, Jean-Anne—see: Avallone, Michael.	
De Reszke, David.	none
De Rouen, Reed.	none
De Secary, Jean.	none
De St. Jorre, John, 1936-	PR6054.E784
De Stefano, Anthony.	none
De Toledano, Ralph, 1916-	PS3554.E85
De Villiers, Dirk.	none
De Villiers, Gerald.	none

De Vries, Anko—see: Vries, Anko de, 1936-
Deal, Babs H.   PS3554.E12
Deal, Borden, 1922-   PS3554.E13
Dean, Amber.   PS3507.E1623
Dean, Robert G. (Robert George), 1930-   none
Dean, S. F. X.   PS3554.E1734
Dean, Spencer—see: Winchell, Prentice.
DeAndrea, William L.   PS3554.E174
Deane, Jim.   none
Deane, Norman—see: Creasey, John.
Deane, Philip.   PR9115.9.D4
Deane, Shirley.   PR6054.E23
Decker, Jake.   none
Decoin, Didier, 1945-   PQ2664.E37
Deford, Frank.   PS3554.E37
DeGrave, Philip.   PS3554.E416
Deighton, Len, 1929-   PR6054.E37
Dekker, Anthony.   PR6054.E38
Dekker, Carl—see: Arden, William, 1924-
Dekobra, Maurice, 1885-1973.   PQ2607.E22
Delacorta—see: Odier, Daniel, 1945-
Delacorte, Peter.   PS3554.E433
Delaney, Laurence.   PS3554.E436
Delap, Richard.   none
Delft, Japhet.   PR6054.E414
Delman, David.   PS3554.E444
DeLuca, Charles.   none
Delving, Michael—see: Williams, Jay, 1914-
Demaine, Christy.   none
DeMarco, Gordon.   PS3554.E448
Demarest, Judith H.   none
Demarest, Phyllis Gordon.   PS3507.E5344
DeMarinis, Rick, 1934-   PS3554.E4554
Demaris, Ovid.   PS3554.E4555
Demijohn, Tom—see: Disch, Thomas M.
DeMille, Nelson.   PS3554.E472
Deming, Richard.   PS3554.E48
Demirjian, Arto.   none
Dempsey, Al.   PS3554.E493
Denbow, William.   none
Denby, Edwin, 1903-   PS3507.E54339
Denham, Bertie, Baron, 1927-   PR6054.E47
Denis, John.   none
Denker, Henry.   PS3507.E5475
Denning, Mark.   PS3554.E534
Dennis, Charles, 1946-   PR9199.3.D44

Dennis, Ralph.	PS3554.E539
Dennis, Robert C.	PS3554.E54
Denniston, Elinor—see: Foley, Rae, 1900-	
Dent, Lester, 1905-1959.	PS3507.E5777
Dentinger, Jane.	PS3554.E587
Denver, Paul.	none
Deptula, Walter.	none
Derleth, August William, 1909-1971.	PS3507.E69 [Z8226.7]
Derrick, Lionel.	none
Derwent, Robert.	none
Des Cars, Guy.	PQ2607.E673
Desmond, Hugh.	none
Desmond, Rachel.	none
Deutcsh, Arthur V.	PS3554.E885
Deutschman, Deborah.	PS3554.E913
Deverell, William, 1937-	PR9199.3.D474
Devi, Shakuntala.	none
Devine, D. M.—see: Devine, Dominic, 1920-	
Devine, Dominic, 1920-	PR6054.E9
Devon, D. G.	PS3554.E9282
Devon, Gary.	PS3554.E92824
Dewar, Evelyn.	PR6054.E93
DeWeese, Gene.	PS3554.E929
DeWeese, Jean—see: DeWeese, Gene.	
Dewey, Thomas Blanchard, 1915-	PS3507.E883
Dewhurst, Eileen.	PR6054.E95
Dexter, Colin.	PR6054.E96
Dexter, Ted.	PR6054.E967
Di Fiore, Frank.	none
Dial, Jean.	none
Diamond, Stephen.	none
Dibb, C. Emily.	none
Dibble, Birney.	none
Dibdin, Michael.	PR6054.I26
Dibner, Martin.	PS3507.I215
Dick, Alexandra—see: Erikson, Sibyl Alexandra.	
Dick, Philip K.	PS3554.I3
Dickens, Charles, 1812-1870.	PR4550-4598 [Z8230]
Dickens, Frank.	none
Dickinson, Peter, 1927-	PR6054.I35
Dickson, Carter—see: Carr, John Dickson, 1906-1977.	
Didelot, Roger Francis, 1902-	PQ2607.I15
Diehl, William	PS3554.I345
Dietrich, Robert—see: Hunt, E. Howard (Everette Howard), 1918-	

Dietz, Lew, 1906-	none
Dillon, Catherine.	none
Dillon, Eilis, 1920-	PR6054.I42
Dillon, Walter.	none
Dilnot, George.	none
Diment, Adam.	PR6054.I45
DiMona, Joseph.	PS3554.I44
Dinesen, Isak, 1885-1962.	PR6003.L545
DiPego, Gerald.	PS3554.I63
Diplomat—see: Carter, John Franklin, 1897-1967.	
Dipper, Alan.	PR6054.I6
Dirckx, John H., 1938-	PS3554.I7
Disch, Thomas M.	PS3554.I8
	[Z8232.5]
Disney, Doris Miles.	PS3507.I75
Disney, Dorothy Cameron.	none
Ditton, James.	none
Divine, Arthur Durham, 1904-	none
Divine, David—see: Divine, Arthur Durham, 1904-	
Dix, Maurice Buxton.	none
Dixon, Harry Vernor.	none
Dixon, Mark.	none
Dixon, Roger.	PR6054.I95
Dixon, Stephen, 1936-	PS3554.I92
Dobbins, Richard.	none
Dobler, Bruce.	PS3554.O16
Dobner, Maeva Park.	none
Dobson, Margaret.	none
Dobson, William—see: Butterworth, Michael, 1924-	
Dobyns, Stephen, 1941-	PS3554.O2
Dodge, David.	PS3507.O248
Dodge, Mary Louise.	none
Dodson, Daniel Boone.	PS3554.O34
Doherty, P. C.	PR6054.O37
Dolan, Patrick.	none
Dold, Gaylord.	none
Doliner, Roy.	PS3554.O45
Dolson, Hildegarde.	PS3507.O662
Domatilla, John.	PR6054.O427
Domenica.	none
Dominic, R. B.	PS3562.A755
Donald, Miles.	PR6054.O459
Donaldson, Norman.	none
Donaldson, Robert, 1919-	PR6054.O46
Donavan, John—see: Morland, Nigel, 1905-	
Dong, Eugene.	PS3554.O4694

Donne, Maxim—see: Duke, Madelaine.	
Donovan, Dick, 1843-1934.	PR5101.M363
Doody, Margaret Anne.	PR9199.3.D556
Dooley, H. H.	PS3554.O57
Dooley, Roger Burke, 1920-	PS3507.O7254
Dorer, Frances.	none
Dorer, Nancy.	none
Dorland, Michael.	none
Dorling, Henry Taprell, 1883-	none
Dorrell, Mike.	none
Doty, William Lodewick, 1919-	PS3507.O748
Doubtfire, Dianne.	PR6054.O78
Douglas, Arthur, 1928-	PR6054.O82
Douglas, Gavin.	none
Douglas, George—see: Brown, George Douglas, 1869-1902.	
Douglas, Graeme.	none
Douglas, Gregory A.	none
Douglas, John, 1947-	PS3554.O8257
Douglass, Donald McNutt.	none
Douthwaite, Louis Charles, 1878-	none
Dowdell, Dorothy.	PS3554.O895
Dowling, Gregory.	PR6054.O862
Dowling, Richard, 1846-1898.	PR4613.D45
Downey, Timothy.	PS3554.O934
Downing, Warwick, 1931-	PS3554.O935
Doxey, William.	PS3554.O974
Doyle, Adrian Conan.	PR6054.O89
Doyle, Arthur Conan, Sir, 1859-1930.	PR4622 [Z8240]
Doyle, James T., 1928-	PS3554.O9744
Doyle, Richard.	none
Drabble, John Frederick, 1906-	PR6054.R23
Drachman, Theodore S.	PS3507.R1723
Drake, Francis.	none
Dramann, Ann.	none
Draper, Alfred.	PR6054.R28
Dresden, Thomas.	none
Drew, John H., 1949-	PS3554.R44
Drew, Mary Anne—see: Cassiday, Bruce.	
Drexler, J. F.—see: Paine, Lauran.	
Driscoll, Peter, 1942-	PR6054.R53
Driver, C. J.	PR6054.R55
Droge, Edward F.	PS3554.R57
Drumm, D. B.	none
Drummond, Charles—see: Giles, Kenneth.	
Drummond, Ivor.	PR6054.R79

Drummond, J.—see: Chance, John Newton.	
Drummond, June.	PR9369.3.D7
Drummond, William.	none
Du Bois, Theodora McCormick, 1890-	none
Du Boisgobey, Fortune Hippolyte Auguste, 1821-	PQ2220.D6
Du Maurier, Daphne, Dame, 1907-	PR6007.U47
Duane, Allan.	PS3554.U23
DuBreuil, Linda.	none
Dudley, Ernest.	none
Duffy, Maureen.	PR6054.U4
Duke, Francis.	none
Duke, Madelaine.	PR6054.U45
Duke, Winifred.	none
Dumas, Claire.	PQ2664.U382
Duncan, David, 1913-	none
Duncan, Francis.	none
Duncan, Lois, 1934-	PS3554.U464
Duncan, Robert Lipscomb, 1927-	PS3507.U629
[both used]	PS3554.U465
Duncan, W. Glenn.	none
Duncan, William Murdoch, 1909-	PR6007.U535
Dunlap, Susan.	PS3554.U46972
Dunleavy, Steve.	PS3554.U46974
Dunmore, Spencer, 1928-	PR6054.U53
Dunn, Joseph Allan Elphinstone, 1872-1941.	PR6007.U5615
Dunne, Bernard.	none
Dunne, John Gregory, 1932-	PS3554.U493
Dunne, Lee, 1934-	PR6054.U555
Dunne, Thomas L.	PS3554.U4936
Dunnett, Alastair MacTavish, 1908-	PR6054.U557
Dunnett, Dorothy.	PR6054.U56
Dunning, John, 1942-	PS3554.U494
Dunning, Lawrence.	none
Dunsany, Edward John Moreton Drax Plunkett, Baron, 1878-1957.	
	PR6007.U6
Duras, Marguerite.	PQ2607.U8245
Durbin, Charles.	PR6054.U66
Durbridge, Francis.	PR6054.U7
Duris, Gene.	none
Durrant, Digby.	PR6054.U73
Dürrenmatt, Friedrich.	PT2607.U493
	[Z8246.2]
Durst, Paul.	PS3554.U695
Dutton, Charles Judson, 1888-	none
Dutton, James S.	none
Dvorkin, David.	PS3554.V67

Dwyer, Deanna—see: Koontz, Dean R. (Dean Ray), 1945-
Dwyer, K. R.—see: Koontz, Dean R. (Dean Ray), 1945-
Dwyer-Joyce, Alice. PR6054.W9
Dykes, Lew. none
Dyson, John. PR9639.3.D9
Eachus, Irv. PS3555.A25
Earl, Lawrence. PR6055.A69
Early, Jack. PS3555.A693
Early, Robert, 1940- PR9369.3.E17
East, Michael—see: West, Morris L., 1916-
East, Roger. none
Easterman, Daniel. PS3555.A697
Eastman, Robert. PS3555.A73
Eastvale, Margaret. none
Eastwood, Helen. none
Eastwood, James, 1918- PR6055.A84
Eatock, Marjorie, 1927- PS3555.A75
Eberhart, Mignon Good, 1899- PS3509.B453
Ebersohn, Wessel. PR9369.3.E24
Ebisch, Glen. none
Echard, Margaret. none
Eco, Umberto. PQ4865.C6
Eddings, David. PS3555.D38
Eden, Dorothy, 1912- PR9639.3.E38
Eden, Francis I. S. none
Eden, Matthew. PR9199.3.E33
Edgar, Josephine, 1907- PR6015.O857
Edgar, Ken, 1924- PS3555.D45
Edgar, Stanley Walter. none
Edgley, Leslie, 1912- PS3509.D472
Edmonds, Harry Moreton Southey, 1891- none
Edson, John Thomas. PR6055.D8
Edwards, Alexander. none
Edwards, Anne, 1927- PS3555.D87
Edwards, Charman—see: Edwards, Frederick Anthony, 1896-
Edwards, Frederick Anthony, 1896- PR6009.D72
Edwards, Gillian Mary, 1918- none
Edwards, Mike. none
Edwards, Paul. PS3555.D96
Edwards, R. T. none
Edwards, Rachelle. none
Edwards, Rex. PR6055.D95
Edwards, Ruth Dudley. PR6055.D98
Edwards, Samuel—see: Gerson, Noel Bertram, 1914-
Effinger, George Alec. PS3555.F4
Egan, Lesley. PS3562.I515

Egerton-Thomas, Christopher.	none
Egleton, Clive.	PR6055.G55
Ehrenfeld, David.	none
Ehrlich, Collis.	none
Ehrlich, Jack.	none
Ehrlich, Max Simon, 1909-	PS3509.H663
Ehrlichman, John.	PS3555.H74
Einstein, Charles.	PS3555.I58
Eisenberg, Hershey.	PS3555.I796
Ekström, Jan, 1923-	PT9876.15.K74
Elder, Mark.	PS3555.L33
Eldridge, Jim, 1944-	PR6055.L29
Elegant, Robert S.	PS3555.L37
Elgin, Mary.	none
Eliade, Mircea, 1907-	PC839.E38
Elias, Albert J.	none
Eliot, Anne, 1902-	PS3553.O473
Eliot, Jessica.	none
Eliot, Marc.	none
Elkins, Aaron J.	PS3555.L48
Eller, John.	PS3555.L53
Ellerbeck, Rosemary.	PR6055.L46
Ellery, Jan.	none
Ellin, Stanley.	PS3555.L56
Elliot, John Michael.	none
Elliott, Bruce.	none
Elliott, Jane.	none
Elliott, Richard.	none
Elliott, Sumner Locke.	PR9619.3.E44
Ellis, Julie.	PS3555.L597
Ellis, Leigh.	none
Ellis, Mel, 1912-	PS3555.L615
Ellis, Ron.	none
Ellis, Scott.	PS3555.L6157
Ellis, William.	PR6055.L52
Ellison, Harlan.	PS3555.L62
Ellroy, James, 1948-	PS3555.L6274
Ellson, Hal.	none
Elman, Richard M.	none
Elsna, Hebe—see: Ansle, Dorothy Phoebe.	
Elward, James.	PS3555.L84
Ely, David, 1927-	PS3555.L9
Emerson, Earl W.	PS3555.M39
Emmerton, Anton.	none
Emmet, E. R. (Eric Revell)	none
Emsley, Lloyd.	none

Endfield, Mercedes.	none
Endore, S. Guy, 1901-1970.	PS3509.N374
Enefer, Douglas.	PR6055.N35
Engel, Howard, 1931-	PR9199.3.E49
England, Edward Harold.	none
England, George Allan, 1877-1936.	PS3509.N4
England, Jane, 1897-	none
Englander, Seymour.	none
Engleman, Paul.	PS3555.N426
English, Ernest I.	none
English, Jean M.	PS3555.N428
Epstein, Edward Jay, 1935-	PS3555.P652
Epstein, Edward Z.	none
Erdman, Paul Emil, 1932-	PS3555.R4
Ericson, Liz.	none
Erikson, Sibyl Alexandra.	none
Erlanger, Michael, 1915-	PS3555.R5
Ernst, Paul, 1886-	none
Erskine, Margaret.	PR6073.I4332
Eskapa, Shirley.	PR6055.S4
Esler, Anthony.	PS3555.S52
Esmond, Harriet.	PR6055.S5
Esser, Robin, 1933-	PR6055.S7
Essex, William.	none
Esteven, John—see: Shellabarger, Samuel, 1888-1954.	
Estey, Dale.	PR9199.3.E8
Estleman, Loren D.	PS3555.S84
Estow, Daniel.	none
Etheridge, Christina.	none
Eulo, Ken.	none
Eustis, Helen.	PS3509.U66
Evans, Alan, 1930-	PR6055.V13
Evans, Cicely Louise.	PS3555.V213
Evans, Elaine.	none
Evans, John P.	none
Evans, Jonathan.	none
Evans, Kenneth.	none
Evans, Kenneth L.	PS3555.V218
Evans, Peter, 1933-	PR6055.V218
Evans, Philip.	PR6055.V22
Evans, Stuart, 1934-	PR6055.V24
Everett, Peter.	PR6055.V34
Everett-Green, Evelyn—see: Green, Evelyn Everett, 1856-1932.	
Everitt, Bridget.	PR6055.V35
Everson, David.	none
Eyerly, Jeannette.	PS3555.Y4

Eyers, John.	PR6055.Y47
Eyre, Katherine Wigmore.	none
Eyre, Marie.	none
Faber, Doris.	none
Fabian, Ruth.	none
Fackler, Elizabeth.	PS3556.A28
Facos, James, 1924-	PS3556.A3
Fadiman, Edwin.	PS3511.A333
Fagyas, M.	PS3556.A34
Fahy, Christopher.	PS3556.A346
Fair, A. A.—see: Gardner, Erle Stanley, 1889-1970.	
Fairbairn, Douglas, 1926-	PS3556.A362
Fairbairn, Roger—see: Carr, John Dickson, 1906-1977.	
Fairburn, Eleanor M.	PR6056.A49
Fairburn, James.	none
Fairchild, William.	PR6011.A395
Fairfax, Jane.	none
Fairlawn, James.	none
Fairlie, Gerard, 1899-	PR6011.A43
Fairman, Paul W.	none
Fairweather, Nancy.	none
Falkirk, Richard—see: Lambert, Derek, 1929-	
Fallon, Martin—see: Higgins, Jack, 1929-	
Fane, Julian, 1927-	PR6056.A57
Fantoni, Barry.	PR6056.A59
Farjeon, Benjamin Leopold, 1838-1903.	PR4699.F17
Farjeon, Joseph Jefferson, 1883-1955	PR6011.A74
Farmer, Joan.	PR6056.A675
Farmer, Philip José.	PS3556.A72
Farnol, Jeffery, 1878-1952.	PR6011.A753
Farnsworth, Mona.	none
Farr, Caroline—see: Brown, Carter, 1923-	
Farrant, Sarah.	PR6056.A736
Farrar, Helen Graham.	none
Farrar, Stewart.	PR6056.A74
Farrère, Claude, 1876-1957.	PQ2611.A78
Farrimond, John.	PR6056.A76
Farrington, Fielden, 1909-	PS3511.A7395
Farris, John.	PS3556.A777
Fast, Howard, 1914-	PS3511.A784
Fast, Jonathan.	PS3556.A779
Fast, Julius, 1918-	PS3556.A78
Faulcon, Robert.	PR6058.O442
Faust, Joe Clifford.	none
Faust, Ron.	PS3556.A98
Fawcett, Edgar, 1847-1904.	PS1657

Fearing, Kenneth, 1902-1961.	PS3511.E115
Fearn, John Russell, 1908-1960.	PR6011.E295
Feegel, John R.	PS3556.E32
Feely, Terence.	PR6056.E35
Feibleman, Peter S., 1930-	PS3556.E4
Feiffer, Jules.	PS3556.E42
Felber, Ron.	none
Felix, Charles.	PR4699.F183
Femling, Jean.	PS3556.E475
Fenady, Andrew J.	PS3556.E477
Fenisong, Ruth.	PS3511.E376
Fenn, George Manville, 1831-1909.	PR4699.F1844
Fennelly, Tony.	PS3556.E49
Fennerton, William.	PR6056.E485
Fenty, Philip.	none
Fenwick, Elizabeth, 1920-	PS3511.E435
Ferguson, Anthony.	PR6056.E57
Ferguson, Austin.	PS3556.E68
Ferguson, Chris.	PS3556.E69
Ferguson, John Alexander, 1873-	PR6011.E64
Ferguson, Pamela.	PR6056.E619
Ferguson, William Blair Morton, 1882-	none
Ferm, Betty.	PS3556.E724
Ferrand, Georgina.	PR6056.E68
Ferrars, E. X.	PR6003.R458
Ferris, Jean Erskine.	none
Ferris, Paul, 1929-	PR6056.E74
Ferris, Wally.	PS3556.E75
Fessier, Michael, 1907-	none
Fick, Carl.	PS3556.I32
Fickling, G. G.	none
Fiedler, Jean.	none
Field, Evan.	PS3556.I374
Field, Penelope.	PS3557.I16
Field, Ruth Baker.	none
Fielding, Archibald E., 1900-	none
Fielding, Joy.	PR9199.3.F518
Fields, Alan.	none
Filgate, Macartney—see: Macartney-Filgate, Terence.	
Finch, Matthew.	none
Finch, Phillip.	PS3556.I456
Findley, Ferguson—see: Frey, Charles Weiser, 1910-	
Findley, Timothy.	PR9199.3.F52
Fine, Peter Heath.	PS3556.I4635
Finlay, Iain.	PR9619.3.F46
Finney, Jack.	PS3556.I52

Fischer, Bruno, 1908-	PS3511.I687
Fischer, Erwin, 1928-	PT2666.I75
Fischer, John.	none
Fish, Robert L.	PS3556.I79
Fisher, Alan E.	none
Fisher, David E., 1932-	PS3556.I813
Fisher, George.	none
Fisher, Graham.	PR6056.I777
Fisher, Norman, 1910-	PR6056.I795
Fisher, Stephen Gould, 1912-	PS3511.I7438
Fishman, Hal.	PS3556.I81455
Fiske, Dorsey.	PS3556.I81463
Fitt, Mary, 1897-1959.	PR6011.I787
Fitz, Jean DeWitt.	PS3556.I82
Fitzgerald, Arlene J.—see: Heath, Monica.	
Fitzgerald, Nigel, 1906-	PR6056.I856
Fitzgerald, Penelope.	PR6056.I86
Fitzgerald, Tom.	PS3556.I84
FitzGibbon, Constantine, 1919-	PR6011.I88
Fitzmaurice, Eugene.	PS3556.I87
Fitzpatrick, Janine.	none
Fitzsimmons, Cortland, 1893-1949.	none
Fitzsimons, Christopher.	PR6056.I916
Flagg, John.	none
Flagg, Jonas.	none
Flaherty, Joe.	PS3556.L28
Flannery, Sean.	none
Fleet, Charles.	none
Fleetwood, Hugh.	PR6056.L38
Fleischman, Sid.	none
Fleming, H. K. (Horace Kingston), 1901-	PS3511.L4417
Fleming, Ian, 1908-1964.	PR6056.L4
Fleming, Jane.	none
Fleming, Joan, 1908-	PR6011.L46
Fleming, May Agnes Early, 1840-1880.	none
Fleming, Nichol, 1939-	PR6056.L42
Fletcher, Aaron.	PR9639.3.F56
Fletcher, Adrian.	none
Fletcher, David, 1940-	PR6056.L43
Fletcher, Dorothy.	none
Fletcher, Frances.	none
Fletcher, Harry Lutf Verne, 1902-	none
Fletcher, Joseph Smith, 1863-1935.	PR6011.L5
Fletcher, Lucille.	PS3556.L424
Fletcher, Mary Mann.	none
Flett, Alfred.	PR9639.3.F57

Fliegel, Richard.	none
Flood, Charles Bracelen.	PS3556.L58
Flood, Robert J.	none
Flora, Fletcher, 1914-	none
Flores, Janis.	PS3556.L586
Flower, Pat.	PR9619.3.F54
Flowers, Charles.	PS3556.L6
Fluke, Joanne.	none
Flynn, Brian, 1885-	none
Flynn, Carol Houlihan, 1945-	PS3556.L78
Flynn, Don.	PS3556.L84
Flynn, J. M.	none
Flynn, Jay.	none
Fogarty, Michael, 1939-	PR6056.O3
Fogelson, Genia.	none
Fokker, Nicholas, 1908-	PS3556.O37
Foley, Helen.	PR6056.O4
Foley, Lorette.	none
Foley, Rae, 1900-	PS3511.O186
Follett, Edwina.	none
Follett, James, 1939-	PR6056.O44
Follett, Ken.	PR6056.O45
Fong, C. K.	none
Fontana, D. C.	PS3556.O48
Foote, Shelby.	PS3511.O348
Foote-Smith, Elizabeth.	PS3556.O63
Footman, Robert.	PS3556.O64
Footner, Hulbert, 1879-1944.	none
Foran, Phil.	none
Forbes, Bryan, 1926-	PR6056.O63
Forbes, Colin, 1923-	PR6069.A94
Forbes, Stanton, 1923-	PS3556.O67
Ford, Florence.	none
Ford, George.	none
Ford, Hilary—see: Christopher, John.	
Ford, Leslie—see: Brown, Zenith Jones, 1898-	
Forde, Nicholas.	none
Fores, John, 1916-	none
Forester, Bruce.	PS3556.O7249
Forester, C. S. (Cecil Scott), 1899-1966.	PR6011.O56
Forma, Warren.	PS3556.O7325
Forrest, David.	PR6056.O684
Forrest, Elizabeth.	none
Forrest, Richard, 1932-	PS3556.O739
Forrest, Wilma.	none
Forrest-Webb, Robert, 1929-	PR6056.O692

Forrester, Larry.	PR6056.O693
Forster, Margaret, 1938-	PR6056.O695
Forsyth, Frederick, 1938-	PR6056.O699
Forvé, Guy.	none
Foster, Iris—see: Posner, Richard.	
Foster, Reginald Francis, 1896-	none
Foster, Richard, 1910-	PS3505.R89224
Foster, Tony.	PR9199.3.F577
Fought, Catherine Anne.	PS3556.O78
Fountain, Nigel.	none
Fowler, Dennis.	none
Fowler, Sydney—see: Wright, Sydney Fowler, 1874-1967.	
Fowles, Anthony.	PR6056.O847
Fowlkes, Frank V., 1941-	PS3556.O873
Fox, Anthony.	PS3556.O877
Fox, Clayton.	PS3556.O8773
Fox, George.	PS3556.O88
Fox, James M., 1908-	PS3561.N55
Fox, Peter F.	PR6056.O865
Foxall, P. A.	PR6056.O875
Foxall, Raymond.	PR6056.O88
Foxx, Jack, 1943-	PS3566.R67
Foy, George.	PS3556.O99
Fraley, Oscar, 1914-	none
Francis, Dick.	PR6056.R27
Francis, Richard, 1945-	PR6056.R277
Frankau, Gilbert, 1884-	PR6011.R26
Frankau, Pamela, 1908-1967.	PR6011.R28
Frankel, Neville.	PS3556.R3355
Frankel, Sandor, 1943-	PS3556.R3356
Frankle, Judith.	none
Franklin, Charles, 1909-1976.	PR6071.S8
Franklin, Donald.	none
Franklin, Eugene.	PS3556.R337
Franklin, Harry.	none
Franklin, June.	none
Franklin, Keith.	none
Franklin, Max—see: Deming, Richard.	
Franklin, Steve.	PS3556.R34
Fraser, Anthea.	PR6056.R286
Fraser, Antonia, 1932-	PR6056.R2863
Fraser, Guy.	none
Fraser, James, 1924-	PR6073.H49
Fraser, Jean.	none
Fraser, John, 1932-	PR6056.R292
Frazee, Steve, 1909-	PS3556.R358

Frazer, Robert Caine—see: Creasey, John.	
Frede, Richard.	PS3556.R37
Fredericks, Harriet.	none
Frederics, Jocko.	none
Frederics, Macdowell—see: Frede, Richard.	
Fredman, John.	PR6056.R38
Fredman, Mike.	PR6056.R383
Freeborn, Brian.	PR6056.R394
Freeborn, Richard.	none
Freed, Donald.	PS3556.R383
Freeling, Nicholas.	PR6056.R4
Freeman, Barbara.	none
Freeman, Jayne.	none
Freeman, Lucy.	PS3556.R392
Freeman, R. Austin (Richard Austin), 1862-1943.	PR6011.R43
Freemantle, Brian.	PR6056.R43
Freivalds, John.	PS3556.R394
Fremlin, Celia.	PR6056.R45
French, Fergus.	none
French, Richard P.	PS3556.R43
Frey, Charles Weiser, 1910-	none
Frey, James N.—see: Washburn, Mark.	
Freytag, Joseph.	none
Freytag, Josephine.	none
Fried, Barbara.	none
Friedman, Bruce Jay, 1930-	PS3556.R5
Friedman, Hal.	PS3556.R52
Friedman, Kinky.	PS3556.R527
Friedman, Mickey.	PS3556.R53
Friedman, Philip, 1944-	PS3556.R545
Friedman, Roy.	PS3556.R56
Friedman, Stuart, 1913-	none
Friend, Oscar Jerome, 1897-	none
Frimmer, Steven.	PS3556.R5687
Frizell, Bernard.	PS3556.R59
Frome, David—see: Brown, Zenith Jones, 1898-	
Frost, G. H.	none
Frost, Jason.	none
Frost, Joan Van Every.	none
Fruchter, Norm, 1937-	PS3556.R77
Fruttero, Carlo.	PQ4866.R8
Fry, Peter, 1914-	PR6061.I44
Fuentes, Roberto.	none
Fuentos, Carlos.	PQ7297.F793
Fulford, Paul A.	none
Fulk, David.	none

Fuller, Dean.	PS3556.U38
Fuller, H. E.	none
Fuller, Jack.	PS3556.U44
Fuller, Peter.	none
Fuller, Roger—see: Tracy, Don, 1905-	
Fuller, Roy Broadbent, 1912-	PR6011.U55
Fuller, Samuel Michael, 1911-	PS3511.U6622
Fulton, E. G.	none
Furness, Audrey.	none
Furst, Alan.	PS3556.U76
Futrelle, Jacques, 1875-1912.	PS3511.U98
Fyhrlund, Eric.	none
Gaboriau, Émile, 1832-1873.	PQ2257.G2
Gadney, Reg, 1941-	PR6057.A294
Gaffney, Marguerite S.	PS3557.A29
Gage, Edwin.	PS3557.A326
Gage, Nicholas.	PS3557.A33
Gainham, Sarah.	PR6057.A34
Galbraith, Ruth.	none
Gall, Sandy, 1927-	PR6057.A386
Gallacher, Tom.	PR6057.A388
Gallagher, P. B.	none
Gallagher, Patricia.	none
Gallagher, Richard.	none
Gallagher, Stephen.	PR6057.A3893
Gallant, Gladys S.	PS3557.A41167
Gallico, Paul, 1897-	PS3513.A413
Gallie, Menna.	PR6057.A394
Gallon, Tom, 1866-1914.	none
Galloway, David D.	PS3557.A4155
Galway, Robert Conington.	none
Gandolfi, Simon.	none
Ganpat—see: Gompertz, Martin Louis Alan, 1886-	
Gant, Jonathan—see: Adams, Clifton.	
Gant, Norman F.	none
Gantzer, Hugh.	PR9499.3.G28
Garbo, Norman.	PS3557.A65
Garden, John—see: Fletcher, Harry Lutf Verne, 1902-	
Gardiner, Dorothy, 1894-	none
Gardiner, Judy, 1922-	PR6057.A627
Gardiner, Wayne J.	none
Gardner, Alan Harold.	none
Gardner, Craig Shaw.	none
Gardner, Erle Stanley, 1889-1970.	PS3513.A6322 [Z8324.15]
Gardner, John E.	PR6057.A63

Gardner, Lee.	none
Garfield, Brian, 1939-	PS3557.A715
Garfield, Leon.	PR6057.A636
Garforth, John.	none
Garland, Bob.	none
Garland, Nicholas—see: Katz, Herbert M.	
Garlington, Philip, 1943-	PS3557.A7163
Garner, Craig C.	none
Garner, David.	none
Garner, Hugh, 1913-	PR9199.3.G3
Garner, James.	none
Garner, William, 1920-	PR6057.A675
Garnet, A. H.	PS3557.A7167
Garnett, Bill.	PS3557.A7165 [sic]
Garrett, Randall.	PS3557.A7238
Garrett, Robert.	PS3557.A724
Garrison, Christian.	none
Garrison, Jim, 1921-	PS3557.A735
Garrity.	none
Garth, David, 1908-	none
Garth, Ed.	none
Garton, Ray.	none
Garve, Andrew, 1908-	PR6073.I56
Garvin, Richard M.	PS3557.A8
Gascar, Pierre, 1916-	PQ2613.A59
Gash, Joe.	PS3557.R256
Gash, Jonathan.	PR6057.A728
Gask, Arthur, 1872-	none
Gaskell, Jane, 1941-	PR6057.A73
Gaskin, Catherine.	PR6057.A75
Gast, Kelly P.	PS3557.A847
Gaston, Bill.	none
Gat, Dimitri V., 1936-	PS3557.A85
Gatenby, Rosemary.	PS3557.A86
Gates, Natalie.	PS3557.A88
Gates, Tudor.	PR6057.A8
Gattzden, Matt.	none
Gault, William Campbell.	PS3557.A948
Gavin, Bernard.	PR6057.A87
Gavin, Catherine Irvine.	PR6013.A83
Gay, Virginia.	PR6057.A97
Gayet, Caroline.	PQ2667.A98
Geary, Patricia.	PS3557.E23
Gebhard, H. Harris.	none
Geddes, Paul.	PR6057.E24
Gee, Maurice.	PR9639.3.G4

Gelb, Alan Lloyd.	none
Gelien, Modena.	PS3557.E378
Geller, Michael.	none
Geller, Stephen.	PS3557.E4
Gellis, Roberta.	PS3557.E42
George, Jonathan—see: Burke, John Frederick, 1922-	
George, Kara.	PS3557.E486
George, Peter, 1924-1966.	PR6057.E54
George, Sara.	PR6057.E55
George, Theodore.	PS3557.E5
Gerahty, Digby George.	PR6013.E68
Gérard, Francis, 1905-	none
Gerard, Morice—see: Teague, John Jessop, 1856-1929.	
Gerard, Ron L.—see: Renauld, Ron.	
Germeshausen, Anna Louise.	none
Geron, Frank.	none
Gerrity, Dave.	none
Gerrity, David J.—see: Gerrity, Dave.	
Gerson, Jack.	PR6057.E72
Gerson, Noel Bertram, 1914-	PS3513.E8679
Gethin, David.	PR6057.E76
Gettel, Ronald E., 1931-	PS3557.E86
Gheorghiu, Virgil, 1916-	PQ2667.H4
Giannetta, Sal.	PS3557.I134
Gibbon, Charles, 1843-1890.	none
Gibbons, Scott.	none
Gibbs, George F.	none
Gibbs, Henry.	PR6013.I254
Gibbs, Mary Ann.	PR6057.I234
Gibson, George.	none
Gibson, Miles.	PR6057.I28
Gibson, Walter Brown, 1897-	PS3513.I2823
Gibson-Jarvie, Clodagh.	PR6057.I3
Gielgud, Val Henry, 1900-	PR6013.I295
Gifford, Barry, 1946-	PS3557.I283
Gifford, Thomas.	PS3557.I284
Gilbert, Anna.	PR6057.I49
Gilbert, Anthony, 1899-	PR6025.A438
Gilbert, Harriett, 1948-	PR6057.I515
Gilbert, Michael A.	PR9199.3.G5244
Gilbert, Michael Francis, 1912-	PR6013.I3335
Gilbert, Stephen, 1912-	PR6013.I3363
Gilchrist, Andrew, Sir, 1910-	none
Gilchrist, Robert Murray, 1868-1917.	none
Giles, Kenneth.	PR6057.I53
Giles, Peter.	none

Giles, Raymond.	none
Gilford, C. B.	PS3557.I345
Gill, B. M.	PR6057.I538
Gill, Bartholomew, 1943-	PS3563.A296
Gill, John.	PR6057.I55
Giller, Norman.	none
Gillespie, Robert B.	PS3557.I3795
Gillette, Paul.	none
Gillette, Paul J.	PS3557.I385
Gillis, Jackson.	PS3557.I394
Gilman, Dorothy, 1923-	PS3557.I433
Gilman, J. D.	PR6057.I63
Gilman, James—see: Gilmore, Joseph L.	
Gilmer, J. Lance.	none
Gilmore, Christopher Cook.	PS3557.I458
Gilmore, Joseph L.	PS3557.I459
Gilmour, H. B. (Harriet B.), 1939-	PS3557.I462
Ginn, R. C. K.	none
Giovannetti, Alberto.	PQ4867.I6348
Gipe, George.	PS3557.I6
Girard, Bernard.	none
Giroux, E. X.—see: Shannon, Doris.	
Giroux, Leo.	PS3557.I73
Givens, John.	PS3557.I85
Glatzer, Hal.	none
Glazner, Joseph Mark.	none
Glemser, Bernard, 1908-	PS3513.L646
Glendinning, Ralph.	PS3557.L443
Gloag, John, 1896-	PR6013.L5
Gloag, Julian.	PR6057.L6
Gluck, Sinclair, 1887-	none
Gluckman, Janet, 1939-	PS3557.L8214
Glut, Donald F.	PS3557.L87
Gluyas, Constance, 1920-	PR6057.L87
Gober, Dom.	none
Goddard, Anthea.	PR6057.O28
Goddard, Harry.	none
Goddard, Kenneth W. (Kenneth William)	PS3557.O285
Godden, Jon, 1906-	PR6013.O18
Goddin, Jeffrey.	none
Godey, John, 1912-	PS3513.O155
Godfrey, Ellen.	PR9199.3.G593
Goff, Oliver.	none
Goines, Donald, 1937-1974.	none
Gold, Don.	PS3557.O327
Gold, Herbert, 1924-	PS3557.O34

Goldberg, Gerald Jay.	PS3557.O357
Goldberg, Marshall.	PS3557.O358
Goldfluss, Howard E.	PS3557.O363
Golding, Louis, 1895-1958.	PR6013.O3
Goldman, James.	PS3513.O337
Goldman, Lawrence.	PS3513.O338
Goldman, William, 1931-	PS3557.O384
Goldsborough, Robert.	PS3557.O3849
Goldsmith, John, 1947-	PR6057.O44
Goldstein, Arthur D.	PS3557.O388
Goldstein, William.	none
Goldthwaite, Eaton K.	PS3513.O355
Goller, Nicholas.	PR6057.O46
Gollin, James.	PS3557.O445
Gombrowicz, Witold.	PG7158.G669
Goodchild, George, 1888-	PR6013.O473
Goodfield, G. J. (G. June), 1927-	PR6057.O537
Gooding, Kathleen.	none
Goodis, David, 1917-1967.	PS3513.O499
Goodman, Jonathan.	PR6057.O55
Goodrich, David L.	PS3557.O588
Goodrum, Charles A.	PS3557.O59
Gordon, A. C.	none
Gordon, Diana.	PR6057.O65
Gordon, Donald—see: Cameron, Ian, 1924-	
Gordon, Ethel Edison.	PS3557.O655
Gordon, Giles, 1940-	PR6057.O67
Gordon, Gordon.	PS3557.O665
Gordon, John V.	none
Gordon, Mildred.	PS3557.O67
Gordon, Noah.	PS3557.O68
Gordon, Peter.	none
Gordon, Richard, 1921-	PR6057.O714
Gordon, Richard Laurence.	PR9199.3.G63
Gordons.	PS3557.O725
Gores, Joe, 1937-	PS3557.O75
Goring, Anne.	PS3557.O757
Gorman, Edward.	PS3557.O759
Goshgarian, Gary.	PS3557.O77
Gosling, Paula.	PR6057.O75
Gottlieb, Annie.	none
Gottlieb, Nathan.	none
Gottlieb, Paul, 1936-	PR9199.3.G6 [sic]
Goulart, Ron, 1933-	PS3557.O85
Gould, Chester.	none
Gould, Heywood.	PS3557.O86

Gover, Robert, 1929-	PS3557.O92
Goyne, Richard.	none
Grace, Alicia.	none
Grady, James, 1949-	PS3557.R122
Grae, Camarin.	PS3557.R125
Graeme, Bruce, 1900-	PR6019.E33
Graeme, Roderic, 1926-	PR6060.E43
Graff, Mab.	PS3557.R128
Grafton, C. W. (Cornelius Warren), 1909-	PS3513.R1457
Grafton, Sue.	PS3557.R13
Graham, Burton.	PR6013.R14
Graham, James—see: Higgins, Jack, 1929-	
Graham, John Alexander, 1941-	PS3557.R2
Graham, Neill—see: Duncan, William Murdoch, 1909-	
Graham, Robert—see: Haldeman, Joe W.	
Graham, Victoria.	PS3557.R224
Graham, Winston.	PR6013.R24
Grainger, Tom.	PR9199.3.G69
Gram, Dewey.	none
Granbeck, Marilyn.	none
Grandower, Elissa—see: Waugh, Hillary.	
Granger, Bill.	PS3557.R256
Grant, Ben—see: Granbeck, Marilyn.	
Grant, Charles L.	PS3557.R265
Grant, David—see: Thomas, Craig.	
Grant, James, 1933-	PR6057.R29
Grant, Maxwell.	PR9619.3.G654
Grant, Maxwell—see: Gibson, Walter Brown, 1897- or Arden, William, 1924-	
Grant, Roderick, 1941-	PR6057.R323
Grant-Adamson, Lesley.	PR6057.R324
Granville, Edgar.	none
Gratus, Jack.	none
Gravatt, Glenn G.	none
Graves, Evelyn.	none
Graves, Geoffrey.	none
Graves, Richard L.	PS3557.R289
Gray, Angela.	none
Gray, Berkeley—see: Brooks, Edwy Searles, 1889-	
Gray, Dulcie.	PR6013.R364
Gray, Linda Crockett.	none
Gray, Malcolm.	PR6069.T77
Gray, Nicholas Stuart.	PR6057.R327
Gray, Simon, 1936-	PR6057.R33
Grayson, Elizabeth.	none
Grayson, Richard.	PR6057.R55

Grayson, Rupert, 1897-	PR6013.R39
Grayson, Ruth.	none
Greatorex, Wilfred, 1921-	PR6057.R337
Greaves, Jimmy.	none
Greeley, Andrew M., 1928-	PS3557.R358
Green, Anna Katherine, 1846-1935.	PS2731-2732
Green, Edith Piñero.	PS3557.R367
Green, Evelyn Everett, 1856-1932.	none
Green, F. L. (Frederick Lawrence), 1902-1953.	PR6013.R414
Green, Gerald.	PS3513.R4493
Green, Janet.	none
Green, Julien, 1900-	PQ2613.R3
Green, Kate.	PS3557.R3729
Green, Maury.	none
Green, Thomas J.	PS3557.R3756
Green, William M., 1936-	PS3557.R3757
Greenan, Russell H.	PS3557.R376
Greenaway, Gladys.	none
Greenbaum, Leonard.	PS3557.R3765
Greenberg, Dave, 1943-	none
Greenburg, Dan.	PS3557.R379
Greene, Graham, 1904-	PR6013.R44
Greene, Harris.	PS3557.R38
Greene, L. Patrick.	none
Greenfield, Irving A.	PS3557.R3942
Greenfield, Richard Pierce.	none
Greenland, Francis.	none
Greenleaf, Stephen.	PS3557.R3957
Greenlee, Sam, 1930-	PS3557.R396
Greenwald, Nancy.	PS3557.R3967
Greenwood, John, 1921- —see: Hilton, John Buxton.	
Greenwood, L. B.	PS3557.R3975
Greer, Ben.	PS3557.R399
Greer, Woody.	none
Gregg, Cecil Freeman, 1898-	none
Gregory, Jackson, 1882-1943.	PS3513.R562
Gregory, James.	none
Greig, Maysie, 1902-	PS3513.R5772
Gresham, Elizabeth.	none
Gresham, Stephen.	none
Grex, Leo, 1908-	none
Grey, Anthony.	PR6057.R454
Grey, Naidra.	PR6057.R456
Gribble, Leonard R. (Leonard Reginald), 1908-	none
Grierson, Edward, 1914-1975.	PR6013.R72
Grierson, Francis Durham, 1888-	none

Griffin, Gerald G.	none
Griffin, John.	none
Griffin, Robert J.	none
Griffin, Samuel Franklin.	none
Griffith, George Chetwynd.	PR4728.G83
Griffiths, Arthur, 1838-1908.	PR4728.G84
Griffiths, Peter, 1944-	PR6057.R517
Grimes, Lee.	none
Grimes, Martha.	PS3557.R48998
Grimsey, Len.	none
Grimwood, Ken.	PS3557.R497
Grindal, Richard—see: Grayson, Richard.	
Grisman, Arnold.	PS3557.R536
Groom, Arthur John Pelham.	none
Gross, Shelly.	PS3557.R62
Gross, Tudor.	none
Grove, Marjorie.	none
Grubb, Davis, 1919-	PS3513.R865
Gruber, Frank, 1904-1969.	PS3513.R866
Gruber, Helmut, 1928-	PS3557.R78
Gruppe, Henry.	PS3557.R85
Guenter, C. H.	none
Guild, Nicholas.	PS3557.U357
Gulik, Robert Hans van, 1910-	PR6057.U45 [Z8375.3]
Gull, Cyril Arthur Edward Ranger, 1876-1923.	PR6013.U54
Gulliver, Hal, 1935-	PS3557.U45
Gulliver, Sam.	PR6057.U46
Guliashki, Andrei.	PG1037.G8
Gunn, James E., 1923-	PS3513.U797
Gunn, John.	none
Gunn, Victor—see: Brooks, Edwy Searles, 1889-	
Gunn, Virginia S.	PS3557.U487
Gunter, Archibald Clavering, 1847-1907.	PS1769.G27
Gunther, Max, 1927-	PS3557.U53
Gurr, David, 1936-	PR9199.3.G795
Guthrie, A. B. (Alfred Bertram), 1901-	PS3513.U855
Gutteridge, Lindsey, 1923-	PR6057.U84
Gwynne, P. N.	PS3557.W95
Haas, Ben.	PS3558.A17
Haas, Charlie.	PS3558.A173
Haas, Joseph, 1929-1971.	PS3558.A177
Habe, Hans, 1911-1977.	PT2615.A18
Habersham, Elizabeth.	none
Hacker, Shyrle.	none
Hackforth-Jones, Gilbert, 1900-	PR6015.A1534

Haddad, C. A.	PS3558.A3117
Hadley, J. B.	none
Hagan, Arthur P.	PS3558.A322
Hagberg, David.	none
Hagenbach, Keith.	PR6058.A365
Haggard, Raymond.	PR6058.A37
Haggard, William.	PR6053.L38
Haiblum, Isidore.	PS3558.A324
Haig, Alec.	PS3558.A326
Haig, Robert.	PR6058.A39
Haïm, Victor.	PQ2668.A36
Haining, Peter.	none
Haldeman, Joe W.	PS3558.A353
Haldimon, Madelaine.	none
Hale, Arlene.	PS3515.A262
Hale, Christopher.	none
Hale, Jennifer.	none
Hale, John.	PR6058.A438
Halegua, Lillian.	PS3558.A3572
Haligon, Richard.	none
Hall, Adam—see: Trevor, Elleston.	
Hall, Angus.	PR6058.A4447
Hall, Douglas, 1929-	PR9199.3.H317
Hall, F. H., 1926-	PS3558.A3666
Hall, Gimone.	none
Hall, Jenni.	none
Hall, Marjory, 1908-	none
Hall, Oakley M.	PS3558.A373
Hall, Parnell.	PS3558.A37327
Hall, Patrick, 1932-	PR6058.A47
Hall, Richard Walter.	PS3558.A3735
Hall, Robert Lee.	PS3558.A3739
Hall, Roger, 1919-	PS3558.A374
Hall, Steven.	PS3558.A375
Hallahan, William H.	PS3558.A378
Halleran, Tucker.	PS3558.A3795
Halley, Laurence.	none
Halliday, Brett, 1904-1977.	PS3507.R615
Halliday, Dorothy—see: Dunnett, Dorothy.	
Halliday, Fred, 1937-	PS3558.A385
Halliday, Michael—see: Creasey, John.	
Halls, Geraldine.	PR9619.3.H29
Hallums, James.	none
Halsey, Harlan Page, 1839?-1898.	PS1784.H24
Halstead, Thayer.	none
Hambly, Barbara.	PS3558.A4215

Hamill, Denis.	PS3558.A4217
Hamill, Desmond.	PR6058.A549
Hamill, Edson T.	none
Hamill, Pete, 1935-	PS3558.A423
Hamill, Stuart.	none
Hamilton, Adam.	none
Hamilton, Alex.	PR6058.A552
Hamilton, Alistair—see: Beattie, Tasman.	
Hamilton, Bruce, 1900-	PR6015.A425
Hamilton, Charles, 1875-1961.	PR6015.A43
Hamilton, Donald, 1916-	PS3515.A42514
Hamilton, Ian, 1935-	PR6058.A553
Hamilton, Jessica.	PS3558.A443
Hamilton, Michael.	none
Hamilton, Nan.	PS3558.A4434
Hamilton, Roger.	none
Hamman, Henry.	PS3558.A4475
Hammett, Dashiell, 1894-1961.	PS3515.A4347 [Z8385]
Hammil, Joel.	PS3558.A4488
Hammond, Gerald.	PR6058.A55456
Hammond, Marc.	none
Hampton, Jay.	none
Hampton, Ruth E.	none
Hancock, Sybil.	none
Handley, Alfred.	none
Hanley, Clifford.	PR6058.A58
Hanley, Elizabeth—see: DuBreuil, Linda.	
Hanley, William.	PS3558.A47
Hanna, David.	none
Hanna, Frances Nichols.	none
Hannah, Barry.	PS3558.A476
Hannon, Ezra—see: Hunter, Evan, 1926-	
Hansen, Joseph, 1923-	PS3558.A513
Hanshew, Thomas W., 1857-1914.	none
Hansl, Arthur.	PS3558.A51363
Hanson, Vic J.	none
Harbinson, W. A. (William Allen), 1941-	none
Harcourt, Palma.	PR6058.A62
Hardin, Robert.	PS3558.A62317
Harding, William Harry.	PS3558.A62344
Hardwick, Michael, 1924-	PR6058.A673
Hardwick, Mollie.	PR6058.A6732
Hardy, Robin.	PR6058.A6754
Hardy, Ronald.	PR6058.A676
Hardy, William M.	PS3558.A624

Hare, Cyril, 1900-	PR6005.L3115
Hargrave, Leonie.	PS3554.I8
Harington, Donald.	PS3558.A6242
Harkins, Sterling.	none
Harknett, Terry.	none
Harling, Robert.	PR6058.A6867
Harmon, Margaret.	none
Harper, David—see: Corley, Edwin.	
Harper, Lynette.	none
Harper, Richard.	none
Harper, Stephen.	PR6058.A6875
Harrington, Denis J.	none
Harrington, Joseph, 1903-	PS3558.A628
Harrington, Joyce.	PS3558.A6284
Harrington, R. E.	PS3558.A6295
Harrington, William, 1931-	PS3558.A63
Harris, Alfred, 1928-	PS3558.A633
Harris, Andrea.	none
Harris, Charlaine.	PS3558.A6427
Harris, Charlie Avery.	none
Harris, Evelyn.	PR6058.A6883
Harris, Herbert.	none
Harris, Hyde.	none
Harris, John, 1916-	PR6058.A6886
Harris, Leonard, 1929-	PS3558.A6467
Harris, MacDonald, 1921-	PS3558.E458
Harris, Marilyn, 1931-	PS3558.A648
Harris, Max F.	none
Harris, Randolph.	none
Harris, Richard, 1926-	PS3558.A653
Harris, Rosemary, 1923-	PR6058.A6915
Harris, Thomas, 1940-	PS3558.A6558
Harris, Timothy, 1946-	PS3558.A657
Harris, Walter.	PR6058.A6919
Harris-Burland, John Burland, 1870-1926.	PR6015.A6473
Harrison, Barbara.	none
Harrison, Chip.	PS3558.A665
Harrison, Harry.	PS3558.A667
Harrison, J. M., 1937-	PS3558.A67
Harrison, Joel.	none
Harrison, Michael.	PR6058.A694
Harrison, Ray.	PR6058.A69424
Harrison, William, 1933-	PS3558.A672
Harriss, Will.	PS3558.A673
Hart, Carolyn G.	PS3558.A676
Hart, Gary, 1936-	PS3558.A6776

Hart, Jon.	none
Hart, Norman Phillip.	none
Hart, Roy.	PR6058.A694857
Hart, Stan.	none
Hart, Ted.	PR6058.A69486
Hart, Tom.	none
Hart-Davis, Duff.	PR6058.A6949
Hartenfels, Jerome, 1934-	PR6058.A69494
Hartland, Michael.	PR6058.A69496
Hartley, Norman.	PR6058.A69497
Hartman, Dane.	none
Hartmann, Michael, 1944 July 24-	PR6058.A6955
Hartshorne—see: Blum, Richard H.	
Harvester, Simon—see: Gibbs, Henry.	
Harvey, John, 1938-	PR6058.A6989
Harwood, Ronald, 1934-	PR6058.A73
Hasluck, Alexandra, Lady.	PR6058.A75
Hasluck, Nicholas P.	PR9619.3.H337
Hastings, Beverly.	none
Hastings, Brook, pseud.	PS3515.A82868
Hastings, Macdonald.	PR6058.A79
Hastings, Michael, 1938 Jan. 30-	PR9510.9.B3
Hastings, Michael, 1938 Sept. 2-	PR6058.A816
Hastings, Phyllis, 1913-	PR6058.A82
Hatch, Denison.	PS3558.A73
Hathaway, Mavis—see: Avery, Ira, 1914-	
Hatton, Joseph, 1841-1907.	PR4759.H78
Haughey, Thomas Brace.	PS3558.A7565
Hauser, Thomas.	PS3558.A759
Hawke, Simon.	none
Hawkes, Ellen.	PS3558.A817
Hawkes, Robert.	PR9199.3.H365
Hawkey, Raymond.	PR6058.A886
Hawkins, Edward H.	PS3558.A823
Hawkins, Frank N.	none
Hawkins, Odie.	none
Hawthorne, Julian, 1846-1934.	PS1845-1848 [Z8392.9]
Hawthorne, Nathaniel, 1804-1864.	PS1850-1898 [Z8393]
Hawthorne, Violet.	PS3558.A824
Hawton, Hector, 1901-	none
Hay, Jacob.	PS3558.A826
Hay, Mary Cecil, 1840?-1886.	none
Hayes, Joseph Arnold, 1918-	PS3515.A942
Hayes, Mary-Rose.	PR6058.A982

94

Hayes, Ralph.	none
Hayes, Roy.	PS3558.A836
Hayles, Brian, 1931-	PR6058.A9853
Haymon, Mark.	none
Haymon, S. T.	PR6058.A9855
Haynes, Brian.	none
Haynes, Conrad.	none
Hays, Lee.	none
Haysom, Derrick.	none
Haythorne, John.	PS3558.A88
Hayward, David.	none
Hazo, Samuel John.	PS3515.A9877
Head, Lee.	PS3558.E15
Head, Matthew—see: Canaday, John, 1907-	
Heal, Anthony.	PR6058.E166
Heald, Tim.	PR6058.E167
Healey, Ben.	PS3558.E23
Healy, J. F. (Jeremiah F.), 1948-	PS3558.E2347
Heaps, Leo.	PS3558.E24
Heard, Nathan C.	PS3558.E25
Hearn, Daniel.	PS3558.E2545
Heath, Catherine.	PR6058.E217
Heath, Monica.	PS3558.E264
Heath, Roy A. K.	PR9320.9.H4
Heath, W. L. (William L.), 1924-	PS3558.E27
Heatter, Basil, 1918-	none
Heaven, Constance.	PR6058.E23
Hebden, Mark, 1916-	PR6058.A6886
Heberden, M. V. (Mary Violet), 1906-1965.	PR6015.E244
Hébert, Anne.	PQ3919.H37
Hecht, Ben, 1893-1964.	PS3515.E18
Heddon, James.	none
Hedges, Joseph—see: Harknett, Terry.	
Heffernan, William, 1940-	PS3558.E4143
Hegner, William.	PS3558.E42
Hehl, Eileen.	none
Heimer, Melvin Leighton, 1915-1971.	PS3558.E453
Heldman, Gladys.	PS3558.E474
Heley, Veronica.	none
Helgerson, Joel.	none
Heller, Keith.	PS3558.E47614
Helm, Eric.	none
Helwig, David, 1938-	PR9199.3.H445
Hemingway, Joan.	none
Hemyng, Bracebridge, 1841-1901.	none
Henaghan, Jim—see: O'Neill, Archie.	

Henderson, James, 1934-	PR6058.E4927
Henderson, Laurence.	PR6058.E493
Henderson, M. R.	PS3558.E487
Hendryx, James Beardsley, 1880-	PS3515.E5
Henege, Thomas.	PS3558.E4954
Henissart, Paul.	PS3558.E4958
Henkin, Harmon.	PS3558.E4959
Henle, Theda O.	PS3558.E496
Henn, Henry.	none
Henrick, Richard P.	none
Henry, O., 1862-1910.	PS2649.P5
Hensley, Joe L., 1926-	PS3558.E55
Henstell, Diana.	none
Hentoff, Nat.	PS3558.E575
Herbert, Ivor, 1925-	PR6058.E6
Herbert, James, 1943-	PR6058.E62
Herbert, Nan.	none
Herbrand, Jan.	none
Herlin, Hans, 1925-	PT2668.E748
Herman, J. B.	none
Heron, James.	none
Herrick, Marian J.	none
Herring, Peter C.	none
Herron, Shaun.	PR6058.E68
Hersey, John, 1914-	PS3515.E7715
Hershatter, Richard L.	none
Hershman, Morris, 1926-	PS3558.E78
Herst, Roger.	PS3558.E793
Hervey, Evelyn—see: Keating, H. R. F. (Henry Reymond Fitzwalter), 1926-	
Hervey, Michael.	none
Herzog, Arthur.	PS3558.E796
Hesky, Olga.	PR6058.E69
Hesla, Stephen.	PS3558.E7965
Hess, Joan.	PS3558.E79785
Hess, Kamelle.	none
Hewens, Frank E.	none
Heyer, Georgette, 1902-1974.	PR6015.E795 [Z8402.4]
Heyman, Evan Lee.	none
Hiaasen, Carl.	PS3558.I217
Hichens, Robert Smythe, 1864-1950.	PR6015.I4
Hickman, Hal.	PR9369.3.H55
Higgins, George V., 1939-	PS3558.I356
Higgins, Jack, 1929-	PR6058.I343
Higgins, Joan.	PS3558.I3573

Higgins, Margaret.	none
Higgs, Eric C.	PS3558.I3623
High, Bernard G.	none
Highland, Dora—see: Avallone, Michael.	
Highsmith, Patricia, 1921-	PS3558.I366
Higman, Dennis J.	none
Hilaire, Frank.	PS3558.I38
Hilary, Richard.	none
Hild, Jack.	none
Hildick, E. W. (Edmund Wallace), 1925-	PR6058.I37
Hill, Albert Fay.	none
Hill, Archie.	PR6058.I376
Hill, Christopher, fl. 1974-	PR6058.I38
Hill, David Campbell.	PS3558.I3855
Hill, Headon—see: Grainger, Francis Edward, 1857-1927.	
Hill, Pamela.	PR6058.I446
Hill, Peter, fl. 1976-	PR6058.I4465
Hill, R. Lance.	PR9199.3.H48
Hill, Reginald.	PR6058.I448
Hill, Susan, 1942-	PR6058.I45
Hilldrup, Robert P., 1933-	none
Hillerman, Tony.	PS3558.I45
Hilliard, Maurice, 1931-	PR6058.I455
Hillstrom, Tom.	PS3558.I4535
Hilton, Christopher.	none
Hilton, James, 1900-1954.	PR6015.I53
Hilton, John Buxton.	PR6058.I5
Himes, Chester B., 1909-	PS3515.I713
Himmel, Richard.	PS3515.I7147
Hinde, Thomas, 1926-	PR6058.I524
Hine, Al.	PS3558.I48
Hines, Jeanne.	PS3558.I527
Hinkel, M. L.	none
Hinkemeyer, Michael T.	PS3558.I54
Hinkle, Vernon.	PS3558.I5445
Hintze, Naomi A.	PS3558.I55
Hinxman, Margaret.	PR6058.I537
Hirschberg, Cornelius.	PS3558.I665
Hirschfeld, Burt, 1923-	PS3558.I67
Hirschhorn, Richard Clark.	PS3558.I675
Hirt, Howard.	PS3558.I73
Hitchcock, Alfred, 1899-	none [Z8408.8]
Hitchcock, Raymond.	PR6058.I7
Hitchens, Dolores Birk, 1907-1972.	PS3515.I955
Hitt, Frisco.	PT2668.I8

Hjortsberg, William, 1941-	PS3558.J6
Hobhouse, Christina, 1941-	PR6058.O18
Hobson, Polly.	PR6058.O24
Hoch, Edward D., 1930-	PS3558.O337
Hochstein, Peter.	none
Hocking, Anne—see: Messer, Mona Naomi Anne Hocking.	
Hocking, Mary.	PR6058.O26
Hodder-Williams, Christopher, 1926-	PR6058.O267
Hoddinott, Derek.	PR6015.O146
Hodel, Michael P.	PS3558.O3419
Hodge, Jane Aiken.	PS3558.O342
Hodgson, William Hope, 1877-1918.	PR6015.O253
Hoffenberg, Jack.	PS3558.O3445
Hoffman, Louise.	PS3558.O3462
Hoffman, William, 1925-	PS3558.O3464
Hogan, James P.	PR6058.O348
Hogan, Robert J.	PS3515.O2469
Hogg, Gil.	PR9639.3.H6
Høgstrand, Olle E., 1933-	PT9876.18.O327
Hoklin, Lonn.	none
Holden, Anne.	PR6058.O426
Holding, Elisabeth Sanxay, 1889-	none
Holicker, Charlotte.	none
Holland, Isabelle.	PS3558.O3485
Holland, Norman.	PR6015.O38
Holland, Rebecca.	none
Holland, Robert—see: Katz, Robert, 1933-	
Holland, Sheila.	none
Holles, Robert, 1926-	PR6058.O446
Holly, Joan Hunter.	none
Holme, Timothy.	PR6058.O45355
Holmes, Beth.	PS3558.O358
Holmes, H. H.—see: Boucher, Anthony, 1911-1968.	
Holt, Gavin.	none
Holt, Glenn.	none
Holt, Henry.	none
Holt, Robert Lawrence.	PS3562.A18
Holt, Samuel.	PS3558.O42
Holt, Victoria—see: Plaidy, Jean, 1906-	
Holt, Will.	none
Holt-White, William Edward Bradden, 1878-	PR6015.O48
Holton, Leonard—see: Wibberley, Leonard, 1915-	
Holzer, Hans, 1920-	none
Homer, Joel.	none
Homes, Geoffrey—see: Mainwaring, Daniel, 1902-	
Homewood, Harry.	PS3558.O45

Hone, Joseph, 1937-	PR6058.O49
Honeycombe, Gordon.	PR6058.O5
Honig, Donald.	PS3558.O5
Hood, Christopher.	PR6058.O536
Hood, William, 1920-	PS3558.O545
Hopkins, Kenneth.	PR6015.O62
Hopkins, Robert S.	PS3558.O636
Hopley, George, 1903-1968.	PS3515.O6455
Hoppe, Joanne.	none
Hopwood, Jim.	none
Horan, Don.	none
Horan, James David, 1914-	PS3558.O65
Horler, Sydney, 1888-1954.	PR6015.O66
Horne, Geoffrey, 1916-	PR6015.O6824
Hornig, Doug.	PS3558.O68785
Hornsby, Wendy.	PS3558.O689
Hornung, E. W. (Ernest William), 1866-1921.	PR6015.O687
Horrock, Nicholas.	none
Horst, Joel.	none
Horstman, Thomas.	none
Horton, John.	none
Horváth, Ödön von, 1901-1938.	PT2615.O865
Horvitz, Leslie.	none
Hosegood, Lewis, 1920-	PR6058.O7197
Hosken, Clifford James Wheeler, 1882-	none
Hoskins, Robert, 1933-	PS3558.O76
Hossent, Harry.	none
Hotchner, A. E.	PS3558.O8
Hougan, Carolyn.	PS3558.O835
Hough, Charlotte Woodyatt, 1924-	PR6058.O79
Hough, John T.	PS3558.O84
Hough, S. B. (Stanley Bennett), 1917-	PR6058.O83
Houghton, Claude—see: Oldfield, Claude Houghton, 1889-	
Household, Geoffrey, 1900-	PR6015.O7885
Houston, David, 1938-	none
Houston, James D.	PS3558.O87
Houston, Margaret Bell.	PS3515.O79
Houston, Robert, 1940-	PS3558.O873
Howard, Clark.	PS3558.O877
Howard, Colin—see: Shaw, Howard.	
Howard, Hartley—see: Ognall, Leopold Horace.	
Howard, James A.	none
Howard, Lesley.	PS3558.O882
Howard, Linden.	PR6058.O884
Howatch, Susan.	PS3558.O884
Howe, J. M.	none

Howe, James.	none
Howell, Jean.	none
Howell, Patricia Hagan.	none
Howlett, John, 1940-	PR6058.O96
Hoyle, Fred, Sir.	PR6058.O98
Hoyle, Geoffrey.	none
Hoyle, Trevor.	PR6058.O99
Hoyt, Edwin Palmer.	PS3558.O97
Hoyt, Richard, 1941-	PS3558.O975
Hrabal, Bohumil, 1914-	PG5039.18.R2
Hubbard, P. M. (Philip Maitland), 1910-	PR6058.U2
Hubbard, Regina—see: Hubbard, Richard.	
Hubbard, Richard.	none
Huber, Frederic Vincent, 1944-	PS3558.U237
Hubert, Tord, 1933-	PT9876.18.U2
Hudson, Christopher.	PR6058.U313
Hudson, John Paul.	none
Huebner, Fredrick D.	none
Huff, Afton.	none
Huff, T. E.	PS3558.U323
Huffman, Laurie.	PS3558.U34
Hufford, Susan.	PS3558.U343
Huggett, William Turner.	PS3558.U345
Hughes, Dorothy Belle Flanagan, 1904-	PS3515.U268
Hughes, Michael.	none
Hughes, Richard E.	PS3558.U388
Hughes, Rodney.	none
Hughes, Terry.	PR6058.U38
Hughes, William.	none
Hugill, Robert.	none
Hugo, Richard, 1947-	PS3558.U396
Hull, Richard, 1896-1973.	PR6015.U43
Hume, David.	none
Hume, Fergus, 1859-1932.	PR9639.2.H84
Humes, Larry R.	none
Humphreys, James.	none
Humphreys, Joel Don.	PS3558.U4654
Hunt, Charlotte.	none
Hunt, E. Howard (Everette Howard), 1918-	PS3515.U5425
Hunter, Alan.	PR6015.U565
Hunter, Evan, 1926-	PS3515.U585
Hunter, Jack D.	PS3558.U48
Hunter, Stephen, 1946-	PS3558.U494
Hunvald, Henry.	PS3558.U53
Hurd, Douglas, 1930-	PR6058.U7
Hurd, Florence.	PS3558.U532

Hurst, Heather Smith.	none
Hurst, Kathryn.	none
Hurt, Freda.	none
Hurwood, Bernhardt J.	none
Huson, Paul.	none
Huston, Fran.	PS3558.U78
Hutchinson, Mary Jane.	none
Hutson, Shaun.	none
Hutter, A. D.	none
Hutton, John, 1928-	PR6058.U859
Hutton, Malcolm.	PR6058.U8598
Huxley, Elspeth Jocelyn Grant, 1907-	PR6015.U92
Hyams, Edward, 1910-1975.	PR6015.Y33
Hyams, Joe.	PS3558.Y33
Hyatt, Betty Hale.	PS3558.Y337
Hyde, Anthony.	PS3558.Y35
Hyde, Christopher.	PS3558.Y36
Hyde, Eleanor.	PR6058.Y4
Hyland, Henry Stanley.	PR6058.Y6
Hylton, Sara.	PR6058.Y63
Hyman, Ann.	PS3558.Y46
Hynd, Noel.	PS3558.Y54
Hyne, Charles John Cutcliffe Wright, 1865-1944.	PR6015.Y6
Iams, Jack, 1910-	none
Iannuzzi, John Nicholas, 1935-	PS3559.A55
Ibargüengoitia, Jorge, 1928-	PQ7298.19.B3
Iles, Francis—see Berkeley, Anthony, 1893-1971.	
Inchbald, Peter.	PR6059.N3
Ind, Allison, 1903-	PS3517.N2
Ing, Dean.	PS3559.N37
Ingate, Mary.	PR6059.N47
Ingersol, Jared—see: Paine, Lauran.	
Ingham, Daniel.	PR6059.N516
Ingham, Richard, 1935-	PR6059.N52
Ingram, Grace.	PR6059.N54
Innes, Hammond, 1913-	PR6017.N79
Innes, Michael, 1906-	PR6037.T466
Innocenzi, Paul Claude.	PQ2669.N63
Ions, Edmund S.	PR6059.O5
Iraldi, James C.	none
Ireland, David, 1927-	PR9619.3.I674
Irish, William, 1903-1968.	PS3515.O6455
Ironside, Elizabeth.	none
Irvine, Patricia McCune.	none
Irvine, R. R. (Robert R.)	PS3559.R65
Irving, Clifford.	PS3559.R79

Irving, Clive.	PR6059.R914
Irving-James, Thomas—see: James, Thomas Irving.	
Irwin, Frances.	PR6059.R92
Irwin, Inez Haynes, 1873-1970.	PS3517.R864
Irwin, Wallace, 1876-1959.	PS3517.R87
Isaacs, Susan, 1943-	PS3559.S15
Isely, Reymoure Keith.	PR9199.3.I8
Israel, Peter, fl. 1967-	PS3559.S74
Ives, John.	PS3559.V44
Jack, Jeremiah.	none
Jackman, Stuart Brooke, 1922-	PR6019.A18
Jacks, Oliver—see: Royce, Kenneth.	
Jackson, Basil, 1920-	PR9199.3.J37
Jackson, Blyden.	PS3560.A18
Jackson, Bruce.	PS3560.A212
Jackson, Clarence L.—see: Bulliet, Richard W.	
Jackson, Eileen.	PR6060.A226
Jackson, Everatt.	none
Jackson, James O.	PS3560.A2157
Jackson, Jon A.	PS3560.A216
Jackson, Ken.	PS3560.A22
Jackson, Olive.	PS3560.A2416
Jackson, Shirley, 1920-1965.	PS3519.A392
Jacobs, Nancy Baker.	none
Jacobs, T. C. H. (Thomas Curtis Hicks), 1899-1976.	none
Jacquemard-Sénécal.	PQ2670.A249
Jaffe, Susanne.	PS3560.A316
Jaffee, Irving.	none
Jaffee, Mary.	none
Jagoda, Robert.	PS3560.A34
Jahn, Mike.	PS3560.A35
Jakes, John, 1932-	PS3560.A37
James, Donald, 1931-	PR6060.A453
James, Leigh, 1918-	PS3560.A395
James, Margaret—see: Bennetts, Pamela.	
James, P. D.	PR6060.A467
James, Rebecca—see: Elward, James.	
James, Robert.	none
James, Susan.	none
James, Thomas Irving.	none
Jamison, Amelia.	none
Jance, Judith A.	none
Janes, J. Robert (Joseph Robert), 1935-	none
Janeshutz, Trish.	none
Janeway, Harriet.	none
Janifer, Laurence M.	PS3560.A52

Jansson, Robert.	none
Japrisot, Sébastien, 1931-	PQ2678.O72
Jarvis, Edward.	PS3560.A6
Jarvis, Fred G.	PS3560.A63
Jarvis, Suzan.	none
Jason, Stuart.	none
Jaunière, Claudette.	none
Javits, Hank.	none
Jay, Charlotte—see: Halls, Geraldine.	
Jay, Simon.	none
Jefferis, Barbara.	PR9619.3.J4
Jeffers, H. Paul (Harry Paul), 1934-	PS3560.E36
Jefferson, Paul.	PS3560.E4
Jeffery, Ransom.	PS3560.E42
Jeffreys, J. G.	PS3560.E45
Jeffries, Roderic.	PR6060.E43
Jenkins, Geoffrey, 1920-	PR9369.3.J38
Jenkins, Jerry B.	PS3560.E485
Jenkins, Will, 1896-	PS3519.E648
Jennifer, Susan—see: Hoskins, Robert, 1933-	
Jensen, Ruby Jean.	none
Jenson, Martin.	none
Jepson, Edgar, 1863-1938.	PR6019.E55
Jepson, Selwyn, 1899-	PR6060.E6
Jerome, Owen Fox—see: Friend, Oscar Jerome, 1897-	
Jesmer, Elaine, 1939-	PS3560.E77
Jessup, Richard.	PS3560.E8
Jeter, K. W.	PS3560.E85
Jevons, Marshall.	PS3560.E88
Jewell, Derek.	PR6060.E94
Jobson, Hamilton.	PR6060.O22
Joensuu, Matti Yrjänä, 1948-	PH355.J553
Joey.	none
John, Hendrix.	PS3560.O32
John, Katherine, d. 1984.	none
John, Owen, 1918-	PR6060.O24
John, Romilly.	PR6019.O39135
Johns, Derek, 1948-	PR6060.O26
Johns, Larry.	none
Johns, W E. (William Earl), 1893-1968.	PR6019.O3914
Johnson, B. B.	PS3560.O3715
Johnson, Diane.	PS3560.O3746
Johnson, E. Richard, 1937-	PS3560.O376
Johnson, James Leonard, 1927-	PS3560.O379
Johnson, Ken, 1942-	PS3560.O3796
Johnson, Mendal W.	PS3560.O3817

Johnson, Sandy.	PS3560.O38635
Johnson, Stanley, 1940-	PR6060.O37
Johnson, William Oscar.	none
Johnston, Clint.	none
Johnston, Jane, 1927-	PS3560.O3893
Johnston, Norma.	PS3560.O3897
Johnston, Ronald, 1926-	PR6060.O43
Johnston, Velda.	PS3560.O394
Johnston, William, 1924-	PS3560.O395
Johnstone, William W.	none
Jon, Montague.	PR6060.O45
Jones, Brian.	none
Jones, Cleo.	PS3560.O465
Jones, Craig.	PS3560.O466
Jones, Dennis, 1945-	PR9199.3.J6276
Jones, Elwyn.	PR6060.O512
Jones, Frank, 1937-	none
Jones, James, 1921-1977.	PS3560.O49
Jones, John Handel.	none
Jones, L. Q.	none
Jones, Madison, 1925-	PS3560.O517
Jones, Mervyn.	PR6060.O56
Jones, Philip M., 1919-	none
Jones, Robert Gerallt.	PB2298.J6142
Jones, Robert Page.	none
Jones, Terry, 1942-	none
Jones, Tristan, 1924-	PR6060.O59
Jones, Victor, 1919-	PR6060.O6
Jontos, Richard.	none
Jopson, Marion.	PR6060.O62
Jordan, Cathleen.	PS3560.O68
Jordan, David.	PR6060.O624
Jordan, Keeling.	PS3560.O74
Joseph, Alan.	none
Joseph, George, 1912 Sept. 19-	PR6060.O634
Joseph, Marie.	PR6060.O636
Joseph, Mark.	PS3560.O776
Joshe, O. K.	PR9499.3.J598
Jost, John.	none
Journet, Terence.	PR6060.O9
Joyce, Cyril.	none
Joyce, T. Robert.	none
Judson, William.	PS3560.U4
Jute, André, 1945-	PR9369.3.J84
Kahn, James.	PS3561.A37
Kahn, Roger.	PS3561.A39

Kahn, Steve.	none
Kail, Robert.	none
Kains, Josephine—see: Goulart, Ron, 1933-	
Kaiser, Ronn.	none
Kalb, Bernard.	PS3561.A41628
Kalb, Marvin L.	PS3561.A4163
Kalish, Robert.	none
Kallen, Lucille.	PS3561.A41662
Kamarck, Lawrence.	PS3561.A417
Kaminsky, Stuart M.	PS3561.A43
Kamitses, Zoë.	PS3561.A434
Kamm, Dorinda.	none
Kane, Abel.	none
Kane, Frank, 1912-1968.	none
Kane, Henry.	PS3521.A4347
Kane, Mark.	none
Kantner, Rob.	none
Kantor, Hal.	PS3561.A48
Kantor, Harry—see: Kantor, Hal.	
Kaplan, Andrew.	PS3561.A545
Kaplan, Arthur.	PS3561.A547
Kaplan, Barry Jay, 1943-	none
Kaplan, Howard, 1950-	PS3561.A558
Karman, Mal.	none
Karney, Jack.	none
Karp, David, 1922-	none
Karr, Lee.	none
Karta, Nat—see: Norwood, Victor George Charles.	
Kartun, Derek.	PR6061.A78
Kassak, Fred.	PQ2671.A78
Kastle, Herbert D.	PS3561.A7
Katcher, Leo.	PS3561.A73
Katkov, Norman.	PS3521.A654
Kato, Arei.	none
Katz, Herbert M.	PS3561.A754
Katz, Michael J., 1951-	PS3561.A772
Katz, Robert, 1933-	PS3561.A773
Katz, William, 1940-	PS3561.A777
Katzenbach, John.	PS3561.A7778
Kauffman, Reginald Wright, 1877-1959.	PS3521.A725
Kauffmann, Lane, 1921-	PS3561.A824
Kaufman, Michael.	PS3561.A8614
Kaufman, Michael T.	none
Kaufman, Pamela.	PS3561.A8617
Kavanagh, Dan, 1946-	PR6061.A898
Kavanagh, Paul—see: Block, Lawrence.	

Kay, George.	none
Kay, Kenneth.	none
Kaye, H. R.	none
Kaye, M. M. (Mary Margaret), 1911-	PR6061.A945
Kaye, Marvin.	PS3561.A886
Keane, Christopher.	PS3561.E23
Kearey, Charles, 1916-	PR6061.E215
Keating, H. R. F. (Henry Reymond Fitzwalter), 1926-	PR6061.E26
Keating, Henry.	none
Keckhut, John.	PS3561.E253
Keeble, John, 1944-	PS3561.E3
Keech, Scott.	PS3561.E333
Keegan, William.	PR6061.E33
Keeler, Harry Stephen, 1890-	none
Keeley, Edmund.	PS3561.E34
Keenan, James.	none
Keene, Carolyn.	none
Keene, Day.	PS3561.E37
Keene, Joseph E.	none
Keene, Tom.	PR6061.E42
Keener, Joyce.	none
Keifetz, Norman.	PS3561.E3753
Keinzley, Frances.	PR6061.E45
Keitges, Julie.	none
Keith, Carlton—see: Robertson, Keith, 1914-	
Kelland, Clarence Budington, 1881-1964.	PS3521.E3524
Kelleher, Ed.	none
Keller, Beverly.	PS3561.E385
Kellerman, Faye.	PS3561.E3864
Kellerman, Jonathan.	PS3561.E3865
Kelley, James.	none
Kelley, Lamar.	none
Kelley, Leo P.	PS3561.E388
Kelley, Patrick A.	none
Kelley, William, 1929-	PS3561.E39
Kelly, Bill.	none
Kelly, George.	none
Kelly, John, 1921-	PS3561.E3944
Kelly, Mary, 1927-	PR6061.E495
Kelly, Nora.	PS3561.E3947
Kelly, Patrick—see: Allbeury, Ted.	
Kelly, Rod.	none
Kelly, Susan.	PS3561.E39715
Kelly, Terence, 1920-	PR6061.E497
Kelly, Tim J.	PS3521.E43225
Kelman, Judith.	none

Kelton, Elmer.	PS3563.A2932
Kemal, Yashar.	none
Kemelman, Harry.	PS3561.E398
Kemp, Sarah—see: Butterworth, Michael, 1924-	
Kempley, Walter.	PS3561.E422
Kendall, David, 1940-	PR9199.3.K4176
Kendrick, Baynard Hardwick, 1894-	none
Keneally, Thomas.	PR9619.3.K46
Kennealy, G. P.	none
Kennealy, Jerry.	PS3561.E4246
Kennedy, Adam.	PS3561.E425
Kennedy, Elliot.	PS3561.E4255
Kennedy, Milward—see: Burge, Milward Rodon Kennedy, 1894-	
Kennedy, Nancy.	none
Kennedy, William, 1928-	PS3561.E428
Kennedy, William P.	PS3561.E429
Kenney, Susan, 1941-	PS3561.E445
Kenny, Paul.	PQ2671.E58
Kenrick, Douglas.	none
Kenrick, Tony, 1935-	PR9619.3.K49
Kent, Fortune.	PS3561.E517
Kent, Graeme.	PR6061.E635
Kent, Paul.	none
Kenyon, Michael.	PR6061.E675
Kernahan, Coulson, 1858-1943.	none
Kerr, Carole.	none
Kerr, James, 1923-	PS3561.E64
Kerr, M. E.	PS3561.E643
Kerr, Michael.	PR6061.E78
Kerr, Michael—see: Hoskins, Robert, 1933-	
Kerr, Robert, 1899-	PS3561.E646
Kerrigan, John.	none
Kerrigan, Philip, 1959-	PR6061.E794
Kersh, Gerald, 1911-1968.	PR6021.E743
Kershaw, John.	PR6061.E84
Ketchum, Jack.	none
Keverne, Richard—see: Hosken, Clifford James Wheeler, 1882-	
Key, Sean A.	none
Keyes, Edward.	PS3561.E7694
Keyes, Frances Parkinson, 1885-1970.	PS3521.E86
Kezer, Glenn.	none
Kidde, Janet.	none
Kiefer, Warren, 1929-	PS3561.I34
Kienzle, William X.	PS3561.I35
Kilgore, Axel.	none
Kilian, Michael, 1939-	PS3561.I368

Killick, Brian, 1928-	PR6061.I36
Killoran, Geraldine.	none
Killough, Lee.	none
Kilpatrick, Sarah.	PR6061.I37
Kim, Don'o.	PR9619.3.K53
Kimbro, Jean, 1929-	PS3561.I417
Kimbro, John M., 1929-	PS3561.I417
Kimbrough, Katheryn, 1929-	PS3561.I417
Kinder, Kathleen.	PR6061.I434
King, Alison.	none
King, Charles Daly, 1895-1963.	PS3521.I514
King, Christopher.	none
King, Francis Henry.	PR6061.I45
King, Frank, 1892-	none
King, Frank, 1936-	PS3561.I4755
King, Graham, 1930-	PR9619.3.K54
King, Harold, 1945 Feb. 27-	PS3561.I476
King, Irene, 1943-	PS3561.I478
King, Rufus, 1893-1966.	PS3521.I5425
King, Sara.	none
King, Stephen, 1947-	PS3561.I483
King, Tabitha.	PS3561.I4835
King, Terry Johnson.	PR6061.I48
Kingsbury, Myra.	none
Kingsley, Bettina—see: Kaplan, Barry Jay, 1943-	
Kingsley, Gerry.	none
Kingsley, Michael J.	PS3561.I49
Kingsley-Smith, Terence.	none
Kinsley, Peter.	none
Kirk, Lydia.	PS3561.I687
Kirk, Michael, 1928-	PR6061.N6
Kirk, Philip.	none
Kirk, Russell.	PS3521.I665
Kirkbride, Ronald de Levington, 1912-	PS3521.I696
Kirkwood, James.	PS3561.I72
Kirkwood, Thomas.	PS3561.I74
Kirsch, Jonathan.	none
Kirst, Hans Helmut, 1914-	PT2621.I76
Kistler, Mary.	PS3561.I82
Kitchin, C. H. B. (Clifford Henry Benn), 1895-1967.	PR6021.I7
Kittredge, Mary, 1949-	PS3561.I868
Klainer, Albert S.	none
Klainer, Jo-Ann.	PS3561.L15
Klasne, William, 1933-	PS3561.L245
Klausner, Lawrence D.	PS3561.L332
Klawans, Harold L.	PS3561.L336

Klein, Dave.	none
Klinger, Henry.	PS3561.L5
Klop, Thomas.	PS3561.L635
Klose, Kevin.	PS3561.L65
Knapp, Gregory Cromwell.	PS3561.N3
Knebel, Fletcher.	PS3561.N4
Knickmeyer, Steve, 1944-	PS3561.N425
Knight, Adam—see: Lariar, Lawrence, 1908-	
Knight, Alanna.	PR6061.N45
Knight, Clifford, 1886-	PS3521.N5335
Knight, Eric Mowbray, 1897-1943.	PR6021.N417
Knight, Kathleen Moore.	none
Knight, Kathryn Lasky.	PS3561.N485
Knight, Leonard Alfred, 1895-	none
Knight, Stephen.	PR6061.N53
Knight, William E.	PS3561.N53
Knipe, J. A.	none
Knister, Barry.	none
Knowler, John, 1932-	PR6061.N55
Knowlton, Edward Rogers.	none
Knox, Alexander.	PR9199.3.K58
Knox, Bill, 1928-	PR6061.N6
Knox, Oliver.	PR6061.N63
Knox, Ronald Arbuthnott, 1888-1957.	PR6021.N6
Kobryn, A. P.	PS3561.O24
Koch, C. J. (Christopher J.), 1932-	PR9619.3.K64
Koch, Eric, 1919-	PR9199.3.K6
Koenig, Joseph.	PS3561.O3345
Koenig, Laird.	PS3561.O335
Koestler, Arthur, 1905-	PR6021.O4
Kolarz, Henry, 1927-	PT2671.O38
Kolb, Ken.	PS3561.O39
Koning, Hans, 1921-	PS3561.O46
Konrad, James.	none
Konvitz, Jeffrey.	PS3561.O53
Koontz, Dean R. (Dean Ray), 1945-	PS3561.O55
Koperwas, Sam.	PS3561.O64
Korman, Keith.	PS3561.O66
Kornbluth, C. M. (Cyril M.), 1924-1958.	PS3561.O67
Korotkin, Judith.	none
Kosinski, Jerzy N., 1933-	PS3561.O8
Kosner, Alice.	none
Kotzwinkle, William.	PS3561.O85
Kowet, Don.	none
Kozhevnikov, Vadim Mikhailovich, 1909-	PG3476.K67
Kozloff, Charles.	PS3561.O9

Kraft, Gabrielle.	none
Kranes, David.	none
Krasner, William, 1917-	PS3561.R283
Krause, Kathalyn.	none
Krentz, Jayne Ann.	none
Krepps, Robert W., 1919-	PS3521.R527
Kroetsch, Robert, 1927-	PR9199.3.K7
Kroll, Steven.	none
Krone, Chester.	none
Kropp, Lloyd.	PS3561.R6
Krüger, Hardy, 1928-	PT2671.R725
Kruger, Paul—see: Sebentall, R. E.	
Kruger, Rayne, 1922-	none
Kuhns, William.	PS3561.U43
Kullar, A.	none
Kummer, Frederic Arnold, 1873-1943.	PS3521.U65
Kuniczak, W. S., 1930-	PS3561.U5
Kurland, Michael.	PS3561.U647
Kuttner, Henry.	PS3521.U87
Kuttner, Paul.	PS3561.U797
Kwitny, Jonathan.	PS3561.W54
Kyle, Duncan.	PR6061.Y4
Kyle, Elisabeth, 1901-	PR6007.U554
Kyle, Sefton—see: Vickers, Roy.	
Kytle, Ray.	PS3561.Y8
La Barre, Harriet.	none
La Bern, Arthur J.	PR6023.A22
La Fountaine, George.	PS3562.A312
La Frenais, Ian.	none
La Plante, Jerry.	none
La Pointe, Diane.	none
La Tourrette, Jacqueline, 1926-	PS3562.A75895
Laborde, Jean, 1918-	PQ2672.A2
Lacy, Ed.	none
Laffin, John.	none
Laflin, Jack.	none
Laforest, Serge.	PQ2672.A286
Laidlaw, Ross.	PR6062.A3585
Laine, Annabel.	PR6062.A359
Lait, Robert.	PR6062.A37
Lake, Jane.	none
Lake, Peter A.	PS3562.A38
Laker, Rosalind.	PS3566.A82615
Lamb, Antonia.	none
Lamb, J. J.	PS3562.A423
Lamb, Lynton.	PR6062.A45

Lamb, Margaret, 1936-	PS3562.A424
Lamb, Max.	none
Lambert, Derek, 1929-	PR6062.A47
Lambert, Eric, 1921-1966.	PR6062.A48
Lambert, Lee.	none
Lambert, Robert, 1930-	PS3562.A458
Lambirth, F. Edwin.	none
Lambot, Isobel.	none
Lamensdurf, Leonard, 1930-	none
Lamont, Stewart, 1947-	none
L'Amour, Louis, 1908-	PS3523.A446
Lamport, Stephen.	none
Lampp, James W.	none
Lancaster, Graham.	PR6062.A486
Land, Jane—see: Borland, Kathryn Kilby.	
Land, Jon.	none
Land, Myrick, 1922-	PS3562.A47
Landers, Gunnard.	PS3562.A4755
Landon, Christopher.	PR6062.A497
Landon, Herman, 1882-1960.	none
Lane, Andrew.	none
Lane, Jim R.	none
Lanford, Mickey.	none
Lang, Brad.	none
Lang, Jack.	none
Lang, Maria, 1914-	PT9875.L275
Langdon, Gee, 1907-	none
Lange, John—see: Crichton, Michael, 1942-	
Lange, Oliver.	PS3562.A485
Langley, Bob.	PR6062.A5328
Langley, Lee—see: Langley, Sarah, 1927-	
Langley, Sarah, 1927-	PR6062.A535
Langton, Jane.	PS3562.A515
Lanham, Edwin, 1904-	PS3523.A612
Lanigan, Catherine.	PS3562.A53
Lansbury, Coral.	PR9619.3.L37
Lansdale, Nina.	PS3562.A56
Lantigua, John.	PS3562.A57
Lapatine, Kenneth A.	PS3562.A58
Lapierre, Dominique.	none
Larany, Daniel.	PQ2672.A64
Lariar, Lawrence, 1908-	none
Larkin, Rochelle.	none
Larner, Celia.	PR6062.A69
LaRosa, Linda J., 1951-	PS3562.A727
Larsen, Ernest, 1946-	PS3562.A733

Larsen, Gaylord, 1932-	PS3562.A734
Larson, Charles.	PS3562.A75
Lartéguy, Jean, 1920-	PQ2672.A73
Lascelles, Esme.	none
Lash, Jennifer.	PR6062.A743
Laski, Marghanita, 1915-	PR6023.A72
Lassiter, Adam.	none
Latham, Aaron.	PS3562.A7536
Latham, Brad.	none
Latham, Lorraine.	PS3562.A7544
Lathen, Emma, pseud.	PS3562.A755
Latimer, John, 1937-	PR9199.3.L327
Latimer, Jonathan, 1906-	PS3523.A773
Latouche, Harriet.	none
Lauben, Philip.	PS3562.A783
Lauder, Peter.	PR6062.A778
Lauder, William.	none
Laumer, Keith, 1925-	PS3562.A84
Launay, André, 1930-	PR6062.A785
Laurens, Marshall.	none
Lauria, Frank.	PS3523.A828
Law, Janice.	PS3562.A86
Lawrence, Alfred.	none
Lawrence, Hilda.	PS3523.A9295
Lawrence, James Duncan, 1918-	none
Lawrence, Margery H.	PR6023.A935
Lawrence, Mary Margaret.	none
Lawrence, Ron.	none
Lawrence, Susannah.	none
Laws, Stephen.	PR6062.A933
Lawson, Steve.	none
Laymon, Richard.	none
Lazarus, Mel, 1927-	PS3562.A98
Le Breton, Auguste, 1913-	PQ2623.E283
Le Carré, John, 1931-	PR6062.E33
Le Fanu, Joseph Sheridan, 1814-1873.	PR4879.L7
Le Grand, Leon.	none
Le Moult, Dolph.	none
Lea, Timothy.	none
Leach, Christopher, 1925-	PR6062.E18
Leach, Douglas.	none
Leacock, Stephen Butler, 1869-1944.	PR9199.3.L367
Leader, Charles—see: Smith, Robert Charles.	
Leader, Mary.	PS3562.E18
Leasor, James.	PR6062.E24
Leather, Edwin.	PR6062.E26

Leavitt, Alan J.	none
Leblanc, Maurice, 1864-1941.	PQ2623.E24
Lecale, Errol—see: McNeilly, Wilfred.	
LeClaire, Anne D.	none
Lecomber, Brian.	PR6062.E34
Lederer, William J., 1912-	PS3562.E3
Ledwidge, Bernard, 1915-	PR6062.E35
Lee, Elsie.	PS3562.E345
Lee, Gypsy Rose, 1914-1970.	PS3523.E3324
Lee, John, 1931-	PS3562.E3537
Lee, Linda.	PS3562.E3544
Lee, Maureen.	none
Lee, Melissa.	none
Lee, Stan.	PS3562.E3648
Lee, Susan.	PS3562.E365
Lee, Walt.	none
Leech, Audrey.	none
Leeds, Geoffrey.	none
Leek, Margaret.	none
Lees, Dan.	PR6062.E418
Lees, Harold P.	none
Leete-Hodge, Lornie.	none
Leffingwell, Albert, 1895-1946.	none
Leffland, Ella.	PS3562.E375
Legaret, Jean.	PQ2623.E3849
Lehman, Ernest, 1915-	PS3562.E4283
Lehmann, R. C. (Rudolf Chambers), 1856-1929.	none
Lehmkuhl, Donald.	PS3562.E437
Leigh, James, 1937-	PR6062.E445
Leigh, Robert, 1933-	PR6062.E4467
Leigh, Susannah.	none
Leigh, Veronica.	none
Leighton, Marie Connor, d. 1941.	PR6023.E46
Leighton, Tom.	none
Leinster, Murray, 1896-	PS3519.E648
Lejeune, Anthony.	PR6062.E465
Lelchuk, Alan.	PS3562.E464
Lem, Stanislaw.	PG7158.L39
Lemarchand, Elizabeth.	PR6062.E5
Lenton, Anthony.	none
Leokum, Leonard.	none
Leonard, Constance.	PS3562.E54
Leonard, Elmore, 1925-	PS3562.E55
Leonard, Frank.	PS3562.E555
Leonard, George, 1946-	PS3562.E557
Leonard, Phyllis G.	PS3562.E57

Leopold, Christopher.	PR6062.E727
Lequeux, William, 1864-1927.	PR6023.E75
Lerner, Richard A. (Richard Alan), 1938-	none
Leroux, Etienne.	PT6592.22.E7
Leroux, Gaston, 1868-1927.	PQ2623.E6
Lescroart, John T.	PS3562.E78
Leslie, Aleen.	PS3562.E817
Leslie, Josephine Aimee Campbell, 1898-	PR6023.E774
Leslie, Peter, 1922-	none
Leslie-Melville, Betty.	PS3562.E83
Lester, Mark.	none
Lestienne, Voldemar, 1932-	PQ2672.E823
Letton, Jennette Dowling.	PS3523.E794
Leuci, Bob, 1940-	PS3562.E857
Levi, Peter.	PR6023.E912
Levin, Ira.	PS3523.E7993
Levine, Larry.	none
Levine, Lawrence.	none
Levine, Robert.	none
Levon, Fred.	PS3562.E923
Levy, Barbara.	PS3562.E925
Levy, D. Lawrence.	PS3562.E926
Levy, Joseph.	none
Lewin, Elsa.	none
Lewin, Leonard C.	PS3562.E928
Lewin, Michael Z.	PS3562.E929
Lewis, Arthur H., 1906-	PS3562.E937
Lewis, Canella.	none
Lewis, Colin.	none
Lewis, David.	none
Lewis, Deborah—see: Grant, Charles L.	
Lewis, Elliott.	none
Lewis, James.	none
Lewis, June R. (June Rosemarie)	PR6062.E944
Lewis, Lange.	PS3503.E97
Lewis, Margo.	none
Lewis, Norman.	PR6062.E948
Lewis, Richard.	none
Lewis, Roy, 1933-	PR6062.E954
Lewis, Roy Harley.	PR6062.E9543
Lewis, Ted, 1940-	PR6062.E955
Lewis, Tom, 1940-	PS3562.E977
Lewis, William.	PS3562.E984
Ley, Alice Chetwynd.	PR6062.E965
Leyton, Patrick.	none
L'Hereux, Maurice.	none

Liddy, G. Gordon.	PS3562.I34
Lieberman, Herbert H., 1933-	PS3562.I4
Liebling, Howard.	PS3562.I45
Lientz, Gerald.	none
Lifson, David S.	PS3562.I4538
Liggett, Hunter—see: Paine, Lauran.	
Lilley, Tom.	PR6062.I36
Lillie, Helen.	none
Linakis, Steven, 1923-	PS3562.I47
Linares, Louisa-Maria.	none
Lincoln, Natalie Sumner, 1881-1935.	none
Lindall, Edward—see: Smith, Edward Ernest.	
Linden, Catherine.	none
Lindley, Erica.	PR6062.I466
Lindop, Audrey Erskine, 1920-	PR6062.I47
Lindquist, Donald.	PS3562.I5116
Lindsay, Joan Weigall, Lady.	PR9619.3.L49
Lindsay, Kathleen.	none
Lindsey, David L.	PS3562.I51193
Lindsey, Dawn.	PS3562.I51194
Linington, Elizabeth.	PS3562.I515
Linn, Edward.	PS3562.I54
Linscott, Gillian.	PR6062.I54
Linzee, David, 1952-	PS3562.I56
Linzner, Gordon, 1949-	PS3562.I565
Lipez, Richard, 1938-	PS3562.I57
Lippincott, Beverly.	none
Lippincott, David.	PS3562.I58
Lipsyte, Marjorie, 1932-	PS3562.I63
Liston, Robert A.	none
Littell, Blaine.	PS3562.I7825
Littell, Robert, 1935-	PS3562.I7827
Little, Constance.	none
Little, Gwenyth.	none
Littlepage, Layne.	PS3562.I786
Litvinoff, Emanuel.	PR6023.I7
Litvinoff, Ivy.	PR6023.I73
Litwak, Leo E., 1924-	PS3562.I79
Litzinger, Boyd.	PS3562.I795
Livingston, Armstrong, 1885-	none
Livingston, Jack.	PS3562.I937
Livingston, M. Jay.	PS3562.I95
Livingston, Nancy.	PR6062.I915
Llewellyn, Richard.	PR6023.L47
Llewellyn, Sam, 1948-	PR6062.L39
Lloyd, A.	none

Lloyd, Elizabeth.	none
Lochte, Dick.	PS3562.O217
Lockridge, Frances Louise Davis.	PS3523.O243
Lockridge, Richard, 1898-	PS3523.O245
Lockwood, Ethel.	none
Lockwood, Mary, 1934-	PS3562.O28
Loder, Vernon—see: Vahey, John George Haslette, 1881-	
Lofts, Norah, 1904-	PR6023.O35
Logan, Don.	none
Logue, John, 1933-	PS3562.O454
Logue, Mary.	none
London, Jack, 1876-1916.	PS3523.O46
	[Z8514.6]
Long, Amelia Reynolds, 1904-	PS3523.O462
Long, Ernest Laurie, 1886-	PR6023.O435
Long, Frank Belknap, 1903-	PS3523.O465
Long, Freda Margaret.	PR6062.O512
Long, John Arthur.	none
Long, Lydia Belknap—see: Long, Frank Belknap, 1903-	
Long, Manning, 1906-	none
Long, Patrick.	none
Longmate, Norman, 1925-	PR6062.O5155
Longrigg, Roger, 1929-	PR6062.O516
Longstreet, Stephen, 1907-	PS3523.O486
Lorac, E. C. R.—see: Rivett, Edith Caroline, 1894-	
Loraine, Philip, pseud.	PR6062.O67
Lord, Gabrielle.	PR9619.3.L63
Lord, Graham, 1943-	PR6062.O72
Lord, J. Edward.	none
Lordahl, Jo Ann.	none
Lore, Phillips—see: Smith, Terrence Lore.	
Lorena.	none
Loring, Ann.	none
Lorrah, Jean.	PS3562.O767
Lorrimer, Claire.	PR6062.O77
Lory, Robert.	PS3562.O78
Lottman, Eileen.	PS3562.O79
Louis, Joseph.	none
Lourie, Richard, 1940-	PS3562.O833
Love, Edmund G.	PS3562.O84
Lovegrove, Peter.	none
Lovell, Marc.	PR6062.O853
Lovesey, Peter.	PR6062.O86
Lowden, Desmond.	PR6062.O88
Lowe, Steve.	PS3562.O884
Lowell, J. R.	PS3562.O885

Lowing, Anne.	PR6062.O92
Lowndes, Marie Adelaide Belloc, 1868-1947.	PR6023.O95
Luard, Nicholas.	PR6062.U12
Luber, Philip.	PS3562.U22
Lucarotti, John.	none
Lucas, J. K.—see: Paine, Lauran.	
Luce, Helen.	PR6062.U16
Luckless, John.	PS3562.U255
Ludlum, Robert, 1927-	PS3562.U26
Lukas, Susan Ries.	PS3562.U45
Luke, Thomas—see: Masterton, Graham.	
Lund, James.	PR6062.U47
Lundy, Mike.	PS3562.U58
Lupica, Mike.	PS3562.U59
Lustbader, Eric Van.	PS3562.U752
Lustgarten, Edgar, 1907-1978.	PR6023.U73
Lutz, John, 1939-	PS3562.U854
Lyall, Gavin.	PR6062.Y3
Lyday, David Paul.	none
Lydecker, J. J.	PR6062.Y37
Lymington, John.	PR6005.H28
Lynch, Frances.	PR6053.O45
Lynch, Jack.	none
Lynch, Lawrence L.—see: Van Deventer, Emma Murdoch.	
Lynch, Miriam.	PS3562.Y434
Lynds, Dennis—see: Arden, William, 1924-	
Lynn, Jack, 1927-	PS3562.Y444
Lynn, Margaret.	PR6052.A83
Lynne, James Broom.	PR6062.Y62
Lyon, Mabel Dana, 1897-	none
Lyons, Arthur.	PS3562.Y446
Lyons, Delphine C.	none
Lyons, Elena.	none
Lyons, Ivan.	none
Lyons, Nan.	PS3562.Y449
Lysaght, Brian.	PS3562.Y4498
Lytton, Edward Bulwer-Lytton, Baron, 1803-1873.	PR4900-4948
Maas, Peter, 1929-	PS3563.A2
Maas, Virginia.	none
MacAlister, Ian.	none
Macao, Marshall.	none
Macartney-Filgate, Terence.	PR6063.A1188
MacBeth, George.	PR6063.A13
Maccabee, John.	none
MacCargo, J. T.	none
MacDonald, Donald.	none

Macdonald, Elizabeth, 1926-	PS3563.A2767
MacDonald, John D. (John Dann), 1916-1986.	PS3563.A28
	[Z8538.383]
Macdonald, John Ross—see: Macdonald, Ross, 1915-	
MacDonald, Patricia J.	none
MacDonald, Philip.	PR6025.A2218
Macdonald, Ross, 1915-	PS3525.I486
	[Z8574.82]
MacDonald, William Colt, 1891-	PS3525.A2122
MacDougall, James K.	PS3563.A2918
MacDougall, Ruth Doan, 1939-	PS3563.A292
MacGowan, Jonathan.	none
MacGrath, Harold, 1871-1932.	PS3525.A2423
MacGregor, Bill.	none
Macgregor, James Murdoch.	PR6063.A234
MacGregor, T. J.	none
MacHardy, Charles.	PR6063.A235
Machin, Meredith Land.	PS3563.A31155
MacInnes, Hamish.	none
MacIsaac, Frederick John, 1886-	none
MacIvers, Donald.	none
MacIvers, Sarah.	none
Mack, Carol K.	PS3563.A3126
MacKay, Alistair McColl.	none
Mackay, Amanda.	PS3563.A31335
MacKellar, Sinclair.	none
MacKenzie, Donald, 1918-	PR9199.3.M325
MacKenzie, Nigel.	none
Mackenzie-Lamb, Eric.	PS3563.A31356
MacKersey, Ian.	none
Mackey, Mary.	PS3563.A3165
MacKinnon, Allan.	none
MacKintosh, Ian.	PR6063.A24635
Mackintosh, May.	PR6063.A2464
Maclaren, Deanna, 1944-	PR6063.A2473
Maclay, John.	none
MacLean, Alistair, 1922-	PR6063.A248
MacLean, Jane.	PS3563.A317983
MacLean, Katherine.	PS3563.A31799
MacLeod, Charlotte.	PS3563.A31865
MacLeod, Robert, 1928-	PR6061.N6
MacLeod, Ruth.	PS3563.A31873
MacManus, Yvonne.	PS3563.A31885
MacNeil, Duncan, 1920-	PR6063.A167
MacNeil, Neil—see: Ballard, Todhunter, 1903-	
Macomber, Daria.	PS3563.A3235

MacPherson, Malcolm.	PS3563.A3254
MacVicar, Angus, 1908-	PR6025.A34
Madden, David, 1933-	PS3563.A339
Madderom, Gary.	PS3563.A3394
Maddock, Stephen—see: Walsh, J. M. (James Morgan), 1897-1952.	
Madsen, Axel.	PS3563.A343
Madsen, David.	PS3563.A344
Magali, pseud.	PQ2625.A63
Maggio, Joe.	PS3563.A345
Magnay, William, Sir, 2d Bart., 1855-	none
Magnuson, James.	PS3563.A352
Magnuson, Teodore.	PS3563.A3523
Magowan, Ronald.	PR6063.A33
Maguire, Michael.	PR6063.A332
Maher, Frank J.	none
Mahoney, Gene, 1923-	none
Mai, Denyse.	none
Mailer, Norman.	PS3525.A4152
Maimane, Arthur, 1932-	PR9369.3.M34
Mainwaring, Daniel, 1902-	none
Mainwaring, Marion.	PS3563.A383
Mainwaring, Michael.	none
Mair, Alistair.	PR6063.A347
Mair, George Brown.	none
Makins, Clifford, 1925-	none
Malcolm, John.	PR6063.A362
Malcolm, Margaret.	PR6063.A363
Malcolm-Smith, George, 1901-	none
Maling, Arthur.	PS3563.A4313
Mallanson, Todd.	none
Mallary, Amos.	none
Mallet, Jacqueline.	PR6063.A3657
Mallett, Richard.	PR6063.A3658
Malloch, Peter.	PR6063.A3664
Mallory, Drew—see: Garfield, Brian, 1939-	
Mallory, Kate.	PS3563.A43166
Mallory, Peter.	none
Mallory, Roosevelt.	none
Malm, Dorothea, 1915-	none
Malone, Michael.	PS3563.A43244
Maloney, J. J., 1940-	PS3563.A4329
Maloney, Mack.	none
Maloney, Ralph.	PS3563.A433
Maltz, Albert, 1908-	PS3525.A49
Malzberg, Barry N.	PS3563.A434
Manchester, Ivy.	none

Mancini, Anthony.	PS3563.A4354
Mandé, Elizabeth Erin—see: Friedman, Stuart.	
Mandelkau, Jamie.	PR6063.A3713
Mandeville, Colin.	PS3563.A4639
Mandeville, D. E.	none
Mandino, Og.	PS3563.A464
Maner, William.	PS3563.A465
Mangat Rai, Edward Nirmal.	PR9499.3.M35
Mankiewicz, Don M., 1922-	none
Mankowitz, Wolf.	PR6025.A4755
Manktelow, Bettine.	PR6063.A3736
Manley, Mark.	none
Mann, Abby.	PS3563.A534
Mann, Anthony, 1914-	PR6063.A3737
Mann, Edward Andrew.	PS3563.A5355
Mann, Jack.	PR6043.I9
Mann, Jessica.	PR6063.A374
Mann, Josephine.	none
Mann, Patrick—see: Waller, Leslie, 1923-	
Mann, Peter.	none
Mann, Roderick, 1922-	PR6063.A375
Manners, Alexandra—see: Rundle, Anne.	
Mannin, Ethel, 1900-	PR6025.A477
Manning, James C.	PS3563.A5367
Manning, Mary.	PR6025.A498
Mannion, John B.	none
Manor, Jason—see: Hall, Oakley M.	
Mansfield, Elizabeth.	none
Manso, Peter.	none
Mantell, Laurie.	PR9639.3.M264
Manville, William H.	PS3563.A58
Marais, Marc.	none
Marasco, Robert.	PS3563.A63
March, Lindsay.	PS3563.A633
March, William, 1893-1954.	PS3505.A53157 [Z8549.8]
Marchant, Catherine—see: Cookson, Catherine.	
Marchant, Herbert.	none
Marchant, William, 1923-	PS3525.A584
Marchetti, Victor.	PS3563.A635
Marchmont, Arthur William, 1852-1923.	PR6025.A612
Marcott, James.	none
Marcus, Joanna.	none
Marcus, Morton.	PS3563.A639
Margolin, Phillip.	PS3563.A649
Marie, Jeanne.	none

Mariel, Anne, 1907-	PQ2625.A787154
Marin, A. C.—see: Coppel, Alfred.	
Mariner, David.	none
Marino, James.	none
Mark, Alane.	PS3563.A662
Markham, Robert—see: Amis, Kingsley.	
Marks, Alan.	none
Marks, Peter.	PS3563.A667
Marks, Walter.	PS3563.A669
Markson, David.	PS3563.A67
Markstein, George.	PR6063.A644
Marler, Michael.	none
Marlett, Melba Balmat Grimes, 1909-	none
Marlow, Edwina.	PS3558.U323
Marlowe, Ann.	PS3563.A6739
Marlowe, Dan J.	none
Marlowe, Derek.	PR6063.A655
Marlowe, Hugh—see: Higgins, Jack, 1929-	
Marlowe, Stephen, 1928-	PS3563.A674
Maron, Margaret.	PS3563.A679
Marquand, John P. (John Phillips), 1893-1960.	PS3525.A6695
Marquis, Max.	none
Marric, J. J.—see: Creasey, John or Butler, William Vivian, 1927-	
Marriner, Brian.	none
Marsh, Geoffrey, 1912-	PS3563.A7145
Marsh, James J.	PS3563.A715
Marsh, John, 1907-	none
Marsh, Ngaio, 1899-	PR9639.3.M27
Marsh, Patrick—see: Hiscock, Leslie, 1902-	
Marsh, Richard, d. 1915.	PR6025.A645
Marsh, Robert W.	none
Marshall, Bruce, 1899-	PR6025.A654
Marshall, James Vance—see: Cameron, Ian, 1924-	
Marshall, Joanne—see: Rundle, Anne.	
Marshall, Lovat—see: Duncan, William Murdoch, 1909-	
Marshall, William Leonard, 1944-	PR9619.3.M275
Marsland, Amy Louise.	PS3563.A7226
Marsten, Richard—see: Hunter, Evan, 1926-	
Martens, Paul—see: Bell, Neil, 1887-1964.	
Martenson, Jan, 1933-	PT9876.23.A69
Martin, David.	none
Martin, Desmond.	PR9619.3.M278
Martin, Dwight.	PS3563.A7236
Martin, Hansjörg, 1920-	PT2673.A55
Martin, Ian Kennedy.	PR6063.A715
Martin, James E., 1936-	PS3563.A7243

Martin, Kay.	PS3563.A7247
Martin, Lee, 1943-	PS3563.A7249
Martin, Robert.	none
Martin, Russ.	PS3563.A7284
Martin, Sheila.	none
Martin, Trevor.	none
Martin, William, 1950-	PS3563.A7297
Martínez, Al.	PS3563.A7333
Martinez, S. A.	none
Martins, Richard.	PS3563.A7345
Marton, George.	PS3563.A738
Martyn, Don.	none
Martyn, Wyndham, 1875-	none
Maryk, Michael, 1935-	PS3563.A76
Mascott, Trina.	PS3563.A782
Masello, Robert.	none
Masiello, Joseph.	none
Mason, A. E. W. (Alfred Edward Woodley), 1865-1948.	PR6025.A79
Mason, Alexander.	none
Mason, Clifford.	PS3563.A7878
Mason, Colin, 1926-	PR9639.3.M28
Mason, David.	none
Mason, F. van Wyck (Francis van Wyck), 1901-	PS3525.A7943
Mason, Lee W.—see: Malzberg, Barry N.	
Mason, Michael, 1939-	PS3563.A793
Mason, Paule.	PS3563.A785 [sic]
Massey, Charlotte.	PR6063.A774
Massie, Chris.	none
Masson, Richard.	none
Masterman, J. C. (John Cecil), 1891-	PR6025.A796
Masterman, Walter Sidney, 1876-	none
Masters, Anthony, 1940-	PR6063.A83
Masters, Doug.	none
Masters, John, 1914-1983.	PS3525.A8314
Masterson, Linda.	none
Masterson, Whit, pseud.	PS3563.A835
Masterton, Graham.	PR6063.A834
Masur, Harold Q., 1909-	PS3525.A835
Matera, Lia.	none
Mather, Arthur R.	PR9619.3.M29
Mather, Berkely.	PR9619.3.M3
Matheson, Don.	PS3563.A83545
Matheson, Richard, 1926-	PS3563.A8355
Mathewson, John.	none
Mathewson, Joseph.	none
Mathis, Edward.	PS3563.A8364

Matranga, Frances Carfi.	none
Matsumoto, Seicho, 1909-	PL856.A8
Matthews, Christopher, 1954-	PR9619.3.M315
Matthews, Clayton.	PS3563.A84
Matthews, Clyde.	PS3563.A842
Matthews, Patricia, 1927-	PS3563.A853
Maudsley, Jere.	PR9199.3.M398
Maugham, Robin, 1916-	PR6025.A858
Maugham, W. Somerset (William Somerset), 1874-1965.	PR6025.A86 [Z8555.3]
Maxfield, Henry S.	PS3563.A896
Maxim, John R.	PS3563.A8965
Maxwell, A. E.	PS3563.A899
Maxwell, Helen K.	PS3563.A9
Maxwell, Patricia.	none
Maxwell, Peter.	none
Maxwell, Richard.	PS3563.A918
Maxwell, Thomas.	PS3563.A926
May, Janis Susan, 1946-	PS3563.A9418
May, Peter, 1951-	PR6063.A884
Maybury, Anne.	PR6025.A943
Mayer, Edward E.	none
Mayer, Martin, 1928-	PS3563.A9525
Mayer, Robert, 1939-	PS3563.A954
Mayfield, Serena.	none
Mayhew, Margaret, 1936-	PR6063.A887
Mayhew, Vic.	PS3563.A963
Mayne, William, 1928-	none
Mayo, James—see: Coulter, Stephen, 1913-	
Mayo, Nick.	PS3563.A964
Mazzaro, Ed.	none
McAfee, Paul K.	none
McAllister, Alister, 1877-	PR6025.A12
McAllister, Amanda.	none
McAllister, Annie Laurie—see: Cassiday, Bruce.	
McAuliffe, Frank.	none
McBain, Ed, 1926-	PS3515.U585
McBriarty, Douglas, 1918-	PS3563.C3336
McCabe, Cameron—see: Borneman, Ernest, 1915-	
McCabe, Eugene.	PR6063.A135
McCaig, Donald.	PS3563.A2555
McCall, Anthony—see: Kane, Henry.	
McCall, Linda Lane.	none
McCammon, Robert R.	PS3563.C3345
McCandless, Anthony.	PR6063.C33
McCann, Thomas.	PR6063.A158

McCarry, Charles.	PS3563.C336
McCartan, Dominic.	PR6063.C34
McCarthy, Dudley.	none
McCarthy, Edward V.	PS3563.A2587
McCarthy, Jane E.	none
McCarthy, Shaun.	none
McCarthy, Wilson, 1930-	PS3563.A2593
McCartney, P.	none
McClean, J. Sloan.	none
McClintick, Malcolm.	PS3563.C3415
McCloy, Helen.	PS3525.A1587
McClure, James, 1939-	PR9369.3.M394
McCombie, J. A. S.	none
McConnell, Frank D., 1942-	PS3563.C3437
McConnell, Malcolm.	PS3563.A2624
McConnor, Vincent.	PS3525.A1653
McCormack, Tom.	none
McCormick, Claire.	PS3563.C3445
McCormick, Jim, 1920-	PS3563.A2645
McCormick, Lois Elizabeth.	none
McCoy, Andrew.	PR9369.3.M396
McCrum, Robert.	PR6063.A1658
McCrumb, Sharyn.	none
McCulley, Johnston, 1883-1958.	PS3525.A17725
McCullough, Andrew.	PS3563.A2677
McCurtin, Peter.	none
McCutchan, Philip, 1920-	PR6063.A167
McCutcheon, Hugh.	PR6025.A216
McDaniel, David.	none
McDermott, John, 1919-1977.	PS3563.A274
McDonald, Cherokee Paul.	none
McDonald, Eva.	PR6063.A16794
McDonald, Frank, 1941-	PS3563.A2768
Mcdonald, Gregory, 1937-	PS3563.A278
McDonald, Hugh C.	none
McDonell, Terry.	PS3563.A29143
McDowell, Michael.	none
McDowell, Rider.	PS3563.C3594
McElroy, Joseph.	PS3563.A293
McErlean, Sheila.	none
McEvoy, Marjorie.	PR6063.A196
McFarlane, Leslie, 1902-	PR9199.3.M3148
McFather, Nelle.	none
McGarrity, Mark—see: Gill, Bartholomew, 1943-	
McGerr, Patricia.	PS3525.A23276
McGhee, Edward.	none

McGill, Gordon, 1943-	PR6063.A2177
McGill, Nancy.	none
McGinley, Patrick, 1937-	PR6063.A21787
McGirr, Edmund—see: Giles, Kenneth.	
McGivern, William P.	PS3525.A236
McGown, Jill.	PS3563.C365
McGrady, Mike.	none
McGraw, Lee.	PS3563.A2997
McGuire, Paul, 1903-	PR9619.3.M324
McGurk, Slater, 1925-	PS3568.O852
McGuyer, Nadine.	none
McHale, Tom.	PS3563.A3115
McHugh, Frances Y.	none
McIlvanney, William, 1936-	PR6063.A237
McInerny, Ralph M.	PS3563.A31166
McInnes, Helen, 1907-	PS3525.A24573
McIntosh, J. T.—see: Macgregor, James Murdoch.	
McIver, N. J.	PS3563.C373
McKay, Kenneth R.	none
McKenney, Kenneth, 1929-	PR6063.A2429
McKenzie, J. Alexander.	PS3563.A31345
McKew, Robert.	none
McKimmey, James.	PS3563.A317
McKnight, Carolyn.	PS3563.A31773
McLachlan, Donald, 1908-1971.	PR6063.A247
McLachlan, Ian, 1938-	PR6063.A2472
McLaughlin, Robert, 1925-	PS3563.A31796
McLeave, Hugh.	PR6063.A249
McLeish, Dougal.	PS3563.A318
McLeish, Roderick, 1926-	PS3563.A3183
McLendon, James.	PS3563.A3184
McMahon, Thomas Patrick.	PS3563.A31883
McManus, Leslie.	none
McMikle, Barbara.	none
McMillan, Dorothy.	none
McMillan, Elsie Mills.	none
McMordie, Taber.	PS3563.A31897
McMullen, Mary, 1920-	PS3563.A31898
McNab, Oliver—see: Frede, Richard.	
McNally, Terrence.	PS3563.A323
McNamara, Joseph D.	PS3563.C3883
McNamara, Michael M., 1940-	PS3563.A3234
McNaughton, Brian.	none
McNear, Robert, 1930-	none
McNeil, John.	PR6063.A2586
McNeile, Herman Cyril, 1888-1937.	PR6025.A317

McNeilly, Wilfred.	none
McQuay, Mike.	none
McQuinn, Donald E.	PS3563.C66
McShane, Mark, 1930-	PR6062.O853
McVean, James.	PR6063.C8
Mead, Robert Douglas.	PS3563.E168
Mead, Russell.	none
Mead, Shepherd.	PS3525.E1147
Meade, Everard.	none
Meade, L. T., 1854-1914.	PS2859
Meade, Richard—see: Haas, Ben.	
Meek, M. R. D.	PR6063.E35
Megahy, Cooper.	none
Meggs, Brown.	PS3563.E34
Meiring, Desmond.	PR9381.9.M44
Meisels, Andrew.	PS3563.E37
Meissner, Hans Otto.	PT2625.E314
Melchior, Ib.	PS3563.E435
Meldrum, James—see: Mitchell, James, 1926-	
Melton, William.	PS3563.E448
Melville, James.	PR6063.E439
Melville, Jennie.	PR6063.E44
Melville-Ross, Antony.	PR6063.E455
Mendelhall, Kitty.	none
Mendelsohn, Felix, 1906-	PS3563.E48
Menegas, Peter.	none
Meredith, D. R. (Doris R.)	PS3563.E7355
Meredith, Richard C.	PS3563.E737
Merle, Robert, 1908-	PQ2625.E5278
Merlin, Christina.	PR6063.E75
Merritt, Abraham, 1884-1943.	PS3525.E676
Merritt, Don, 1945-	PS3563.E74538
Mertz, Barbara.	PS3563.E747
Messer, Mona Naomi Anna Hocking.	PR6025.E744
Messick, Hank.	none
Messmann, Jon.	none
Metcalfe, Susan.	none
Mettler, George B.	none
Mewshaw, Michael, 1943-	PS3563.E87
Meyer, Lawrence, 1941-	PS3563.E875
Meyer, Lynn.	PS3563.E878
Meyer, Nicholas.	PS3563.E88
Meyers, Manny, 1930-	PS3563.E94
Meyers, Martin.	none
Meynell, Laurence, 1899-	PR6025.E93
Miall, Robert—see: Burke, John Frederick, 1922-	

Michael, David J., 1944-	PS3563.I25
Michaels, Alan.	PS3563.I268
Michaels, Barbara, 1927-	PS3563.E747
Michaels, Bill, 1946-	none
Michaels, Jan.	none
Michaels, Philip.	none
Michelson, Bennett.	none
Middlemass, Jean.	none
Middlemiss, Robert.	none
Midgley, John.	none
Miehe, Ulf, 1940-	PT2673.I3
Migliore, John.	none
Mikes, George.	PR6025.I37
Mikolowski, Ken.	PS3563.I37156
Milán, Victor.	PS3563.I371568
Milburn, Ellen.	none
Miles, John—see: Bickham, Jack M.	
Miles, Richard.	none
Millar, Jeff, 1942-	PS3563.I3723
Millar, Kenneth—see: Macdonald, Ross, 1915-	
Millar, Margaret.	PS3563.I3725
Millard, Joe.	none
Millard, Oscar E.	PR6063.I355
Miller, David C.	none
Miller, Denis.	PR6063.I358
Miller, Geoffrey, 1945-	PS3563.I3776
Miller, Hugh, 1937-	PR6063.I373
Miller, J. M. T.	none
Miller, Judi.	none
Miller, Lanora.	none
Miller, Lauritz, 1927-	PS3563.I4136
Miller, Rex.	none
Miller, Victor B.	none
Miller, Wade.	none
Millhiser, Marlys.	PS3563.I4225
Milligan, Spike, 1918-	PR6063.I3777
Mills, Arthur Hobart, 1887-	none
Mills, James, 1932-	PS3563.I423
Mills, John, 1930-	PR9199.3.M48
Mills, Osmington.	none
Mills, Robert E.	none
Milne, A. A. (Alan Alexander), 1882-1956.	PR6025.I65
Milne, John.	PR6063.I3787
Milton, David Scott, 1934-	PS3563.I448
Minahan, John.	PS3563.I4616
Minchin, Devon George, 1919-	PR9619.3.M5

Miner, Valerie.	PS3563.I4647
Minick, Michael.	none
Minton, Paula.	none
Miron, Charles.	none
Mitchell, Gladys, 1901-	PR6025.I832
Mitchell, Ian.	none
Mitchell, James, 1926-	PR6063.I793
Mitchelson, Austin.	none
Mitcheltree, Tom.	none
Mitford, Bertram, 1855-1914.	none
Moffat, Gwen.	PR6063.O4
Moffatt, James.	none
Moffitt, Ian.	PR9619.3.M55
Monahan, Brent.	none
Monahan, George.	none
Monette, Paul.	PS3563.O523
Monig, Christopher, 1910-	PS3505.R89224
Monigle, Martha.	none
Monnow, Peter—see: Croudace, Glynn.	
Monro, Gavin.	PR6063.O496
Monsarrat, Nicholas, 1910-	PR6025.O36
Monsky, Mark.	PS3563.O534
Montague, J. J.	none
Montalbán, Manuel Vázquez—see: Vázquez Montalbán, Manuel.	
Montalbano, William D.	PS3563.O5377
Montana, Ron.	none
Montandon, Pat.	none
Montano, Pablo.	none
Monteilhet, Hubert.	PQ2625.O384
Montgomerie, James.	none
Montgomery, Yvonne.	PS3563.O5458
Montrose, Graham.	none
Moody, Ron.	PR6063.O574
Moody, Susan.	none
Moor, Emily—see: Deming, Richard.	
Moorcock, Michael, 1939-	PR6063.O59
Moore, Andrew.	none
Moore, Arthur.	none
Moore, Barbara, 1934-	PS3563.O57
Moore, Brian, 1921-	PR9199.3.M617
Moore, Clayton—see: Granbeck, Marilyn.	
Moore, Dan Tyler.	none
Moore, Donald Lloyd.	PS3563.O614
Moore, Dorinne.	none
Moore, Leo.	none
Moore, Maureen.	PR9199.3.M619

Moore, Richard A.	none
Moore, Robin, 1925-	PS3563.O644
Moore, Ruth.	PS3525.O5666
Moorhouse, Frank.	PR9619.3.M6
Morales, Pablo.	none
Moran, Richard, 1942-	PS3563.O767
Moray, Helga.	PR6025.O62
Moreau, Daniel.	none
Morella, Joe.	none
Morgan, Al, 1920-	PS3563.O78
Morgan, Allan.	none
Morgan, Claire—see: Highsmith, Patricia, 1921-	
Morgan, Jason.	none
Morgan, John—see: Paine, Lauran.	
Morgan, John S.	none
Morgan, Maybeth.	none
Morgan, Patrick.	none
Morgan, Robert.	none
Morgan, Stanley.	PR6063.O734
Morgan, Ted, 1932-	PS3563.O87149
Morgan, Wesley.	none
Morgan, Wynn L.	none
Morgulas, Jerrold.	PS3563.O87158
Morice, Anne.	PR6063.O743
Morison, B. J. (Betty Jane), 1924-	PS3563.O87167
Morland, Catherine.	none
Morland, Nigel, 1905-	PR6025.O683
Morley, Ellen.	none
Morrell, David.	PR9199.3.M65
Morris, Chris, 1946-	none
Morris, Goodall Varne.	none
Morris, Ira.	none
Morris, Janet, 1946-	PS3563.O87435
Morris, Jim, 1940-	PS3563.O87436
Morris, John.	PR6063.O75
Morris, Thomas Baden, 1900-	PR6025.O754
Morris, W. R., 1934-	none
Morrison, Arthur, 1863-1945.	PR5089.M7
Morrison, James W. R.	none
Morrow, Susan.	PS3563.O878
Morse, L. A.	none
Mortensen, Niels.	none
Mortimer, John Clifford, 1923-	PR6025.O7552
Morton, Anthony—see: Creasey, John.	
Mosiman, Billie Sue.	none
Moss, Baron.	none

Moss, Jack.	none
Moss, Robert, 1946-	PR6063.O83
Moss, Roger.	none
Moss, Rose.	PS3563.O8848
Mounce, David R.	none
Mowatt, Ian.	PR6063.O87
Moyes, Patricia.	PR6063.O9
Muir, Augustus, 1892-	PR6025.U55
Muir, Jean.	PS3563.U38
Mulisch, Harry, 1927-	PT5860.M85
Mulkeen, Thomas P.	PS3563.U395
Mullally, Frederic.	PR6063.U38
Muller, Marcia.	PS3563.U397
Muller, Mary.	none
Muller, Paul, 1924-	PR6063.U39
Munder, Laura.	PS3563.U453
Mundy, Talbot, 1879-1940.	PR6025.U66
Munro, Hugh.	none
Munro, James—see: Mitchell, James, 1926-	
Murari, Timeri.	PR9499.3.M85
Murdoch, Graham.	none
Murfi, Lidie.	none
Murphy, Brian, 1939 May 25-	PS3563.U7278
Murphy, Christopher.	PR6063.U729
Murphy, Dallas.	PS3563.U7283
Murphy, Gloria.	PS3563.U7297
Murphy, Haughton.	PS3563.U734
Murphy, James F., 1932-	PS3563.U737
Murphy, John, 1921-	PS3563.U74
Murphy, Ken, 1935-	PR6063.U733
Murphy, Robert Franklin.	none
Murphy, Tom, 1935-	PS3563.U762
Murphy, Warren.	PS3563.U7634
Murray, David Christie, 1847-1907.	PR5101.M45
Murray, Fiona.	none
Murray, Helen.	none
Murray, John, 1923-	PS3563.U77
Murray, Max, 1901-1956.	PR9619.3.M84
Murray, W. H. (William Hutchinson)	PR6063.U78
Murray, William, 1926-	PS3563.U8
Muse, Patricia.	PS3563.U834
Musto, Barry.	PR6063.U87
Myers, Mary Ruth.	PS3563.Y44
Mykel, A. W.	PS3563.Y49
Myles, Symon—see: Follett, Ken.	
Nabb, Magdalen, 1947-	PR6064.A18

Naha, Ed.	none
Nahum, Lucien.	PR6064.A32
Names, Larry D.	PS3564.A545
Napier, Mary, 1932-	PR6073.R54
Napier, Melissa.	none
Narcejac, Thomas, 1908-	PQ2627.A675
Nash, Jay Robert.	PS3564.A823
Nash, N. Richard.	PS3527.A6365
Nash, Simon—see: Chapman, Raymond.	
Nastase, Ilie, 1946-	PR9170.R63.N37+
Nathan, Robert Stuart.	PS3564.A8495
Nathenson, Joseph.	PS3564.A864
Natsuki, Shizuko, 1938-	PL857.A85
Naughton, Edmund.	none
Nava, Michael.	none
Nazel, Joseph.	none
Nebrensky, Alex—see: Cooper, Parley J.	
Neebel, Richard.	none
Neely, Esther.	none
Neely, Richard.	PS3564.E25
Neggers, Carla.	none
Neiderman, Andrew.	PS3564.E38
Neilan, Sarah.	PR6064.E43
Neill, Robert.	PR6064.E44
Neilson, Andrew.	none
Neilson, Marguerite.	PR6064.E46
Nelson, Jack A.	none
Nelson, Kent, 1943-	PS3564.E467
Nelson, Mark—see: Johnston, Ronald, 1926-	
Nelson, Mildred.	none
Nelson, Walter Henry.	PS3564.E479
Nemec, David.	PS3564.E4797
Nessen, Ron, 1934-	PS3564.E82
Netzen, Klaus.	none
Neuman, Fredric.	PS3564.E846
Neville, Margot.	none
Nevins, Francis M.	PS3564.E854
New, Christopher.	PR6064.E847
New, William Sloane.	none
Newcomb, Kerry.	PS3564.E875
Newell, Rosemary.	none
Newman, Bernard, 1897-1968.	PR6027.E914
Newman, Christopher.	none
Newman, G. F. (Gordon F.)	PR6064.E925
Newman, Robert, 1909-	none
Newton, Mike.	none

Newton, Wilfred Douglas, 1884-	none
Newton, William.	none
Neznanskii, Fridrikh.	PG3549.N45
Nichols, Aeleta.	none
Nichols, Beverley, 1899-	PR6027.I22
Nichols, Fan—see: Hanna, Frances Nichols.	
Nichols, Leigh—see: Koontz, Dean R. (Dean Ray), 1945-	
Nichols, Peter.	none
Nichols, Sarah.	none
Nicholson, Michael.	PR6064.I228
Nicholson, Robin.	none
Nickolay, Michael.	PS3564.I3315
Nicolaysen, Bruce.	PS3564.I334
Nicole, Christopher.	PR9320.9.N5
Nicole, Claudette.	none
Nicole, Claudia.	none
Nielsen, Helen.	PS3564.I35
Nielsen, Torben, 1918 Apr. 22-	PT8176.24.I36
Niesewand, Peter.	PR6064.I33
Nightingale, Ursula.	none
Nile, Dorothea—see: Avallone, Michael.	
Nisbet, Helen C.	none
Nisbet, Hume, 1849-1921?	none
Nisbet, Jim.	PS3564.I7
Niven, Larry.	PS3564.I9
Nixon, Alan, 1937-	PR6064.I83
Nixon, Allan.	none
Nizza, Paul.	PS3564.I97
Noël, Atanielle Annyn.	PS3564.O29
Noël, Denise.	PQ2674.O3
Noel, Jeffrey.	none
Noel, Sterling.	none
Nolan, Frederick W., 1931-	PR6064.O413
Nolan, Madeena Spray.	none
Nolan, William F., 1928-	PS3564.O39
Noone, Carl.	none
Noone, Edwina—see: Avallone, Michael.	
Noone, John.	PR6064.O49
Norden, Eric.	none
Nordhoff, James.	PS3564.O56
Norham, Gerald.	none
Norman, Barry.	none
Norman, Elizabeth, 1924-	PS3564.O564
Norman, Frank.	PR6064.O74
Norman, Yvonne.	none
Noro, Fred.	none

Norris, Carolyn B.	PS3564.O645
Norris, Kathleen Thompson, 1880-1966.	PS3527.O5
Norst, Joel.	none
North, Anthony—see: Koontz, Dean R. (Dean Ray), 1945-	
North, Elizabeth, 1932-	PR6064.O764
North, Gil—see: Horne, Geoffrey, 1916-	
North, Howard.	PS3564.O74
North, Jessica.	PS3564.O763
North, Sam.	PR6064.O765
North, Sara.	none
Norton, Andre.	PS3527.O632
Norton, Michael C.	none
Norton, Olive.	PR6064.O767
Norwood, Elliott.	none
Norwood, Frank.	none
Norwood, Victor George Charles.	PR6064.O79
Nottingham, Poppy.	none
Novak, Robert.	none
Nowak, Jacquelyn.	PS3564.O936
Noyes, Stanley.	PS3564.O98
Nuelle, Helen S.	none
Nuetzel, Charles.	none
Nugent, James.	none
Null, Gary.	none
Nuttall, Anthony.	none
Nuttall, Jeff.	PR6064.U8
Oakes, Philip, 1928-	PR6065.A38
Oakroyd, Simon.	none
Oates, Joyce Carol, 1938-	PS3565.A8
O'Brien, Edna.	PR6065.B7
O'Brien, Fitz James, 1828-1862.	PS2485
O'Brien, Flann, 1911-1966.	PR6029.N56
O'Brien, Lee.	none
O'Brien, Robert C.	PS3565.B74
O'Brien, Saliee.	none
O'Brine, Manning, 1913-1977.	PR6065.B75
Obstfeld, Raymond.	none
O'Callaghan, Maxine.	none
O'Connor, Dermot.	none
O'Connor, Richard, 1915-1975.	PS3529.C63
OCork, Shannon.	PS3565.C66
Odier, Daniel, 1945-	PQ2675.D5
O'Donnell, Lillian.	PS3565.D59
O'Donnell, Margaret.	PR6065.D577
O'Donnell, Peter.	PR6029.D55
O'Donohoe, Nick.	none

O'Farrell, William, 1904-	none
Offord, Lenore Glen, 1905-	none
Offutt, Andrew J.	PS3565.F4
O'Flaherty, Louise.	none
Ogan, George.	none
Ogan, Margaret.	none
Ogilvie, Elisabeth, 1917-	PS3529.G39
Ognall, Leopold Horace.	PR6029.G6
O'Grady, Anne.	PR9619.3.O33
O'Grady, Leslie.	PS3565.G68
O'Grady, Rohan, 1922-	PR9199.3.O343
O'Hagan, Joan.	PR9619.3.O38
O'Hara, Kenneth.	PR6065.H28
O'Hara, Patrick.	none
Ohnet, Georges, 1848-1918.	PQ2378.O3
Okun, Lawrence E., 1929-	PS3565.K8
Olbrich, Freny.	PR6065.L35
Olcott, Anthony, 1950-	PS3565.L28
Old Sleuth—see: Halsey, Harlan Page, 1839?-1898.	
Olden, Marc.	PS3565.L29
Oldsey, Bernard Stanley, 1923-	PS3565.L35
O'Leary, Ed.	none
Olesker, J. Bradford, 1949-	PS3565.L44
Oliver, Anthony.	PR6065.L47
Olivy, D. J.	PS3565.L54
Olsen, D. B.—see: Hitchens, Dolores Birk, 1907-	
Olsen, Jack.	PS3565.L77
Olson, Donald.	PS3565.L825
O'Malley, Mary Dolling Saunders, Lady, 1889-1974.	PR6029.M35
O'Marie, Carol Anne.	PS3565.M347
O'Neil, Russell.	PS3565.N45
O'Neil, Will.	PS3565.N47
O'Neill, Archie.	PS3565.N48
O'Neill, Edward A.	PS3565.N49
O'Neill, Frank.	PS3565.N495
O'Neill-Barna, Anne.	none
Onyeama, Dillibe, 1951-	PR9387.9.O54
Oppenheim, E. Phillips (Edward Phillips), 1866-1946.	PR6029.P5
Oran, Dan.	PS3565.R3
Orczy, Emmuska Orczy, Baroness, 1865-1947.	PR6029.R25
Orde, Lewis.	PS3565.R38
Orenstein, Frank.	PS3565.R39
Orford, Ellen.	none
Organ, Perry.	PS3565.R45
Orgill, Douglas, 1922-	PR6065.R68
Oriol, Laurence.	PQ2672.O7

Ormerod, Roger.	PR6065.R688
O'Rourke, Andrew P.	none
O'Rourke, Frank, 1916-	PS3529.R58
Orr, Mary.	PS3529.R66
Ørum, Poul.	PT8176.25.E7
Orvis, Kenneth—see: Lemieux, Kenneth.	
Osborn, David, 1923-	PS3565.S37
Osborn, John Jay.	PS3565.S38
Osborne, Beresford.	none
Osborne, Dorothy.	none
Osborne, Geoffrey.	none
Osborne, Helena.	PR6065.S17
Osborne, Louise.	none
Osier, John, 1938-	PS3565.S55
Osmond, Andrew.	PR6065.S6
Oster, Jerry.	PS3565.S813
Ostlere, Gordon—see: Gordon, Richard, 1921-	
Ostrander, Isabel Egenton, 1883-1924.	none
Ostrander, Kate.	PS3565.S83
O'Sullivan, James Brendan, 1919-	none
O'Toole, G. J. A. (George J. A.), 1936-	PS3565.T6
Ottum, Bob.	PS3565.T8
Oursler, Fulton, 1893-1952.	PS3529.U65
Ovalov, Lev, 1905-	PG3476.O89
Overgard, William.	PS3565.V427
Overholser, Stephen.	PS3565.V43
Owen, Dean.	PS3565.W53
Owen, Philip—see: Pentecost, Hugh, 1903-	
Owen, Ray.	PR6065.W44
Owen, Richard, 1942-	PS3565.W56
Ozaki, Milton K.	none
Pace, Eric, 1936-	PS3566.A24
Pace, Tom.	PS3566.A26
Packard, Frank Lucius, 1877-1942.	PS3531.A2154
Packer, Bernard.	PS3566.A316
Packer, Joy Peterson, Lady, 1905-	PR6031.A215
Packer, Vin—see: Kerr, M. E.	
Padden, Ian.	none
Page, Emma.	PR6066.A29
Page, Jake.	PS3566.A333
Page, Martin, 1938-	PR6066.A34
Page, Spider.	none
Page, Thomas, 1942-	PS3566.A335
Paier, Robert.	PS3566.A339
Paige, Leslie.	none
Pain, Barry, 1864-1928.	PR6031.A25

Paine, Lauran.	PS3566.A34
Palin, Michael.	PR6066.A42
Palmer, Lilli, 1914-	PT2631.A36
Palmer, P. K.	none
Palmer, Stuart, 1905-	PS3531.A3868
Palmer, Will.	none
Palmtag, Dinah.	none
Panati, Charles, 1943-	PS3566.A558
Pangborn, Edgar.	PS3566.A56
Panger, Daniel.	PS3566.A57
Papazoglou, Orania, 1951-	PS3566.A613
Pape, Gordon.	PR9199.3.P33
Pape, Sharon.	none
Paradis, Vincent A.	none
Paretsky, Sara.	PS3566.A647
Pargeter, Edith—see: Peters, Ellis, 1913-	
Paris, Ann.	none
Paris, Matthew, 1938-	PS3566.A66
Park, Jacqueline.	none
Park, Jordan—see: Kornbluth, C. M. (Cyril M.), 1924-1958.	
Park, Owen, 1932-	none
Parker, Beatrice.	PS3558.U323
Parker, Bob.	none
Parker, Claire.	PS3566.A677
Parker, Lee.	none
Parker, M. M.	PS3566.A68
Parker, Michael, 1941-	PR6066.A65
Parker, Norman.	PS3566.A684
Parker, Percy Spurlark.	PS3566.A685
Parker, Richard, 1915-	PR6066.A67
Parker, Robert B., 1932-	PS3566.A686
Parker, T. Jefferson.	PS3566.A6863
Parkes, Roger.	PR6066.A6953
Parkhurst, Jane.	none
Parkman, Sydney Müller, 1895-	none
Parrish, Barney.	none
Parrish, Frank.	PR6066.A713
Parry, James, 1943-	PS3566.A76
Parry, Michel.	none
Parvin, Brian.	none
Patrick, Q.	PR6033.U43
Patrick, Vincent.	PS3566.A7869
Patten, Brian, 1946-	PR6066.A86
Patterson, Harry—see: Higgins, Jack, 1929-	
Patterson, James, 1947-	PS3566.A822
Patterson, John M.	PS3566.A823

Patterson, Richard North.	PS3566.A8242
Pattinson, James, 1915-	PR6066.A877
Pattison, Ruth—see: Abbey, Ruth.	
Patton, Cliff.	none
Paul, Barbara, 1931-	PS3566.A82615
Paul, Charlotte.	PS3531.A8519
Paul, Elliot, 1891-1958.	PS3531.A852
Paul, Raymond.	PS3566.A8266
Paul, William.	none
Pauley, Barbara Anne.	PS3566.A828
Paull, Jessyca.	none
Paulsen, Gary.	PS3566.A834
Paxton, Lois.	PR6066.A885
Payes, Rachel Cosgrove.	none
Payn, James, 1830-1898.	PR5154
Payne, Donald Gordon—see: Cameron, Ian, 1924-	
Payne, Laurence.	PR6066.A93
Pearl, Jack.	PS3566.E218
Pearlman, Gilbert.	none
Pearsall, Ronald, 1927-	PR6066.E168
Pearson, Ann.	none
Pearson, Edmund Lester, 1880-1937.	PS3531.E2358
Pearson, John, 1930-	PR6066.E2
Pearson, Peter.	PR6066.E225
Pearson, Ridley.	PS3566.E234
Pearson, William, 1922-	PS3566.E237
Peart, Jane.	none
Peck, Leonard, 1906-	none
Peck, Robert Newton.	PS3566.E254
Pedler, John Branfroot Simpson.	PR6066.E3
Pedneau, Dave.	none
Peel, Colin D.	PR6066.E36
Peeples, Samuel A. (Samuel Anthony), 1917-	PS3531.E286
Pell, Robert.	none
Peltz, Rosemonde.	PS3566.E44
Pember, Ron.	none
Pemberton, Margaret.	PR6066.E488
Pemberton, Max, Sir, 1863-1950.	PR6031.E4
Pembroke, Peter.	none
Pendleton, Don.	none
Pendleton, Tom—see: Van Zandt, Edmund.	
Pendower, Jacques, 1899-1976.	none
Penn, H.	none
Penn, John.	PR6066.E496
Pennant-Rea, Rupert.	PR6066.E497
Penoyre, Mary.	none

Pentecost, Hugh, 1903-	PS3531.H442
Penzler, Otto.	none
Perdue, Lewis.	PS3566.E69122
Pereira, Michael, 1928-	PR6066.E63
Perowne, Barry.	PR6031.E54
Perrault, E. G. (Ernest G.)	PR9199.3.P43
Perrault, Gilles.	PQ2676.E7
Perrett, Geoffrey.	PS3566.E6952
Perrin, Robert, 1939-	PR6066.E684
Perry, Anne.	PR6066.E693
Perry, Patricia.	none
Perry, Ritchie, 1942-	PR6066.E72
Perry, Robin.	PS3566.E716
Perry, Roland, 1946-	PR9619.3.P376
Perry, Thomas.	PS3566.E718
Perry, V. M.	none
Perry, Will.	PS3566.E722
Persico, Joseph E.	PS3566.E727
Pertwee, Roland, 1885-	PR6031.E6
Peter, John Desmond.	PR6066.E73
Peters, Bryan—see: George, Peter, 1924-1966.	
Peters, Elizabeth.	PS3563.E747
Peters, Ellis, 1913-	PR6031.A49
Peters, L. T.—see Klainer, Jo-Ann and Klainer, Albert S.	
Peters, Ludovic—see: Brent, Peter Ludwig.	
Peters, Othello.	none
Peters, Ron.	none
Peterson, Bernard.	PS3566.E766
Peterson, Jim.	none
Peterson, Margaret, 1883-	none
Petievich, Gerald.	PS3566.E773
Petrakis, Harry Mark.	PS3566.E78
Petrie, Glen.	PR6066.E755
Petrie, Rhona.	PR6066.E756
Pettit, Mike.	none
Petty, Barbara.	none
Peyrou, Manuel.	PQ7797.P534
Pfefferle, Seth.	none
Philbin, Tom, 1934-	none
Philbrick, W. R. (W. Rodman)	PS3566.H474
Philips, Judson—see: Pentecost, Hugh, 1903-	
Phillifent, John T.	none
Phillips, Clyde B.	none
Phillips, David Atlee.	PS3566.H477
Phillips, Dennis—see: Chambers, Peter, 1924-	
Phillips, Edward, 1931-	PR9199.3.P476

Phillips, James Atlee.	none
Phillips, Leon.	none
Phillips, Meredith, 1943-	PS3566.H488
Phillips, Mike, 1911-	PS3566.H494
Phillips, R. B., 1943-	PS3552.R2298
Phillips, Stella.	PR6066.H493
Phillips, Steven.	PS3566.H52
Phillpotts, Eden, 1862-1960.	PR5177 [Z8684.5]
Philo, Thomas.	none
Picano, Felice, 1944-	PS3566.I25
Picard, Sam.	none
Pici, J. R.	none
Pickard, Nancy.	PS3566.I274
Picton, Bernard.	none
Pieczenik, Steve R.	PS3566.I3813
Pierce, Noel, 1907-	PS3531.I412
Pifer, Drury L.	PS3566.I43
Pike, Christopher.	none
Pike, Robert L.—see: Fish, Robert L.	
Pikser, Jeremy.	PS3566.I47
Pilcher, Rosamunde.	PR6066.I38
Pileggi, Nicholas.	none
Pilgrim, David, pseud.	PR6003.E3
Pincher, Chapman.	PR6066.I47
Pines, Paul.	PS3566.I522
Pinget, Robert.	PQ2631.I638
Pinkerton, A. Frank.	none
Pinkerton, Allan, 1819-1884.	none
Pintoro, John.	none
Piper, Evelyn.	PS3531.I76
Piper, H. Beam.	PS3566.I58
Pirie, David, 1946-	none
Pirkis, Catherine Louisa.	PR5185.P57
Pitt, Ingrid.	none
Pitt, Roxane.	none
Pittinger, Virginia.	none
Pitts, Denis.	PS3566.I86
Plagemann, Bentz, 1913-	PS3566.L25
Plaidy, Jean, 1906-	PR6015.I3
Plante, Edmund.	none
Platt, Charles.	PS3566.L285
Platt, Kin.	PS3566.L29
Player, Robert.	PR6031.L36
Plum, Josephine—see: Kurland, Michael.	
Plummer, T. Arthur.	none

Poe, Edgar Allan, 1809-1849.	PS2600-2648 [Z8699]
Polk, Dora.	PS3566.O476
Pollak, Richard.	PS3566.O512
Polland, Madeleine A.	PR6066.O38
Pollard, Alfred Oliver, 1893-	none
Pollitz, Edward A., 1937-	PS3566.O534
Pollock, J. C.	PS3566.O5348
Pollock, Robert.	PR6066.O42
Pollock, Ted.	PS3566.O535
Ponder, Patricia.	none
Pons, Maurice.	PQ2631.O6443
Ponthier, François.	PQ2631.O6476
Pope, Leo.	none
Popescu, Petru.	PC840.26.O57
Popplewell, Jack.	PR6031.O625
Porter, Anna.	PR9199.3.P624
Porter, Joyce.	PR6066.O72
Portnoy, Howard N.	PS3566.O664
Portway, Christopher.	none
Posey, Carl A., 1933-	PS3566.O67
Posner, Richard.	PS3566.O673
Posnick, Paul.	none
Post, Melville Davisson, 1871-1930.	PS3531.O76427
Postgate, Raymond William, 1896-	PR6066.O74
Potter, Dan.	PS3566.O696
Potter, Jeremy.	PR6066.O78
Potter, Jerry Allen.	PS3566.O698
Potts, Jean.	PS3531.O789
Potts, Ron.	none
Potts, Ruth.	none
Pournelle, Jerry, 1933-	PS3566.O815
Powell, John D.	none
Powell, Michael.	PR6066.O935
Powell, Richard Pitts.	PS3531.O966
Power, Patricia.	PR6066.O99
Powers, Elizabeth, 1944-	PS3566.O837
Powers, James.	PS3566.O838
Pownall, David, 1938-	PR6066.O995
Poyer, David.	PS3566.O978
Poyer, Joe.	PS3566.O98
Praed, Campbell, Mrs., 1851-1935.	PR5189.P6
Prather, Richard S.	PS3531.R14
Pratt, Theodore, 1901-	PS3531.R248
Preedy, George R.—see: Bowen, Marjorie, pseud.	
Preiss, Byron.	none

Prescott, Casey.	PS3566.R368
Prest, Thomas Peckett.	PR5189.P95
Preston, James, 1913-	PR6066.R4
Preston, T.	none
Price, Anthony.	PR6066.R5
Price, John-Allen.	none
Price, Richard, 1949-	PS3566.R544
Priestley, Brian, 1946-	none
Priestley, J. B. (John Boynton), 1894-	PR6031.R6 [Z8713.535]
Prince, Peter, 1942-	PR6066.R564
Prior, Allan, 1922-	PR6066.R57
Pritchett, Ariadne.	none
Prochnau, William W., 1937-	PS3566.R587
Procter, Maurice.	PR6031.R74
Proffitt, Nicholas, 1943-	PS3566.R643
Pronin, Barbara.	none
Pronzini, Bill.	PS3566.R67
Propper, Milton Morris, 1906-	none
Proud, Franklin M., 1920-	PR6066.R625
Pryce, Larry.	none
Pryce-Jones, David, 1936-	PR6066.R88
Pryor, Larry.	PS3566.R86
Puccetti, Roland.	PS3566.U25
Pugh, Marshall.	PR6066.U4
Puig, Manuel.	PQ7798.26.U4
Pulman, Jack.	PR6066.U45
Pulver, Mary Monica.	PS3566.U47
Punshon, Ernest Robertson, 1872-	none
Purser, Philip, 1925-	PR6066.U78
Purtell, Joseph.	PS3566.U7
Purvis, James L.	none
Putnam, Sean.	none
Puzo, Mario, 1920-	PS3566.U9
Pyle, A. M. (Albert M.)	PS3566.Y53
Quarry, Nick—see: Albert, Marvin H.	
Quartermain, James.	PR6067.U3
Queen, Ellery.	PS3533.U4
Queneau, Raymond, 1903-1976.	PQ2633.U43
Quentin, Patrick.	PR6033.U43
Quest, Erica.	PR6067.U347
Quest, Rodney.	PR6067.U35
Quigley, Aileen.	PR6067.U38
Quigley, John.	PR6067.U4
Quilici, Folco.	none
Quill, Monica—see: McInerny, Ralph M.	

Quilty, Rafe.	PR6067.U47
Quinn, Derry.	PR6067.U54
Quinn, Jake.	none
Quinn, Olga.	none
Quinn, Patrick.	PR6067.U55
Quinn, Seabury, 1889-1969.	PS3533.U69
Quinn, Simon—see: Smith, Martin Cruz, 1942-	
Quinn, Terry, 1945-	PS3567.U3543
Quinnell, A. J.	PS3567.U36
Quintano, Dorothy.	PS3533.U697
Rabe, Peter.	none
Rabinowitz, Max.	none
Racina, Thom, 1947-	PS3568.A25
Radano, Gene.	none
Radcliffe, Ann Ward, 1764-1823.	PR5200-5204
Radcliffe, Janette—see: Roberts, Janet Louise, 1925-1982.	
Radcliffe, Jocelyn.	none
Radford, Edwin, 1891-	none
Radford, John P.	PS3568.A33
Radley, Edward.	none
Radley, Sheila.	PR6068.O846
Rae, Hugh C.	PR6068.A25
Raef, Laura C.	none
Rafferty, S. S.	PS3568.A38
Ragosta, Millie J.	PS3568.A413
Raine, Richard—see: Forbes, Colin, 1923-	
Ralston, Gilbert A., 1912-	PS3568.A435
Ramm, Carl.	PS3568.A4465
Ramrus, Al.	PS3568.A448
Ramsay, Diana.	PR6068.A48
Ramsay, Jack.	none
Ranbern, James.	none
Rance, Joseph.	PR6068.A53
Randall, Bob.	PS3568.A489
Randall, Florence Engel, 1917-	PS3568.A493
Randall, Rona, 1911-	PR6035.A58
Randell, Christine.	none
Randisi, Robert J.	PS3568.A53
Randle, Kevin D.	none
Randolphe, Arabella.	none
Rankin, Ian.	PR6068.A57
Ransom, Daniel.	none
Ransome, Stephen—see: Davis, Frederick C., 1902-	
Raphael, Frederic, 1931-	PR6068.A6
Raphael, Rick.	PS3568.A614
Raskin, Ellen.	none

Raskin, Jonah, 1942-	PS3568.A713
Rathbone, Julian, 1935-	PR6068.A8
Rattray, Simon—see: Trevor, Elleston.	
Rauch, Constance.	PS3568.A788
Raven, James.	none
Raven, Simon, 1927-	PR6068.A9
Ravenswood, Fritzen.	none
Ravin, Neil.	PS3568.A84
Rawlings, Paul.	none
Rawls, Philip.	none
Rawson, Clayton, 1906-	PS3535.A848
Ray, Robert J. (Robert Joseph), 1935- [both used]	PS3568.A92178
	PS3568.A9218
Raymond, Diana.	PR6068.A947
Raymond, Ernest, 1888-	PR6035.A9
Raymond, Patrick.	PR6068.A948
Rayner, Claire.	PR6068.A949
Rayner, William.	PR6068.A95
Raynes, Jean.	PS3568.A95
Reach, James.	PS3535.E12
Read, Piers Paul, 1941-	PR6068.E25
Reade, Bill.	PR6068.E258
Reade, Hamish, 1936-	none
Readus, James-Howard.	none
Ready, Stuart.	PR6035.E244
Reagan, Thomas B.	PS3568.E225
Reakes, Paul.	PR6068.E28
Reasoner, James M.	none
Reaves, Michael.	PS3568.E269
Reddoch, Jennifer.	none
Redfield, Malissa.	PS3568.E345
Redgate, John—see: Kennedy, Adam.	
Redwood, Alec—see: Sava, George, 1903-	
Reed, Christine, 1947-	none
Reed, Dana.	none
Reed, Harry.	none
Reed, Ishmael, 1938-	PS3568.E365
Reed, J. D., 1940-	PS3568.E366
Reed, Kit.	PS3568.E367
Reed, Rex.	PS3568.E3694
Rees, Arthur John, 1872-	none
Rees, Eloise Rodkey.	none
Rees, Joan.	PR6068.E38
Reese, John Henry.	PS3568.E43
Reese, Judith.	none
Reese, Ralph.	none

Reese, Sammy.	PS3568.E433
Reeve, Arthur Benjamin, 1880-1936.	PS3535.E354
Reeves, John, 1926-	PR9199.3.R425
Reeves, Robert Nicholas.	PS3568.E472
Regan, Mark.	none
Regester, Seeley—see: Victor, Metta Victoria Fuller, 1831-1885.	
Reginald, R.	PS3568.E4754
Reid, Desmond.	none
Reid, James (James W.)	PR6068.E44
Reid, Jamie.	PR6068.E45
Reid, Philip.	PR6068.E454
Reiffel, Leonard.	PS3568.E4795
Reilly, Helen Kieran.	none
Reinsmith, Richard.	none
Reisman, John.	none
Reisner, Mary.	none
Reiss, Bob.	PS3568.E517
Reit, Seymour V.	none
Reiter, B. P., 1945-	PS3568.E525
Rellas, Dorothy.	none
Relling, William.	none
Rémy, Pierre-Jean, 1937-	PQ2678.E42
Renauld, Ron.	none
Rendell, Ruth, 1930-	PR6068.E63
Renek, Morris.	PS3568.E58
Renn, Chris.	PS3568.E595
Rennert, Maggie.	PS3568.E6
Reno, Marie R.	PS3568.E65
Resnicow, Herbert.	PS3568.E69
Resnick, Michael D.	none
Resnick, Mike—see: Resnick, Michael D.	
Reston, James, 1941-	PS3568.E75
Revelli, George.	PR6068.E9
Rey, Pierre.	PQ2678.E888
Reybold, Malcolm.	PS3568.E86
Reynolds, Baillie, Mrs.—see: Reynolds, Gertrude M. Robins, d. 1939.	
Reynolds, Bonnie Jones.	PS3568.E887
Reynolds, Catherine.	none
Reynolds, George W. M. (George William MacArthur), 1814-1879.	PR5221.R35
Reynolds, Gertrude M. Robins, d. 1939.	PR6035.E73
Reynolds, Mack.	PS3568.E895
Reynolds, William J.	PS3568.E93
Rhea, Nicholas.	PR6068.H4
Rhode, John, 1884-1964.	PR6037.T778
Rhodes, Evan H.	PS3568.H57

Rhodes, Richard.	PS3568.H64
Rhodes, Russell L.	PS3568.H65
Rice, Craig.	none
Rice, Jeff.	none
Rich, Nicholas.	none
Rich, Virginia.	PS3568.I298
Richard, James L.	none
Richard, Susan.	none
Richards, Clay, 1910-	PS3505.R89225
Richards, Curtis.	none
Richards, Guy, 1905-	none
Richards, Judith.	PS3568.I3155
Richards, Leslie.	none
Richards, Nat, 1942-	PS3568.I316
Richards, Paul.	none
Richards, Tad.	none
Richards, Tony.	none
Richardson, Carl.	none
Richardson, Mozelle.	PS3568.I319
Richardson, Robert.	PR6068.I2467
Richmond, Donald.	PS3568.I3515
Richmond, Mary.	none
Rickard, Jessie Louise Moore, 1879-	none
Rico, Don.	none
Riddell, J. H., Mrs., 1832-1906.	PR5227.R33
Rider, Anne, 1924-	PR6068.I282
Rider, J. W.	PS3568.Y398
Rider, Warrick W.	none
Ridyard, Richard D.	none
Riefe, Alan.	none
Riefe, Barbara—see: Riefe, Alan.	
Rife, Ellouise A.	none
Rifkin, Shepard, 1918-	PS3568.I365
Rigg, Jennifer, 1939-	PR6068.I336
Riggs, John R., 1945-	PS3568.I372
Riis, David Allen.	none
Riley, Dick.	PS3568.I3778
Riley, Frank, 1927-	PS3568.I378
Riley, Joe.	none
Rilla, Wolf Peter.	PR6035.I597
Rimmer, Robert H., 1917-	PS3568.I4
Rinehart, Mary Roberts, 1876-1958.	PS3535.I73
Ripley, H. A. (Harold Austin), 1896-	none
Ripley, Jack—see: Wainwright, John William, 1921-	
Rippon, Marion.	PR6068.I6
Risku, Cillay.	none

Ritchie, Rita.	none
Ritchie, Simon.	PR9199.3.R524
Ritner, Peter, 1927-	PS3568.I82
Ritter, Margaret.	PS3568.I827
Rivera, William L.	none
Rivers, Anne.	PR6068.I93
Rivers, Gayle.	PR6068.I94
Rivett, Edith Caroline, 1894-	none
Roadarmel, Paul.	PS3568.O16
Robbe-Grillet, Alain, 1922-	PQ2635.O117
Robbins, David.	none
Robbins, Norman.	PR6068.O13
Robens, Howard.	PR9199.3.R5266
Roberts, Gillian.	PS3568.O2384
Roberts, James Hall—see: Duncan, Robert Lipscomb, 1927-	
Roberts, Jan.	PS3568.O2386
Roberts, Janet Louise, 1925-1982.	PS3552.R656
Roberts, Lee—see: Martin, Robert Lee.	
Roberts, Lillian.	none
Roberts, Morley, 1857-1942.	PR6035.O532
Roberts, Patricia (Patricia Flora Clementina)	PS3568.O246
Roberts, Rinalda.	none
Roberts, Suzanne, 1925-	PS3568.O2474
Roberts, Thomas A., 1947-	PS3568.O2475
Roberts, Willo Davis.	PS3568.O2478
Robertson, Brian.	none
Robertson, Charles.	none
Robertson, Colin.	none
Robertson, Keith, 1914-	none
Robertson, Netta.	none
Robeson, Kenneth.	PS3507.E5777
Robin, Liliane, 1925-	PQ2635.O182
Robinett, Stephen.	PS3568.O274
Robinson, Abby.	PS3568.O2775
Robinson, Derek, 1932 Apr. 12-	PR6068.O1954
Robinson, Edward L.	PS3568.O288
Robinson, Jeffrey.	none
Robinson, Leonard Wallace, 1912-	PS3568.O3
Robinson, Richard.	none
Robinson, Robert, 1927-	PR6068.O197
Robinson, Sondra Till.	PS3568.O3154
Robson, James, 1944 or 5-	PR6068.O23
Roby, Adelaide Q.	none
Roby, Mary Linn.	PS3568.O319
Roche, Arthur Somers, 1883-1935.	PS3535.O2678
Rochester, George E.	none

Rock, Phillip, 1927-	PS3568.O33
Rockwood, Harry—see: Young, Ernest A.	
Roderus, Frank.	PS3568.O346
Roeburt, John.	PS3535.O383
Roffman, Jan.—see: Summerton, Margaret.	
Rogers, Barbara, 1935-	PS3568.O39
Rogers, David, 1927-	PS3568.O43
Rogers, J. Trumbell.	none
Rogers, James Cass.	none
Rogers, Joel Townley.	none
Rogers, Ray Mount.	PS3568.O455
Rohan, Donald.	PS3568.O495
Rohmer, Richard H.	PR9199.3.R58
Rohmer, Sax, 1883-1959.	PR6045.A37 [Z8949.27]
Roland, Betty.	PR9619.3.R615
Romaine, Dallas.	none
Roman, Eric, 1926-	PS3568.O545
Roman, Howard.	PS3568.O546
Romanes, Julian.	PR6068.O43
Romano, Deane.	PS3568.O547
Romano, Don.	PS3568.O548
Rome, Tony.	none
Ronns, Edward—see: Aarons, Edward S. (Edward Sidney), 1916-1975.	
Ronson, Mark.	none
Rook, Tony.	PR6068.O53
Rooke, Rebecca.	none
Roos, Kelley.	PS3535.O54665
Roosevelt, Elliott, 1910-	PS3535.O549
Roosevelt, James, 1907-	PS3568.O638
Roote, Mike.	none
Rooth, Anne Reed.	PS3568.O67
Roper, Gayle G.	PS3568.O68
Roper, L. V.	none
Roscoe, Theodore.	PS3535.O6423
Rose, Elizabeth.	none
Rose, Geoffrey, 1932-	PR6068.O66
Rose, Patricia.	none
Rosen, Dorothy.	PS3568.O7648
Rosen, Norma Stahl.	PS3568.O77
Rosen, Richard Dean, 1949-	PS3568.O774
Rosen, Sidney.	none
Rosenbaum, Ron.	PS3568.O778
Rosenberg, Philip, 1942-	PS3568.O7877
Rosenberg, Stuart.	PS3568.O7883
Rosenberger, Joseph.	none

Rosenblum, Robert J.	PS3568.O795
Rosenfeld, Lulla.	PS3568.O815
Rosner, Joseph, 1922-	PS3568.O8419
Ross, Albert—see: Goldstein, Arthur D.	
Ross, Angus, 1927-	PR6068.O817
Ross, Ann B.	PS3568.O84198
Ross, Barnaby—see: Queen, Ellery.	
Ross, Cameron.	none
Ross, Clarissa—see: Ross, W. E. D. (William Edward Daniel), 1912-	
Ross, Dan—see: Ross, W. E. D. (William Edward Daniel), 1912-	
Ross, Dana—see: Ross, W. E. D. (William Edward Daniel), 1912-	
Ross, Frank, 1938-	PR6068.O8187
Ross, Hal, 1941-	PR9199.3.R598
Ross, Ian—see: Rossmann, John F.	
Ross, Jonathan, 1916-	PR6068.O835
Ross, Kathleen.	none
Ross, Marilyn—see: Ross, W. E. D. (William Edward Daniel), 1912-	
Ross, Paul.	none
Ross, Paul B.	none
Ross, Philip, 1932-	PS3568.O8439
Ross, Regina—see: Mackintosh, May.	
Ross, Robert.	PS3568.O8443
Ross, Sam, 1912-	PS3535.O7493
Ross, Sheila.	PR6068.O825
Ross, W. E. D. (William Edward Daniel), 1912-	PR9199.3.R5996
Ross, William, 1923-	PS3568.O845
Rossi, Bruno.	none
Rossiter, John.	PR6068.O835
Rossmann, John F.	none
Rossner, Judith.	PS3568.O848
Rossner, Robert.	PS3568.O849
Rostand, Robert—see: Hopkins, Robert S.	
Rosten, Leo Calvin, 1908-	PS3535.O7577
Rostov, Mara.	PS3568.O8493
Roth, Arthur J., 1925-	PS3568.O852
Roth, Holly.	none
Rothberg, Abraham.	PS3568.O857
Rothblatt, Henry B.	none
Rothman, Judith.	none
Rothrock, Ken.	none
Rothstein, Allan.	none
Rothstein, Raphael.	none
Rothweiler, Paul R., 1931-	PS3568.O869
Rothwell, H. T.	PS3568.O87
Rotsstein, Aaron Nathan.	PS3568.O874
Rouch, James.	none

Roudybush, Alexandra.	PS3568.O88
Roueché, Berton, 1911-	PS3535.O845
Rouverol, Jean.	none
Rovin, Jeff.	PS3568.O8884
Rowan, Deirdre—see: Williams, Jeanne, 1930-	
Rowan, Hester.	PR6068.O846
Rowden, Dick.	none
Rowe, James N., 1938-	PS3568.O93
Rowe, John.	PR9619.3.R6277
Roy, A. E. (Archie E.), 1924-	PR6068.O95
Royce, Kenneth.	PR6068.O98
Ruark, Eric B.	none
Rubel, Marc.	PS3568.U18
Ruben, William S.	none
Rubens, Bernice.	PR6068.U2
Rubens, Robert.	none
Rubin, Ron.	PS3568.U285
Rubinstein, Paul, 1935-	none
Rudd, Colin.	none
Rudorff, Raymond.	PR6068.U3
Ruell, Patrick—see: Hill, Reginald.	
Rumanes, George N.	PR9115.9.R8
Rundle, Anne.	PR6068.U7
Runyon, Charles W., 1928-	PS3568.U53
Ruse, Gary Alan, 1946-	PS3568.U72
Ruse, Paul.	none
Russell, Andrew Joseph.	PS3568.U7655
Russell, Agnes.	none
Russell, Charles—see: Kelly, Terence, 1920-	
Russell, Charlotte Murray, 1899-	none
Russell, Enid S.	PS3568.U766
Russell, Martin James, 1934-	PR6068.U86
Russell, Ray.	PS3568.U77
Russell, Richard.	none
Russell, William.	PR5271.R8
Russell, William Clark, 1844-1911.	PR5280-5283
Russo, John, 1939-	none
Rutherford, Cecile.	none
Rutherford, Douglas, 1915-	PR6025.A1697
Rutherford, Ward.	PR6068.U87
Ruuth, Marianne.	none
Ruyle, John.	PS3568.U88
Ryan, Alan, 1943-	PS3568.Y26
Ryan, Donald.	none
Ryan, J. M.—see: McDermott, John, 1919-1977.	
Ryan, Jim.	none

Ryan, Peter.	none
Ryan, Thomas Joseph, 1942-	PS3568.Y394
Ryck, Francis.	PQ2678.Y3
Rydell, Forbes, pseud.	none
Ryder, Jonathan, 1927-	PS3562.U26
Ryland, Clive.	none
Sabatini, Rafael, 1875-1950.	PR6037.A2
Saberhagen, Fred, 1930-	PS3569.A215
Sachar, Howard Morley, 1928-	PS3569.A225
Sackett, Jeffrey.	none
Sadler, Barry, 1940-	PS3569.A24
Sadler, Mark—see: Arden, William, 1924-	
Saffron, Robert.	PS3569.A282
Sagola, Mario J.	PS3569.A365
Saint-Lambert, Patrick.	PQ2679.A478
Sakol, Jeannie.	PS3569.A455
Salcido, Craig.	none
Sale, Medora.	none
Sale, Richard, 1911-	PS3537.A413
Salinger, Pierre.	PS3569.A4595
Salisbury, Carola—see: Butterworth, Michael, 1924-	
Salisbury, Harrison Evans, 1908-	PS3569.A4596
Salisbury, John.	PR6069.A474
Salt, Jonathan.	none
Salvato, Sharon Anne.	PS3569.A46233
Samson, Joan, 1937-	PS3569.A4667
San-Antonio.	PQ2607.A558
Sanchez, Thomas.	PS3569.A469
Sand, Margaret.	PS3569.A4694
Sandberg, Berent.	PS3569.A4696
Sandberg, Peter Lars, 1934-	PS3569.A4697
Sanders, David.	PR6069.A512
Sanders, James, 1911-	PR9619.3.S25
Sanders, Lawrence, 1920-	PS3569.A5125
Sanders, Leonard.	PS3569.A5127
Sandford, Jane.	none
Sandroff, Ronni.	PS3569.A5196
Sandulescu, Jacques.	PS3569.A5198
Sanford, Harry.	none
Sanford, Ursula.	none
Sang, Bob.	PS3569.A5267
Sang, Dusty.	none
Sangster, Jimmy.	PR6069.A53
Sann, Paul.	PS3569.A54
Santiago, V. J.	none
Saperstein, David.	PS3569.A584

Sapir, Richard.	PS3569.A59
Sarabande, William.	none
Saralegui, Jorge.	nonef
Sarasin, J. G.	none
Sargent, Craig.	none
Sargent, Patricia.	none
Sariola, Mauri.	PH355.S27
Sarrantonio, Al.	PS3569.A73
Satterthwait, Walter.	none
Saul, John.	PS3569.A787
Saul, John Ralston.	PR6069.A78
Saul, Oscar.	PS3537.A87
Sauter, Eric.	none
Savage, David—see: Hossent, Harry.	
Savage, Ernest, 1918-	PS3569.A8235
Savage, Jenny.	PR6069.A936
Savage, Richard Henry, 1846-1903.	PS2779.S5
Savage, Thomas.	PS3569.A83
Savage, Wallace.	PS3569.A835
Sawkins, Raymond H.—see: Forbes, Colin, 1923-	
Sawn, David.	none
Sax, Andre.	none
Saxon, Alex, 1943-	PS3566.R67
Saxon, Peter.	none
Saxon, Van.	none
Sayers, Dorothy L. (Dorothy Leigh), 1893-1957.	PR6037.A95
Scaduto, Anthony.	PS3569.C24
Scanlon, Noel.	PR6069.C33
Scannell, Vernon.	PR6037.C25
Scarborough, Chuck.	PS3569.C32
Scarpetta, Frank.	none
Scerbanenco, Giorgio, 1911-1969.	PQ4841.C4
Schaefer, Frank, 1936-	none
Scherf, Margaret.	PS3537.C3214
Schier, Norma.	PS3569.C4855
Schiff, Barry J.	PS3569.C486
Schleifer, Gerry.	PR6069.C516
Schnurr, William.	none
Schock, T. A.	none
Schoell, William.	none
Scholefield, Alan.	PR9369.3.S3
Scholey, Jean.	PR9399.9.S36
Schorr, Mark.	PS3537.C598
Schrader, Leonard.	none
Schubert, John D.	none
Schuler, Frank.	none

Schulman, Sarah, 1958-	PS3569.C5393
Schutz, Benjamin M.	PS3569.C5556
Schwartz, Alan.	PS3569.C5648
Schweitzer, Gertrude, 1909-	PS3537.C816
Sciascia, Leonardo.	PQ4879.C54
Scoppettone, Sandra.	PS3569.C586
Scortia, Thomas N., 1926-	PS3569.C587
Scott, Annjeanette.	none
Scott, Antonia.	none
Scott, Chris, 1945-	PR9199.3.S32
Scott, Deborah.	none
Scott, Douglas, 1926-	PR6069.C586
Scott, Gavin, 1950-	PR6069.C588
Scott, Genevieve.	none
Scott, Jack Denton, 1915-	PS3569.C63
Scott, Jack S.	PR6069.C589
Scott, James Maurice.	PR6037.C927
Scott, Jeffry.	none
Scott, Jeremy.	PR6054.I29
Scott, Jody.	none
Scott, June Meindl.	PS3569.C64
Scott, Justin.	PS3569.C644
Scott, Margerie.	PR9199.3.S36
Scott, Milton.	none
Scott, Reginald Thomas Maitland, 1882-	none
Scott, Steve.	none
Scott, Virgil, 1914-	PS3537.C92937
Scott, Warwick—see: Trevor, Elleston.	
Scott-Heron, Gil, 1949-	PS3569.C7
Scotter, John.	none
Scotti, R. A.	PS3569.C72
Scowcroft, Richard.	PS3537.C954
Sea-Lion—see: Bennett, Geoffrey Martin.	
Seaman, Donald.	PR6069.E154
Seamark—see: Small, Austin J.	
Searle, Weston.	none
Searls, Hank, 1922-	PS3569.E18
Sears, Ruth McCarthy.	none
Sebastian, Margaret, 1921-	PS3569.E28
Sebentall, R. E.	PS3537.E1884
Sederberg, Arelo.	PS3569.E315
Seeley, Mabel, 1903-	none
Segal, Alan.	none
Segal, Don.	none
Seidman, Robert J.	PS3569.E532
Sela, Owen.	PR9440.9.S4

Selby, Hubert.	PS3569.E547
Selig, Elaine Booth.	none
Seligson, Tom.	PS3569.E573
Sellar, Maurice.	none
Sellers, Con.	PS3569.E575
Sellers, Mary.	none
Sellers, Michael, 1941-	PR6069.E3695
Selmark, George—see: Truss, Seldon, 1892-	
Selwyn, Francis.	PR6069.E382
Semenov, IUlian, 1931-	PG3486.E45
Semprún, Jorge.	PQ2679.E4
Serafín, David.	PR6069.E6
Sergeant, Adeline, 1851-1904.	none
Serling, Robert J.	PS3569.E7
Serling, Rod, 1924-	PS3537.E654
Serrian, Michael.	none
Settle, Mary Lee.	PS3569.E84
Seuffert, Muir.	none
Severn, Richard.	none
Seward, Jack.	PS3569.E88
Sewart, Alan.	none
Seymour, Gerald.	PR6069.E734
Seymour, Henry.	none
Shabtai, Sabi H.	PS3569.H23
Shaffer, A. (Anthony), 1926-	PR6069.H258
Shagan, Steve.	PS3569.H313
Shah, Diane K.	PS3569.H314
Shannon, Dell, 1921-	PS3562.I515
Shannon, Doris.	PR9199.3.S49
Shankman, Sarah.	PS3569.H3327
Shapiro, Milton J.	none
Sharkey, Jack.	PS3569.H3427
Sharland, Mike.	PR6069.H336
Sharman, Miriam.	none
Sharman, Nick.	none
Sharp, Alan.	none
Sharp, Marilyn.	PS3569.H3434
Shattuck, Dora.	none
Shavelson, Melville, 1917-	PS3569.H357
Shaw, David, 1943-	none
Shaw, Howard.	PR6069.H375
Shaw, Irwin, 1913-	PS3537.H384
Shaw, Robin.	PS3569.H386
Shea, Robert.	PS3569.H39125
Shealy, Larry.	none
Shearing, Joseph—see: Bowen, Marjorie, pseud.	

Sheckley, Robert, 1928-	PS3569.H392
Shedley, Ethan I.	PS3569.H39214
Shelby, Brit.	PS3569.H39257
Sheldon, Sidney.	PS3569.H3927
Sheldon, Walter J.	PS3569.H3928
Shellabarger, Samuel, 1888-1954.	PS3537.H64
Shelley, Sidney, 1921-	none
Shelynn, Jack.	none
Shenton, Alan.	none
Shepard, Sam, 1943-	PS3569.H394
Shepherd, John—see: Ballard, Todhunter, 1903-	
Shepherd, L. P.	none
Shepherd, Michael, 1927-	PS3562.U26
Sheppard, Stephen, 1945-	PR6069.H4553
Sherburne, James, 1925-	PS3569.H399
Sheridan, Anne-Marie.	PR6069.H456
Sherman, Charlotte A.—see: Sherman, Jory.	
Sherman, Dan.	PS3569.H416
Sherman, David.	none
Sherman, Jory.	PS3569.H43
Sherman, Patricia J.	none
Sherman, Robert, 1931-	none
Sherman, Robin.	none
Sherman, Roger.	none
Sherman, Steve, 1938-	PS3569.H4337
Sherman, William.	none
Sherriff, R. C. (Robert Cedric), 1896-1975.	PR6037.H513
Sherry, Edna.	none
Sherwood, John, 1913-	PR6037.H517
Sherwood, Pete.	none
Shiel, Matthew Phipps, 1865-1947.	PR6037.H524
Shimer, Ruth H.	PS3569.H49
Shingler, William G.	none
Shipway, George, 1908-	PR6069.H5
Shoebridge, Marjorie.	PR6069.H56
Shoesmith, Kathleen A.	none
Shore, Norman.	none
Shore, Valery.	none
Short, Christopher.	none
Shreve, Susan Richards.	PS3569.H74
Shroyer, Frederick B.	PS3569.H744
Shryack, Dennis.	none
Shub, Joyce L.	PS3569.H75
Shubin, Seymour.	PS3569.H754
Shulman, Irving.	PS3537.H99185
Shulman, Sandra.	PS3569.H775

Shura, Mary Francis.	PS3553.R226
Shute, Nevil, 1899-1960.	PR6027.O54
Sibley, Patricia.	PR6069.I25
Siddons, Anne Rivers.	PS3569.I28
Siegel, Benjamin, 1914-	PS3569.I37
Siegel, Jack.	none
Sigel, Efrem.	PS3569.I412
Siegrist, Robert R.	none
Silbersky, Leif.	PT9876.29.I39
Silberstang, Edwin, 1930-	PS3569.I415
Siller, Van—see: Van Siller, Hilda.	
Silver, Alfred.	none
Silver, Victoria.	none
Silverman, Robert M.	none
Silverman, Robert S.	none
Silverwood, Roger.	PR6069.I365
Simart, Hélène.	PQ2679.I45
Simenon, Georges, 1903-	PQ2637.I53
	[Z8819.I47]
Simmel, Johannes Mario.	PT2639.I63
Simmons, Diane, 1948-	PS3569.I47293
Simmons, Geoffrey S.	PS3569.I4732
Simmons, John.	none
Simmons, Mary Kay.	PS3569.I476
Simmons, Steven.	PS3569.I4768
Simon, Angela.	none
Simon, Leonard, 1937-	PS3569.I4825
Simon, Roger Lichtenberg.	PS3569.I485
Simon, S. J., d. 1948.	none
Simons, Roger, pseud.	PR6069.I42
Simpson, Dorothy, 1933-	PR6069.I422
Simpson, George E.	PS3569.I4895
Simpson, Howard R., 1925-	PS3569.I49
Simpson, M. E.	none
Simpson, Margaret, 1913-	PR6069.I427
Sims, George, 1923-	PR6037.I715
Sims, George Robert, 1847-1922.	PR5452.S4
Sims, L. V.	none
Sinclair, Andrew.	PR6069.I5
Sinclair, Dennis.	none
Sinclair, Michael.	PR6069.I54
Sinclair, Murray.	PS3569.I525
Sinclair, Olga.	PR6069.I55
Singer, Loren.	PS3569.I545
Singer, Norman.	PS3569.I55
Singer, Rochelle—see: Singer, Shelley.	

Singer, Sally M.	PS3569.I57
Singer, Shelley.	PS3569.I565
Singleton, James R.	PS3569.I575
Siodmak, Kurt, 1902-	PR6037.I775
Sjöwall, Maj, 1935-	PT9876.29.J63
Skehan, Everett M.	PS3569.K38
Skinner, Ainslie.	PR6069.K48
Skinner, Michael.	none
Skipp, John.	none
Skirrow, Desmond.	PR6069.K54
Skoggard, Bruno.	PS3569.K6
Škvorecky, Josef.	PG5038.S527
Slabber, I. G.	none
Slade, Michael.	PR9199.3.S55115
Sladek, John Thomas.	PS3569.L25
Slater, Ian, 1941-	PR9199.3.S5512
Slater, Nigel, 1944-	PR6069.L334
Slavitt, David R., 1935-	PS3569.L3
Slawson, Evan.	none
Slear, Genevieve.	PS3569.L35
Slesar, Henry.	PS3569.L38
Sloan, Sarah.	none
Sloane, William Milligan, 1906-1974.	PS3537.L59
Slovo, Gillian, 1952-	PR6069.L56
Small, Austin J.	none
Smart, Hawley, 1833-1893.	none
Smiley, Jane.	PS3569.M39
Smith, A. C. H. (Anthony Charles H.), 1935-	PR6069.M42
Smith, Alison, 1932-	PS3569.M46
Smith, Caesar—see: Trevor, Elleston.	
Smith, Charles Merrill.	PS3569.M5156
Smith, Colin.	PR6069.M428
Smith, D. W.	none
Smith, Dan.	PR6069.M444
Smith, Dave.	none
Smith, David, 1936-	PS3569.M51718
Smith, Dennis, 1940-	PS3569.M52
Smith, Dodie, 1896-	PR6037.M38
Smith, Don, 1909-	none
Smith, Edgar, 1934-	PS3569.M534
Smith, Edward Ernest.	PR9619.3.S57
Smith, Evelyn E.	PS3569.M53515
Smith, Frank A.	PR6069.M47
Smith, Frank E., 1919-	none
Smith, Frederick E. (Frederick Escreet), 1919-	PR6069.M482
Smith, Godfrey, 1926-	PR6069.M483

Smith, Guy N.	none
Smith, J. C. S.	PS3569.M5374
Smith, Jack Nickle.	PR6069.M487
Smith, Jasper.	none
Smith, John, 1943-	PR6069.M495
Smith, Julie, 1944-	PS3569.M537553
Smith, Kay Nolte.	PS3569.M537554
Smith, L. Neil.	none
Smith, Laura.	none
Smith, Lou.	PR6069.M52
Smith, Mark, 1935-	PS3569.M53766
Smith, Martin Cruz, 1942-	PS3569.M5377
Smith, Michael A., 1942-	PS3569.M53783
Smith, Mitchell, 1935-	PS3569.M537834
Smith, Nancy Carolyn.	none
Smith, Nancy Taylor.	none
Smith, Naomi Gladish.	none
Smith, Neville.	none
Smith, Robert Arthur, 1926-	none
Smith, Robert Charles.	PR6069.M53
Smith, Robert Kimmel, 1930-	PS3569.M53795
Smith, Shelley, 1912-	PR6037.M57
Smith, Steven.	PR9199.3.S5615
Smith, Surrey.	none
Smith, Sydney, 1912-	PR6069.M554
Smith, Terrence Lore.	PS3569.M538
Smith, Vern E.	PS3569.M5394
Smith, Wilbur A.	PR9405.9.S5
Smithies, Richard H. R.	none
Smitten, Richard.	none
Smoke, Stephen L., 1949-	PS3569.M645
Snell, David, 1942-	PS3569.N35
Snell, Edmund.	none
Snelling, Laurence, 1933-	PS3569.N4
Snellings, John.	none
Snodgress, G. M.	none
Snow, C. P. (Charles Percy), 1905-	PR6037.N58
Snow, Kathleen.	PS3569.N623
Snow, Lyndon—see: Ansle, Dorothy Phoebe.	
Snyder, Gene.	none
Snyder, Zilpha Keatley.	PS3569.N97
Sobel, Irwin Philip.	PS3569.O2
Sobol, Donald J., 1924-	none
Sodaro, Craig.	none
Soderberg, Dale L.	none
Sohl, Jerry.	PS3569.O4

Solomon, Brad.	PS3569.O595
Somers, Suzanne.	PS3569.O652
Somerville-Large, Peter.	PR6069.O43
Soutar, Andrew, 1879-1941.	none
Southcott, Audley.	PR6069.O87
Southworth, Emma Dorothy Eliza Nevitte, 1819-1899.	PS2892
Southworth, Louis.	none
Souvestre, Pierre, 1874-1914.	PQ2637.O84
Spain, Peter.	PR6069.P28
Spann, Weldon.	none
Spark, Muriel.	PR6037.P29
Sparkia, Roy.	none
Sparks, Christine.	none
Spector, Craig.	none
Speicher, Helen Ross.	none
Speight, T. W. (Thomas Wilkinson), 1830-1915.	PS2894.S54
Spencer, Ross H.	PS3569.P454
Spetz, Steven N.	none
Spicer, Bart.	PS3569.P464
Spicer, Dorothy Gladys.	PS3569.P465
Spicer, Michael.	none
Spike, Paul, 1947-	PS3569.P53
Spilken, Aron, 1939-	PS3569.P54
Spillane, Mickey, 1918-	PS3537.P652
Spinrad, Norman.	PS3569.P55
Spooner, John D.	PS3569.P6
Spore, Keith.	none
Spouse, Mary.	none
Sprague, Joyce Claypool.	none
Spruill, Steven G.	PS3569.P733
Squerent, Will—see: Bradbury, Wilbur.	
Squire, Robin.	PR6069.Q5
St. Clair, David.	PS3569.A425
St. Clair, Elizabeth.	none
St. Clair, Jeananne.	none
St. Clair, Katherine.	PS3558.U323
St. Clair, Leonard.	PS3569.A43
St. George, Geoffrey.	PS3569.A452
St. George, Judith, 1931-	none
St. James, Bernard.	PS3569.A4533
St. James, Ian.	PR6069.A423
St. John, Barnett.	none
St. John, Cheryl.	none
St. John, David—see: Hunt, E. Howard (Everette Howard), 1918-	
St. John, Nicole—see: Johnston, Norma.	
St. Martin, Thomas.	none

Stacey, Tom, 1930-	PR6069.T18
Stacpoole, H. De Vere (Henry De Vere), 1863-1951.	PR6037.T15
Stacy, Ryder.	none
Stade, George.	PS3569.T145
Stadley, Pat.	PS3569.T15
Stafford, Caroline.	PS3569.T165
Stagge, Jonathan, pseud.	none
Stahl, Norman.	PS3569.T313
Stall, Mike.	none
Stam, Paul Justin.	none
Stand, Marguerite.	PR6069.T25
Stander, Siegfried.	PR9369.3.S77
Standish, Burt L., 1866-1945.	none
Standish, Robert—see: Gerahty, Digby.	
Stang, JoAnne.	PS3569.T3318
Stanley, John.	none
Stanley, Michael.	none
Stanley, Ray.	none
Stanley, Sandra.	none
Stansberry, Domenic.	PS3569.T3335
Stanton, Coralie, pseud.	none
Stanton, Ken.	none
Stanton, Martin.	none
Stanton, Paul—see: Beaty, David.	
Stanwood, Brooks.	PS3569.T3342
Stanwood, Donald A.	PS3569.T3343
Stapp, Robert.	PS3569.T3355
Stark, Richard—see: Westlake, Donald E.	
Starks, Richard.	none
Starnes, Richard.	PS3569.T336
Starrett, Vincent, 1886-1974.	PS3537.T246
Stashover, Daniel.	PS3569.T33635
Stead, C. K. (Christian Karlson), 1932-	PR9639.3.S7
Stead, Christina, 1902-1983.	PR9619.3.S75
Stearn, Jess.	PS3569.T338
Stebel, S. L.	PS3569.T33815
Steed, Neville.	PR6069.T387
Steegmuller, Francis, 1906-	PS3537.T267
Steele, Curtis.	PS3537.T2687
Steeley, Robert Derek.	none
Steen, Marguerite.	PR6069.T4
Stein, Aaron Marc, 1906-	PS3537.T3184
Stein, Benjamin, 1944-	PS3569.T36
Stein, Gertrude, 1874-1946.	PS3537.T323
Stein, Herbert, 1916-	none
Stein, Peter, 1932-	none

Stein, Sol.	PS3569.T375
Steinberg, Harriet.	none
Steirman, Hy.	none
Stephan, Leslie.	PS3569.T3827
Stephens, Casey.	none
Stephens, Edward Carl, 1924-	PS3569.T384
Stephens, Reed.	PS3554.O469
Stephenson, Maureen.	none
Sterling, Stewart—see: Winchell, Prentice, 1895-	
Sterling, Thomas L.	none
Stern, Daniel, 1928-	PS3569.T3887
Stern, Richard G., 1928-	PS3569.T39
Stern, Richard Martin, 1915-	PS3569.T394
Stern, Stuart—see: Rae, Hugh C.	
Sternberg, Cecilia.	PR6069.T442
Stevens, Christian D.	PS3569.T45114
Stevens, Curtis.	none
Stevens, Diane.	PS3569.T4512
Stevens, Gus.	none
Stevens, Jon.	none
Stevens, Lucile Vernon.	none
Stevens, Robert Tyler, 1911-	PR6069.T296
Stevens, Shane.	PS3569.T453
Stevenson, Anne.	PR6069.T449
Stevenson, Burton Egbert, 1872-1962.	PS3537.T476
Stevenson, D. E. (Dorothy Emily), 1892-1973.	PR6037.T458
Stevenson, Florence.	PS3569.T455
Stevenson, John.	none
Stevenson, Richard.	PS3569.T4567
Stevenson, Robert Louis, 1850-1894.	
Stevermer, C. J.	none
Steward, Barbara.	PS3569.T458
Steward, Dwight.	PS3569.T459
Stewart, Alfred W. (Alfred Walter), 1880-	PR6037.T4627
Stewart, Desmond, 1924-	PR6069.T4584
Stewart, Edward, 1938-	PS3569.T46
Stewart, Fred Mustard, 1932-	PS3569.T464
Stewart, Gary.	PS3569.T4644
Stewart, Ian, 1928-	PS3569.T4647
Stewart, Kerry—see: Stewart, Linda.	
Stewart, Linda.	PS3569.T46527
Stewart, Mary, 1916-	PR6069.T46
Stewart, Michael, 1946-	PS3569.T4653
Stewart, Ramona, 1922-	PS3569.T468
Stewart, Sam—see: Stewart, Linda.	
Stimson, Robert G.	none

Stine, Hank.	none
Stine, R. L.	none
Stinson, Jim.	PS3569.T53
Stitt, Milan.	PS3569.T55
Stivers, Dick.	none
Stockbridge, Grant.	none
Stoddard, Charles—see: Strong, Charles Stanley, 1906-	
Stohlman, Richard.	none
Stoker, Bram, 1847-1912.	PR6037.T617
Stokes, Arthur M.	none
Stokes, Robert S.	none
Stone, Eddie.	none
Stone, Elna.	PS3569.T633
Stone, George.	PS3569.T6348
Stone, Hampton, 1906-	PS3537.T3184
Stone, Nick.	none
Stone, Scott C. S.	PS3569.T642
Stone, Thomas H.—see: Harknett, Terry.	
Stone, Zachary—see: Follett, Ken.	
Storey, Anthony.	PR6069.T63
Storey, Michael, 1941-	PR6069.T664
Storm, Michael.	none
Story, Jack Trevor.	PR6037.T7144
Stout, Rex, 1886-1975.	PS3537.T733 [Z8849.34]
Stovall, Walter.	PS3569.T673
Stowe, James L.	PS3569.T675
Straker, J. F. (John Foster)	PR6069.T675
Strange, John Stephen—see: Tillett, Dorothy Stockbridge, 1896-	
Stratford, Michael—see: Bingham, Carson.	
Stratton, Chris.	none
Stratton, Ted.	PS3569.T69134
Stratton, Thomas.	none
Straub, Peter.	PS3569.T6914
Street, Bradford.	none
Street, Cecil J. C. (Cecil John Charles), 1884-1964.	PR6037.T778
Streib, Dan.	none
Stribling, T. S. (Thomas Sigismund), 1881-1965.	PS3537.T836
Strieber, Whitley.	PS3569.T6955
Stringer, Arthur John Arbuthnott, 1874-1950.	PS3537.T845
Strong, Charles Stanley, 1906-	none
Strong, L. A. G. (Leonard Alfred George), 1896-1958.	PR6037.T845
Strong, Michael, 1929-	PR6069.T73
Strother, Elsie W., 1912-	none
Strutton, Bill.	PR9619.3.S86
Stuart, Anne.	PS3569.T78

Stuart, Anthony, 1940-	PR6058.A4385
Stuart, Blair.	none
Stuart, Ian—see: MacLean, Alistair, 1922-	
Stuart, Ian.	PR6069.T77
Stuart, Jane.	PS3569.T82
Stuart, John.	none
Stuart, Ruth McEnery, 1856-1917.	PS2960
Stuart, Sidney—see: Avallone, Michael.	
Stuart, Vivian.	none
Stubbs, Jean, 1926-	PR6069.T78
Sturgeon, Theodore.	PS3569.T875
Sturrock, Jeremy.	PS3558.E23
Styles, Showell, 1908-	PR6037.T96
Subond, Valerie.	none
Sugar, Andrew.	none
Sullivan, Lewis W.	none
Sullivan, Sean Mei.	none
Sullivan, Tim.	none
Sulzberger, C. L. (Cyrus Leo), 1912-	PS3569.U36
Summerton, Margaret.	PR6069.U4
Summers, Dennis.	none
Summerscales, Rowland.	none
Sumner, Cid Ricketts, 1890-	PS3537.U732
Sunagel, Lois A.	none
Sundman, Per Olof, 1922-	PT9876.29.U5
Surr, T. S. (Thomas Skinner), 1770-1847.	PR5499.S36
Süskind, Patrick.	PT2681.U74
Sussman, Barth Jules.	none
Sutton, Henry—see: Slavitt, David R., 1935-	
Sutton, Jeff.	PS3569.U89
Svedelid, Olov, 1932-	PT9876.29.V34
Swaim, Lawrence.	PS3569.W22
Swan, Phyllis.	none
Swann, Francis.	none
Swann, Ingo, 1933-	none
Swanton, Scott.	none
Swarthout, Glendon Fred.	PS3537.W3743
Swazee, Ruth.	none
Swerdlow, Joel L.	PS3569.W413
Swift, Bryan.	none
Swift, Graham, 1949-	PR6069.W47
Swinnerton, Frank, 1884-	PR6037.W85
Symons, Julian, 1912-	PR6037.Y5
Syvertsen, Ryder.	none
Szanto, George H., 1940-	PR9199.3.S99
Tabor, Margaret.	PR6070.A2

Tabori, Paul, 1908-	PR6039.A15
Tack, Alfred.	PR6070.A25
Taffrail—see: Dorling, Henry Taprell, 1883-	
Taggart, Donald Gilbert.	PS3570.A3
Taillet, Edmond.	none
Takagi, Akimitsu, 1920-	PL862.A4
Talbot, Hake—see: Nelms, Henning, 1900-	
Talbot, Michael, 1953-	PR6070.A36
Talmy, Shel.	none
Tanenbaum, Barry, 1944-	none
Tanous, Peter.	PS3570.A56
Tapply, William G.	PS3570.A568
Tarmey, Martin.	PR6070.A56
Tarrant, John—see: Egleton, Clive.	
Taschdjian, Claire.	PS3570.A69
Tate, Richard—see: Masters, Anthony, 1940-	
Tattersall, Jill.	PR6070.A68
Taube, Lester S., 1920-	PS3570.A87
Tavis, Alec.	PR6070.A75
Taylor, Andrew, 1951-	PR6070.A79
Taylor, Bernard, 1934-	PR6070.A884
Taylor, Bonnie.	none
Taylor, Charles D.	PS3570.A92723
Taylor, Domini.	PR6070.A913
Taylor, Edith.	PS3570.A9284
Taylor, Elizabeth Atwood.	PS3570.A9286
Taylor, Fred.	PR9619.3.T318
Taylor, Georgia Elizabeth.	PS3570.A929
Taylor, Gordon, 1943-	PS3570.A9292
Taylor, H. Baldwin—see: Waugh, Hillary.	
Taylor, L. A. (Laurie Aylma), 1939-	PS3570.A943
Taylor, Mary Ann.	none
Taylor, Matt.	PS3570.A946
Taylor, Phoebe Atwood, 1909-1976.	PS3539.A9635
Taylor, Roger.	none
Teague, John Jessop, 1856-1929.	none
Teilhet, Darwin L.	none
Teixeira, Bernardo.	none
Telford, Don.	none
Telushkin, Joseph, 1948-	none
Temmey, Bob.	none
Temple, Richard.	none
Templeton, Charles Bradley, 1915-	PR9199.3.T42
Tennant, Emma.	PR6070.E52
Tepperman, Emile C.	PS3537.T2687
Teresa, Vincent Charles.	PS3570.E675

Terhune, Albert Payson, 1872-1942.	PS3539.E65
Terman, Douglas, 1933-	PS3570.E676
Terrall, Robert.	PS3539.E69
Tessier, Thomas.	PS3570.E84
Teta, Jon A.	none
Teweles, Claude.	none
Tey, Josephine, 1896-1952.	PR6025.A2547
Thackeray, Alec.	none
Thackeray, Kit.	PR6070.H34
Thatcher, Julia, 1952-	PS3552.E54765
Thayer, James Stewart.	PS3570.H347
Thayer, Lee, 1874-	none
Thelwell, Michael.	PR9265.9.T5
Themerson, Stefan.	PR6039.H37
	PG7179.H4
Theroux, Paul.	PS3570.H4
Thesman, Jean.	none
Thirkell, Angela Mackail, 1890-1961.	PR6039.H43
Thom, Robert, 1930-	none
Thomas, Alan Ernest Wentworth, 1896-	PR6039.H48
Thomas, Basil Home, Sir, 1861-1939.	none
Thomas, Bob, 1922-	PS3570.H562
Thomas, Craig.	PR6070.H56
Thomas, D.	none
Thomas, Donald Serrell.	PR6070.H6
Thomas, Dylan, 1914-1953.	PR6039.H52
Thomas, Frank.	none
Thomas, Jack.	none
Thomas, Jack W.	none
Thomas, Jim—see: Reagan, Thomas B.	
Thomas, Leslie, 1931-	PR6070.H647
Thomas, Michael M.	PS3570.H574
Thomas, Ross, 1926-	PS3570.H58
Thomey, Tedd.	none
Thompson, Ann Lorraine.	none
Thompson, Anne Armstrong.	PS3570.H593
Thompson, Arthur Leonard Bell.	PR6070.H66
Thompson, Estelle.	PR9619.3.T447
Thompson, Gene.	PS3570.H614
Thompson, Harrison R.	none
Thompson, Jim, 1906-1977.	PS3539.H6733
Thompson, Raymond, 1949-	PS3570.H6433
Thompson, Steven L.	PS3570.H6437
Thompson, W. Crawford.	none
Thomsen, Frieda.	none
Thomson, David, 1941-	PR6070.H678

Thomson, June.	PR6070.H679
Thoreau, David.	PS3570.H6477
Thorn, Ronald Scott, 1920-	PR6039.H77
Thornburg, Newton.	PS3570.H649
Thorndike, Arthur Russell, 1885-	PR6039.H78
Thorne, Guy—see: Gull, Cyril Arthur Edward Ranger, 1876-1923.	
Thorne, Jim.	none
Thorne, Ramsay.	none
Thornton, Francis John.	PS3570.H667
Thorp, Roderick.	PS3570.H67
Thorpe, Edward.	PR6070.H698
Thum, Marcella.	PS3570.H75
Thurlow, David.	none
Thynn, Alexander.	PR6070.H95
Tibble, Ann Northgrave.	PR6039.I2
Tidyman, Ernest.	PS3570.I3
Tiger, John—see: Wager, Walter H.	
Tigges, John.	none
Tillett, Dorothy Stockbridge, 1896-	PS3539.I522
Tilton, Alice, 1909-1976.	PS3539.A9635
Timperley, Rosemary, 1920-	PR6070.I4
Tindall, Gillian.	PR6070.I45
Tine, Robert.	PS3570.I48
Tippette, Giles.	PS3570.I6
Tippin, G. Lee, 1935-	PS3570.I62
Todd, Ian.	PR6070.O36
Todd, Paul—see: Posner, Richard.	
Todd, Peter—see: Hamilton, Charles, 1875-1961.	
Todd, Ruthven, 1914-	PR6039.O26
Toepfer, Ray Grant.	none
Tofte, Arthur.	PS3570.O424
Togawa, Masako, 1933-	PL862.O3
Tokson, Elliot H.	none
Toma, David.	none
Tomerlin, John, 1930-	none
Tomlinson, Gerald, 1933-	PS3570.O458
Tone, Teona.	none
Tonkin, Peter.	PR6070.O498
Toombs, Jane Jenke.	none
Topol, Allan.	PS3570.O64
Topol, B. H.	none
Topol, Eduard.	PS3570.O643
Topor, Tom, 1938-	PS3570.O65
Torgov, Morley.	PR9199.3.T613
Torr, Dominic—see: Pedler, John Branfroot Simpson.	
Torres, Edwin.	PS3750.O697

Torrie, Malcolm—see: Mitchell, Gladys, 1901-	
Torrio, Vincente.	none
Tourney, Leonard D.	PS3570.O784
Tower, Diana—see: Reinsmith, Richard.	
Townend, Peter, 1935-	PR6070.O89
Townsend, Guy M.	PS3570.O935
Tracey, Grant.	PR6070.R23
Tracy, Don, 1905-	PS3539.R124
Tracy, Hugh.	PR6070.R27
Tracy, Louis, 1863-1928.	PS3539.R15
Tracy, Margaret.	none
Train, Arthur Cheney, 1875-1945.	PS3539.R23
Tranter, Nigel G.	PR6070.R34
Traugot, Leanore.	none
Traver, Robert, 1903-	PS3570.R339
Travis, Gretchen.	PS3570.R35
Treat, Lawrence, 1903-	PS3570.R36
Tremayne, Peter.	PR6070.R366
Tremonte, Julia.	none
Trenhaile, John.	PR6070.R367
Trent, Lawrence.	none
Trent, Lee.	none
Trent, Paul.	none
Trevanian.	PS3570.R44
Trevelyan, Julia.	none
Trevelyan, Robert—see: Forrest-Webb, Robert, 1929-	
Trevor, Elleston.	PR6039.R518
Trevor, James.	none
Trevor, Leslie—see: Wilmot, James Reginald, 1897-.	
Trevor, Ralph.	none
Trevor, William, 1928-	PR6070.R4
Trew, Antony, 1906-	PR9369.3.T7
Trieschman, Charles.	none
Trimble, Louis, 1917-	none
Tripp, Miles, 1923-	PR6070.R48
Trollope, Thomas Adolphus, 1810-1892.	PR5699.T4
Tronson, Robert.	none
Trott, Susan.	PS3570.R594
Trow, M. J.	PR6070.R598
Troy, Simon.	PR6045.A8143
Truman, Margaret, 1924-	PS3570.R82
Truscott, Lucian K., 1947-	PS3570.R86
Truss, Seldon, 1892-	PR6039.R8
Tryon, Thomas.	PS3570.R9
Tucker, Allan James, 1929-	PR6070.U23
Tucker, Wilson, 1914-	PS3539.U324

Tullett, Tom.	none
Tully, Andrew, 1914-	PS3570.U43
Turland, Eileen.	none
Turnbull, Agnes Sligh, 1888-	PS3539.U76
Turnbull, Peter.	PR6070.U68
Turner, Elaine.	none
Turner, James, 1909-1975.	PR6039.U64
Turner, Pearl.	none
Turner, Ray.	none
Turner, Robert, 1915-	PS3570.U73
Turner, William Price.	PR6070.U75
Turpin, Allan.	PR6070.U77
Tute, Warren.	PR6070.U79
Tutt, Mervyn C.	none
Tuttle, Gene.	none
Tuttle, Lisa, 1952-	none
Tuttle, W. C. (Wilbur C.), 1883-	PS3539.U988
Twedt, Jerry L.	none
Tyler, Alison.	none
Tyler, Anne.	PS3570.Y45
Tyler, W. T.	PS3570.Y53
Tynan, Kathleen.	PR6070.Y57
Tyndall, John.	PR6070.Y63
Tyner, Paul, 1939-	none
Tyre, Nedra.	PS3539.Y68
Tyrer, Walter.	PR6070.Y78
Uccello, Linda.	PS3571.C24
Uhnak, Dorothy.	PS3571.H6
Ullman, Betty E.	PS3571.L55
Ullman, James Michael.	none
Ulsh, Wayne C.	PS3571.L78
Underwood, James.	none
Underwood, Michael, 1916-	PR6055.V3
Unsworth, Barry, 1930-	PR6071.N8
Upchurch, Boyd—see: Boyd, John, 1919-	
Upfield, Arthur William, 1888-1964.	PR9619.3.U6 [Z8913.86]
Upton, Peter.	PR6071.P87
Upton, Robert.	PS3571.P5
Upward, Allen, 1863-1926.	none
Urquhart, Paul—see: Black, Ladbroke Lionel Day, 1877-	
Usher, Frank Hugh, 1909- —see: Franklin, Charles, 1909-1976.	
Utechin, Nicholas.	none
Vacha, Robert.	PR6072.A3
Vachss, Andrew H.	PS3572.A33
Vaculík, Ludvík.	PG5039.32.A2

Vahey, John George Haslette, 1881-	none
Valcour, Gary F.	none
Vale, Rena Marie, 1898-	none
Valin, Jonathan.	PS3572.A4125
Vallance, Douglas.	none
Valley, Mel.	none
Van Ash, Cay.	PR6072.A55
Van Atta, Winfred.	PS3572.A416
Van de Wetering, Janwillem, 1931-	PS3572.A4292
	PT5881.32.A5
Van der Zee, John.	PS3572.A429
Van Deventer, Emma Murdoch.	PS3114.V78
Van Dine, S. S.	PS3545.R846
Van Dyke, Henry.	PS3572.A43
Van Greenaway, Peter, 1929-	PR6072.A65
Van Gulik, Robert Hans—see: Gulik, Robert Hans van, 1910-1967.	
Van Hazinga, Cynthia.	none
Van Itallie, Jean Claude, 1935-	PS3572.A45
Van Orsdell, John.	PS3572.A496
Van Rjndt, Philippe, 1950-	PR9199.3.V36
Van Siller, Hilda.	PS3543.A648
Van Slyke, Helen, 1919-	PS3572.A54
Van Zandt, Edmund.	PS3572.A55
Van Zyl, P. R.	PR9369.3.V35
Vance, Charles C.	none
Vance, Ethel, 1891-	PS3537.T667
Vance, Jack, 1916-	PS3572.A424
Vance, John Holbrook—see: Vance, Jack, 1916-	
Vance, Louis Joseph, 1879-1933.	none
Vandergriff, Aola.	none
Vardre, Leslie—see: Davies, L. P. (Leslie Purnell)	
Varley, John, 1947-	PS3572.A724
Vasilikos, Vasiles, 1934-	PA5633.A46
Vasquez, Richard.	PS3572.A85
Vassilikos, Vassilis—see: Vasilikos, Vasiles, 1934-	
Vaughan, Gary.	none
Vaughan, Julian.	none
Vaughan, Matthew.	PR6072.A9
Vaughan, Robert, 1937-	PS3572.A93
Vázquez Montalbán, Manuel.	PQ6672.A92
Veiga, José J.	PQ9697.V292
Veley, Charles, 1943-	PS3572.E4
Venables, Hubert.	PS3572.E46
Venters, Archie.	none
Veraldi, Attilio, 1925-	PQ4882.E63
Veraldi, Gabriel, 1926-	PQ2643.E46

Vermandel, Janet Gregory.	PS3572.E7
Verner, Gerald.	none
Vernier, Patricia.	none
Vernon, Kay R.	PS3572.E763
Vernon, Marjorie.	none
Vicary, Jean.	none
Vicas, Victor.	PQ2682.I243
Vickers, Ralph.	none
Vickers, Roy.	PR6043.I183
Victor, Metta Victoria Fuller, 1831-1885.	PS3129.V58
Victor, Roger.	none
Victor, Sam.	none
Vida, Nina.	PS3572.I29
Vidal, Gore, 1925-	PS3543.I26
Vidal, Harriette.	none
Vignant, Jean François.	PQ2682.I33
Villiers, Margot.	none
Vincent, Claire.	none
Vine, Barbara—see: Rendell, Ruth, 1930-	
Vinter, Michael.	none
Violett, Ellen.	PS3572.I587
Vipond, Don.	PR9199.3.V5
Vivian, Evelyn Charles H.	PR6043.I9
Voldeng, Karl E.	none
Von Block, B. W.	PS3572.O42
Von Block, Bela.	none
Von Elsner, Don, 1909-	PS3572.O44
Von Hoffman, Nicholas.	PS3572.O46
Von Horváth, Ödön—see: Horváth, Ödön von, 1901-1938.	
Voss Bark, Conrad.	PR6072.O8
Vowell, David.	none
Vries, Anko de, 1936-	none
Waddell, Martin.	PR6073.A25
Wade, Bob, 1920-	PS3573.A3
Wade, Henry, 1887-1969.	PR6001.U3
Wade, Jennifer—see: Wehen, Joy DeWeese.	
Wade, Jonathan.	PR6073.A29
Wager, Walter H.	PS3573.A35
Wagner, Elaine.	PS3573.A383
Wagner, Karl Edward.	none
Wagner, Sharon.	PS3573.A387
Wahlöö, Per, 1926-1975.	PT9876.33.A35
Wainwright, John William, 1921-	PR6073.A354
Wakefield, Maureen E.	none
Wald, Malvin.	none
Waldman, Frank, 1919-	PS3545.A4337

Waldron, Simon.	none
Walker, David Harry, 1911-	PR9199.3.W33
Walker, Gerald, 1928-	none
Walker, Gertrude.	none
Walker, Irma, 1921-	PS3573.A4253327
Walker, Mark.	PS3573.A42535
Walker, Martin, 1947-	PR6073.A413
Walker, Max.	none
Walker, Paul, 1942-	none
Walker, Peter.	none
Walker, Peter Norman.	none
Walker, Robert W. (Robert Wayne), 1948-	none
Walker, T. Mike, 1937-	PS3573.A4254
Walker, Thomas P.—see: Page, Thomas, 1942-	
Walker, Walter.	PS3573.A425417
Wall, William.	none
Wallace, David Rains, 1945-	PS3573.A42564
Wallace, Edgar, 1875-1932.	PR6045.A327
	[Z8947.46]
Wallace, Ian.	PS3573.A4258
Wallace, Irving, 1916-	PS3573.A426
Wallace, Marilyn.	PS3573.A4266
Wallace, Pat.	none
Wallace, Patricia—see: Wallace, Pat.	
Waller, Leslie, 1923-	PS3545.A565
Walling, Robert Alfred John, 1869-1949.	PR6045.A3375
Wallmann, Jeffrey M.	PS3573.A4395
Walpole, Hugh, Sir, 1884-1941.	PR6045.A34
Walsh, J. M. (James Morgan), 1897-1952.	PR9619.3.W29
Walsh, Ray, 1949-	PR9144.9.W34
Walsh, Thomas, 1908-	none
Waltch, Lilla M.	PS3573.A47227
Walter, Elizabeth.	PR6073.A4285
Walter, Shelly—see: Sheldon, Walter J.	
Walton, Alan Hull.	PR6073.A446
Walton, Marion.	none
Walton, Todd.	PS3573.A474
Walz, Audrey.	none
Wambaugh, Joseph.	PS3573.A475
Warby, Marjorie.	none
Ward, Dewey Comstock.	none
Ward, Edmund, 1928-	PR6073.A72
Ward, Elizabeth C.	PS3573.A7314
Ward, I. E.	none
Ward, Robert, 1943-	PS3573.A735
Warden, Florence, 1857-1929.	PR4821.J3

Warden, Gertrude.	none
Warden, Mike.	none
Wardman, Gordon.	PR6073.A72235
Warga, Wayne.	PS3573.A755
Warner, Douglas.	PR6073.A723
Warner, Mignon.	PR6073.A7275
Warner, Peter, 1942-	PS3573.A767
Warren, Bill.	none
Warren, Doug.	none
Warren, George, 1934-	PS3573.A773
Warren, Paulette—see: Fairman, Paul W.	
Warren, Robert Penn, 1905-	PS3545.A748
Warren, Samuel, 1807-1877.	PR5730-5734
Warthen, Ron.	none
Warwick, John.	none
Washburn, L. J.	none
Washburn, Mark.	PS3573.A788
Wassermann, Jack.	none
Waters—see: Russell, William.	
Waters, T. A.	PS3573.A82
Watkins, Ivor.	none
Watkins, Leslie.	PR6073.A84
Watkins, Ron.	none
Watson, Clarissa.	PS3573.A848
Watson, Colin.	PR6073.A86
Watson, Geoffrey, 1942-	PR6073.A862
Watson, Jack.	PR9390.9.W3
Watson, James L.	none
Watson, Lawrence.	PS3573.A853
Watson, Marjorie.	PR6073.A874
Watson, Patrick, 1929-	PR9199.3.W376
Watson, Sterling.	PS3573.A858
Watts, John.	none
Waugh, Alec, 1898-	PR6045.A95
Waugh, Harriet, 1944-	PR6073.A916
Waugh, Hillary.	PS3573.A9
Way, Isabel Stewart.	
Way, John H.	none
Way, Peter.	PR6073.A93
Waynar, Chris.	none
Weatherby, William J.	PR6073.E13
Weaver, Graham.	PR6073.E143
Webb, Forrest—see: Forrest-Webb, Robert, 1929-	
Webb, Jack.	none
Webb, Jean Francis.	PS3545.E322
Webb, Jonathan, 1950-	PR9199.3.W394

Webb, Martha G.	PS3573.E196
Webb, Michael.	none
Webb, Victoria—see: Baker, Will, 1935-	
Webster, Ernest.	none
Webster, Frederick Annesley Michael, 1886-	none
Webster, Henry Kitchell, 1875-1932.	PS3545.E362
Webster, Noah, 1928-	PR6061.N6
Wees, Frances Shelley, 1902-	PR6045.E43
Wehen, Joy DeWeese.	PS3573.E37
Weidman, Jerome, 1913-	PS3545.E449
Weil, Barry.	PR6073.E26
Weil, Jerry.	none
Weill, Gus.	PS3573.E388
Wein, Jacqueline.	PS3573.E3913
Wein, Len.	none
Weiner, Jack B., 1929-	PS3573.E3934
Weinman, Irving, 1937-	PS3573.E3963
Weinstein, Sol.	PS3573.E397
Weisman, John.	PS3573.E399
Weiss, David.	PS3573.E415
Weiss, Melford S.	none
Weiss, Mike.	PS3573.E4162
Weissman, Jerry.	none
Welcome, John, 1914-	PR6073.E373
Weldon, David.	none
Wellard, James Howard, 1909-	PR6073.E38
Welles, Orson, 1915-	PS3545.E522
Welles, Elizabeth.	none
Welles, Patricia.	PS3573.E46
Wells, Anna Mary.	none
Wells, Carolyn, d. 1942.	PS3545.E533
Wells, Elaine F.	none
Wells, Lee.	PS3573.E4925
Wells, Tobias—see: Forbes, Stanton, 1923-	
Wells, William K.	none
Wellsley, Julie.	none
Welsh, Ken.	none
Wender, Theodora.	none
Wentworth, Patricia, pseud.	PR6045.E66
Werlin, Marvin.	PS3573.E67
Wernick, Saul.	none
Werry, Richard R.	PS3545.E8254
Wesley, Mary.	PR6073.E753
West, Charles.	none
West, Elliot.	PS3573.E817
West, Morris L., 1916-	PR9619.3.W4

West, Owen—see: Koontz, Dean R. (Dean Ray), 1945-	
West, Pamela Elizabeth.	PS3573.E8246
West, Richard F.	none
Westall, Sheila.	none
Westall, William, 1835-1903.	none
Westbrook, Robert.	PS3573.E827
Westerly, Daniel.	none
Westheimer, David.	PS3573.E88
Westlake, Donald E.	PS3573.E9
Westminster, Aynn.	none
Weston, Carolyn.	PS3573.E92
Weston, John, 1932-	PS3573.E924
Wetherell, June Pat.	PS3545.E917
Weverka, Robert.	PS3573.E96
Wexler, Warren.	none
Whaley, Barton.	none
Wharton, Althea.	none
Wheat, Carolyn.	PS3573.H35
Wheatley, Dennis, 1897-	PR6045.H127 [Z8969.28]
Wheeler, Gordon.	PS3573.H432
Wheeler, Keith.	PS3545.H294
Wheeler, Paul, 1934-	PR6073.H4
Whelton, Clark.	none
Whishaw, Frederick James, 1854-1934.	none
Whitaker, Leo.	PS3573.H445
Whitby, Sharon.	none
White, Alan, 1924-	PR6073.H49
White, Alicen.	none
White, David Fairbank, 1951-	PS3573.H458
White, Ethel Lina.	PR6045.H1565
White, Fred Merrick, 1859-	none
White, Grace Miller.	none
White, James Dillon—see: White, Stanley, 1913-	
White, James P.	PS3573.H4727
White, Jon Ewbank Manchip, 1924-	PR6073.H499
White, Lionel.	PS3573.H4738
White, Osmar.	PR9639.3.W47
White, Reginald James.	PR6073.H52
White, Stanley, 1913-	PR6045.H196
White, Stewart Edward, 1873-1946.	PS3545.H6
White, Terence De Vere.	PR6073.H53
White, Teri.	PS3573.H47495
Whitechurch, Victor L. (Victor Lorenzo), 1868-1933.	PR6045.H227
Whited, Charles.	none
Whitelaw, David.	PR6045.H24

Whitfield, Raoul.	PS3545.H656
Whiting, Charles, 1926-	none
Whitlatch, John.	none
Whitman, Charles, 1916-	PR6073.H64
Whitney, Alec, 1924-	PR6073.H49
Whitney, Phyllis A., 1903-	PS3545.H8363
Whitney, Steven.	PS3573.H535
Whitten, Les, 1928-	PS3573.H566
Whittington, Harry, 1915-	none
Wibberley, Leonard, 1915-	PS3573.I2
Wick, Carter—see: Wilcox, Collin.	
Widdemer, Margaret.	PS3545.I175
Wieselberg, Helen.	PS3573.I376
Wilcox, Collin.	PS3573.I395
Wilcox, Ronald.	none
Wilden, Theodore, 1936-	PR9115.9.W5
Wilder, Robert, 1901-	PS3545.I343
Wiles, Domini.	PR6073.I4159
Wiles, Frank.	none
Wiley, Edward.	none
Wiley, Hugh, 1884-	PS3545.I3587
Wilhelm, Kate.	PS3573.I434
Wilk, Max.	PS3545.I365
Wilkinson, Sandra.	PS3573.I44255
Willeford, Charles Ray, 1919-	PS3545.I464
Williams, Alan, 1935-	PR6073.I4258
Williams, Ben Ames, 1889-1953.	
Williams, Brad.	PS3573.I4476
Williams, Charles, 1909-	PS3573.I448
Williams, David, 1926-	PR6073.I42583
Williams, David, 1939-	PS3573.I44843
Williams, Gordon M., 1934-	PR6073.I426
Williams, Jay, 1914-	PS3545.I528455
Williams, Jeanne, 1930-	PS3573.I44933
Williams, John Ellis.	PR6073.I4322
Williams, Lawrence.	none
Williams, Lynn—see: Hale, Arlene.	
Williams, Mary.	PR6073.I4323
Williams, Mona Goodwyn, 1906-	PS3545.I533525
Williams, Neil.	none
Williams, Raymond.	PR6073.I4329
Williams, Ruth.	none
Williams, T. Jeff.	none
Williams, Thomas, 1926-	PS3573.I456
Williams, Timothy.	PR6073.I43295
Williams, Valentine, 1883-1946.	PR6045.I5464

Williams, Wynn.	none
Williamson, Alice Muriel Livingston, 1869-1933.	PS3319.W7
Williamson, Audrey, 1913-	PR6073.I43325
Williamson, Charles Norris, 1859-1920.	PR5834.W6
Williamson, J. N.	none
Williamson, Moncrieff.	PR9199.3.W493
Williamson, Sherman.	PR6073.I43342
Williamson, Tony.	PR6073.I43344
Willis, Anthony Armstrong, 1897-	PR6045.I565
Willis, Maud—see: Lottman, Eileen.	
Willis, Ted.	PR6045.I567
Willock, Ruth, 1904-	PS3545.I578
Wills, Cecil Melville, 1891-	none
Wills, Garry, 1934-	PS3573.I45658
Willsdon, Andrew.	none
Wilmot, James Reginald, 1897-	none
Wilson, Barbara, 1950-	PS3573.I45678
Wilson, Colin, 1931-	PR6073.I44
Wilson, David.	none
Wilson, F. Paul (Francis Paul)	PS3573.I45695
Wilson, Gar.	none
Wilson, Gertrude Mary Bryant, 1899-	PR6073.I465
Wilson, Jacqueline.	PR6073.I46737
Wilson, Joyce.	none
Wilson, Mary—see: Roby, Mary Linn.	
Wilson, R. McNair (Robert McNair), 1882-	none
Wilson, Sloan, 1920-	PS3573.I475
Wilson, Steve, 1943-	PR6073.I4752
Wilson, Trevor Edward.	PR9639.3.W56
Wilson, William, 1935-	PS3573.I476
Wiltse, David.	PS3573.I478
Wiltz, Chris.	PS3573.I4783
Winch, Arden.	PR6073.I4755
Winchell, Prentice, 1895-	none
Winchester, Jack.	PR6073.I4759
Winchester, Stanley.	PR6073.I48
Windsor, Patricia.	PS3573.I52
Wingard, Alan.	none
Wingate, John.	PR6073.I53
Wingate, William.	PR9369.3.W55
Wingfield, R. D.	none
Wings, Mary.	none
Winnington, Alan.	none
Winslow, Pauline Glen.	PR6073.I553
Winsor, Diana.	PR6073.I554
Winsor, George McLeod.	PR6045.I723

Winsor, Roy.	none
Winstead, Rebecca Noyes.	none
Winston, Daoma, 1922-	PS3545.I7612
Winston, Peter.	none
Winter, Abigail—see: Schere, Monroe.	
Winters, J. C.—see: Cross, Gilbert B.	
Winters, Jon—see: Cross, Gilbert B.	
Winward, Walter.	PR6073.I58
Wise, Ardath.	PS3573.I78
Wise, Arthur, 1923-	PR6073.I75
Wise, David.	PS3573.I785
Wise, William, 1923-	none
Wiseman, Richard.	PR6073.I766
Wiseman, Thomas.	PR6073.I77
Wishart, Nan.	none
Wishman, Seymour.	PS3573.I874
Wissmann, Ruth H.	PS3573.I88
Witting, Clifford.	PR6045.I95
Wittman, George.	PS3573.I94
Wlaschin, Ken.	none
Wodehouse, P. G. (Pelham Grenville), 1881-1975.	PR6045.O53
Wohl, Burton.	PS3573.O38
Wohl, James P.	PS3573.O39
Wolf, Gary K.	PS3573.O483
Wolf, Joyce.	none
Wolf, Sarah.	PS3573.O489
Wolfe, Carson.	PS3573.O496
Wolfe, John.	none
Wolfe, Jonathan.	none
Wolfe, Linda.	PS3573.O523
Wolfe, Michael.	PS3573.O525
Wolff, Benjamin.	none
Wolff, Geoffrey, 1937-	PS3573.O53
Wolfman, Marv.	none
Wolfson, Vi.	PS3573.O5619
Wolk, George.	PS3573.O565
Wolman, David.	none
Wood, Andrew, 1890-	none
Wood, Barbara.	PS3573.O5877
Wood, Bari, 1936-	PS3573.O588
Wood, Deborah.	none
Wood, H. F. (H. Freeman)	PR5842.W92
Wood, Henry, Mrs., 1814-1887.	PR5842.W8
Wood, James, 1918-	PR6073.O58
Wood, Samuel Andrew, 1890-	none
Wood, Ted.	PR9199.3.W57

Wood, William P.	PS3573.O599
Woodford, Jack, 1894-1971.	PS3545.O765
Woodhouse, Martin, 1932-	PR6073.O616
Woodley, Richard.	PS3573.O626
Woodman, Michael.	none
Woods, Sara, pseud.	PR6073.O63
Woods, Stockton—see: Forrest, Richard, 1932-	
Woods, Stuart.	PS3573.O642
Woolfolk, William.	PS3573.O65
Woolrich, Cornell, 1903-1968.	PS3515.O6455
Worboys, Anne.	PR6073.O667
Wormser, Richard Edward, 1908-	PS3545.O88
Worsley, Thomas Cuthbert.	PR6045.O78
Worts, George Frank, 1892-	none
Wren, M. K.	PS3573.R43
Wren, Percival Christopher, 1885-1941.	PR6045.R35 [Z8965.6]
Wright, Eric.	PR9199.3.W66
Wright, Glover.	PR6073.R488
Wright, Joseph E.	none
Wright, L. R.—see: Wright, Laurali, 1939-	
Wright, Laurali, 1939-	PR9199.3.W68
Wright, Laurie Robeson—see: Wright, Laurali, 1939-	
Wright, Richard Bruce, 1937-	PR9199.3.W7
Wright, T. M., 1947-	PS3573.R544
Wright, Wade.	none
Wright, Wilbur.	PR6073.R58
Wulffson, Don L.	none
Wuorio, Eva-Lis, 1918-	none
Wylie, Philip, 1902-1971.	PS3545.Y46
Wyllie, John, 1914-	PR6073.Y58
Wynd, Oswald, 1913-	PR6073.Y65
Wynne, Anthony, 1882-	none
Wynne, Barry.	none
Wynne-Jones, Tim.	PR9199.3.W95
Yablonsky, Yabo.	none
Yaeger, Carl H.	none
Yarborough, Charlotte.	none
Yarbro, Chelsea Quinn, 1942-	PS3575.A7
Yardley, James.	PR6075.A7
Yariv, Fran Pokras.	none
Yarrow, Arnold.	none
Yates, Alan—see: Brown, Carter, 1923-	
Yates, Brock W.	PS3575.A76
Yates, Dornford, 1885-1960.	PR6047.A73
Yates, Edmund Hodgson, 1831-1894.	PR5899.Y3

Yerby, Frank, 1916-	PS3547.E65
York, Andrew, 1930-	PR9320.9.N5
York, Carol Beach.	none
York, Elizabeth.	none
York, Helen.	PS3575.O6
York, Jeremy—see: Creasey, John.	
York, Rebecca.	none
York, Vickie.	none
Yorke, Margaret.	PR6075.O7
Young, Al, 1939-	PS3575.O68
Young, Carter Travis.	PS3575.O7
Young, Collier, 1908-	PS3575.O75
Young, David, 1946-	PR9199.3.Y58
Young, Ernest A.	none
Young, Francis Brett, 1884-1954.	PR6047.O47
Young, Marsha.	none
Young, Phyllis Brett.	PR6047.O58
Younger, Jack.	none
Yourcenar, Marguerite.	PQ2649.O8
Yuill, P. B.	PR6075.U4
Yurick, Sol, 1925-	PS3575.U7
Zachary, Hugh.	PS3576.A23
Zackel, Fred.	PS3576.A27
Zake, S. Joshua L.	PR9402.9.Z3
Zangwill, Israel, 1864-1926.	PR5920-5924
Zaremba, Eve.	none
Zaroulis, N. L.	PS3576.A74
Zawadsky, Patience.	none
Zec, Donald.	PR6076.E25
Zeiger, Henry A.	PS3576.E38
Zelazny, Roger.	PS3576.E43
Zeno, pseud.	PR6076.E5
Ziemann, Hans Heinrich, 1944-	PT2688.I367
Zimmerman, R. D.	none
Zindel, Paul.	PS3576.I518
Ziren, Goland.	none
Zochert, Donald.	PS3576.O23
Zodrow, John Rester.	none
Zuckerman, Albert.	PS3576.U23
Zumwalt, Eva.	PS3576.U5

LC LITERATURE TABLES

In determining the cutters of individual literary works by one author, one must take into account certain numbers reserved for other purposes. A1-6 are reserved for collected works: A11-13 for collected works, A15 for collected fiction, A16 for collected essays, A17 for collected poems, A19 for collected plays, A6 for selected works (by date). A6 is the most commonly used of these "dump" numbers, often being used for omnibus collections of novels by one author (*e.g.*, a book called *Three novels* by Robert A. Heinlein might be classed in PS3515.E288A6 1987). The cutter stays the same for all books of this type, only the year of publication changing; if more than one title is published in the same year, they are differentiated by additional letters (*e.g.*, PS3515.E288A6 1987b). Similarly, Z459-999 is reserved for criticism (Z459 for dictionaries and indexes, Z46-479 for autobiographies, journals, and memoirs, Z48 for collections of letters, Z481-499 for letters to and from specific correspondents, and Z5-999 for general criticism (in alphabetical order by main entry). Because of these reserved numbers, literary works by one author beginning with the letters "A" and "Z" must be squeezed into A61-99 and Z11-458, respectively, and spread across the alphabet. Thus, the paperback edition of Peter Tremayne's *Zombie* might be classed in PR6070.R366Z37 1987, *not* in PR6070.R366Z65 1987 (Z65 being reserved for criticism). Moreover, AACR2's revised filing rules require that titles whose first words consist of numbers file *before* the letter "A"; thus, LC classed Richard Lamm's novel *1988* in PS3562.A4643A615, near the beginning of the "A" section reserved for individual titles (A61-99).

The national literature tables for authors are arranged by language, nationality, and period (usually a century or half-century), in that order, the authors being classed in each period in strict alphabetical order according to AACR2 filing rules. The major literatures (English, French, German, American, etc.), have two spans of numbers each reserved for twentieth-century authors, the demarcation line being 1960 (but in practice, often the 1950s). Smaller literatures may reserve one number for the entire twentieth century. The tables below provide detailed comparisons between the major literatures reflected in this manual.

AUTHOR NUMBERS BY NATIONALITY AND DATE

	19th cent.	1900-60	1961-
Afrikaans literature	PT6590 A-Z	PT6590 A-Z	PT6592-.36

American literature	PS991-3369	PS3500-49	PS3550-76
Argentine literature	PQ7797 A-Z	PQ7797 A-Z	PQ7798-.36
Bohemian literature	PG5038 A-Z	PG5038 A-Z	PG5039-.36
Brazilian literature	PQ9697 A-Z	PQ9697 A-Z	PQ9698-.36
Bulgarian literature	PG1037 A-Z	PG1037 A-Z	PG1038-.36
Chilean literature	PQ8097 A-Z	PQ8097 A-Z	PQ8098-.36
Columbian literature	PQ8179 A-Z	PQ8179 A-Z	PQ8180-.36
Cuban literature	PQ7389 A-Z	PQ7389 A-Z	PQ7390 A-Z
Danish literature	PT8100-8167	PT8175 A-Z	PT8176-.36
Dutch literature	PT5800-5880	PT5800-80	PT5881-.36
Ecuadorean literature	PQ8219 A-Z	PQ8219 A-Z	PQ8220-.36
English literature	PR3991-5925	PR6000-49	PR6050-76
Finnish literature	PH355 A-Z	PH355 A-Z	PH355 A-Z
French literature	PQ2149-2551	PQ2600-51	PQ2660-86
French Canadian lit.	PQ3919 A-Z	PQ3919 A-Z	PQ3919.2 A-Z
German literature	PT1799-2592	PT2600-53	PT2660-88*
Guatemalan literature	PQ7499 A-Z	PQ7499 A-Z	PQ7499.2 A-Z
Hungarian literature	PH3201-3381	PH3201-3381	PH3201-3381
Italian literature	PQ4675-4734	PQ4800-51	PQ4860-86
Japanese literature	PL800-820	PL821-843	PL844-866*
Mexican literature	PQ7297 A-7	PQ7297 A-Z	PQ7298-.36
Norwegian literature	PT8800-8942	PT8950 A-Z	PT8951-.36
Polish literature	PG7158 A-Z	PG7158 A-Z	PG7159-85
Romanian literature	PC839 A-Z	PC839 A-Z	PC840-.36
Russian literature	PG3450-3470	PG3476 A-Z	PG3477-90*
Spanish literature	PQ6500-6576	PQ6600-47	PQ6650-76
Swedish literature	PT9725-9850	PT9875 A-Z	PT9876-.36
Welsh literature	PB2298 A-Z	PB2298 A-Z	PB2298 A-Z
Yiddish literature	PJ5129 A-Z	PJ5129 A-Z	PJ5129 A-Z

*[German literature: 1700-1860/70; 1860/70-1960; 1961- ; Japanese literature: 1868-1926; 1926-1945; 1945- ; Russian literature: 1870-1917; 1917-1960; 1961- .]

TWENTIETH-CENTURY AUTHOR NUMBERS
BY INITIAL LETTER OF LAST NAME

Names	PS	PS	PR	PR	PQ	PQ	PT	PT	PT
A.	3501	3551	6001	6051	2601	2661	2601	2661	9876.1
B.	3503	3552	6003	6052	2603	2662	2603	2662	9876.12
C.	3505	3553	6005	6053	2605	2663	2605	2663	9876.13
D.	3507	3554	6007	6054	2607	2664	2607	2664	9876.14
E.	3509	3555	6009	6055	2609	2665	2609	2665	9876.15
F.	3511	3556	6011	6056	2611	2666	2611	2666	9876.16
G.	3513	3557	6013	6057	2613	2667	2613	2667	9876.17

H.	3515	3558	6015	6058	2615	2668	2615	2668	9876.18
I.	3517	3559	6017	6059	2617	2669	2617	2669	9876.19
J.	3519	3560	6019	6060	2619	2670	2619	2670	9876.2
K.	3521	3561	6021	6061	2621	2671	2621	2671	9876.21
L.	3523	3562	6023	6062	2623	2672	2623	2672	9876.22
M.	3525	3563	6025	6063	2625	2673	2625	2673	9876.23
N.	3527	3564	6027	6064	2627	2674	2627	2674	9876.24
O.	3529	3565	6029	6065	2629	2675	2629	2675	9876.25
P.	3531	3566	6031	6066	2631	2676	2631	2676	9876.26
Q.	3533	3567	6033	6067	2633	2677	2633	2677	9876.27
R.	3535	3568	6035	6068	2635	2678	2635	2678	9876.28
S.	3537	3569	6037	6069	2637	2679	*	*	9876.29
T.	3539	3570	6039	6070	2639	2680	2642	2682	9876.3
U.	3541	3571	6041	6071	2641	2681	2643	2683	9876.31
V.	3543	3572	6043	6072	2643	2682	2645	2684	9876.32
W.	3545	3573	6045	6073	2645	2683	2647	2685	9876.33
X.	3546	3574	6046	6074	2647	2684	2649	2686	9876.34
Y.	3547	3575	6047	6075	2649	2685	2651	2687	9876.35
Z.	3549	3576	6049	6076	2651	2686	2653	2688	9876.36

[*German authors whose last names begin with S: PT2637 (S-Scg), 2638 (Sch), 2639 (Sci-Sudd), 2640 (Sudermann, Hermann), 2641 (Sudf-Sz); PT2679 (Sa-Scg), 2680 (Sch), 2681 (Sci-Sz).]

OTHER ENGLISH LANGUAGE AUTHOR NUMBERS (A-Z)
(Authors writing in English)

PR9105.9	France.
PR9115.9	Greece.
PR9144.9	Norway.
PR9170.R63	Romania.
PR9199.3	Canada—20th century (PR9199.2=19th century).
PR9265.9	Jamaica.
PR9369.3	South Africa—20th century.
PR9381.9	Kenya.
PR9387.9	Nigeria.
PR9390.9	Zimbabwe.
PR9399.9	Tanzania.
PR9402.9	Uganda.
PR9405.9	Zambia.
PR9440.9	Sri Lanka.
PR9499.3	India—20th century.
PR9510.9	Israel.
PR9550.9	Philippine Islands
PR9619.3	Australia—20th century (PR9619.2=19th century).
PR9639.3	New Zealand—20th century (PR9639.2=19th century).

IV
MOTION PICTURE MAIN ENTRIES AND CLASSIFICATION NUMBERS

INTRODUCTION

    Books about individual motion pictures, or motion picture screenplays themselves, are classed in PN1997. Each film receives a unique cutter number derived from the first letter of the title; a second cutter for main entry completes the classification for a particular book. Relatively few mystery and suspense films have received individual numbers. The subject heading for each film is the motion picture title plus the appellation (Motion picture); these may be subdivided further as required. Films produced at different dates with the same title (remakes, for example) are identified by adding dates to the appellation—see the film *Dracula* below.

Blade runner (Motion picture)	none
Cabinet der Dr. Caligari (Motion picture)	PN1997.C18
Diamonds are forever (Motion picture)	PN1997.D4593
Dr. Jekyll and Mr. Hyde (Motion picture)	PN1997.D55
Dracula (Motion picture : 1931)	none
Frankenstein (Motion picture)	none
From Russia with love (Motion picture)	PN1997.F7473
Goldfinger (Motion picture)	PN1997.G56863
King Kong (Motion picture : 1933)	PN1997.K437
King Kong (Motion picture : 1976)	PN1997.K4374
Live and let die (Motion picture)	PN1997.L5953
Night of the living dead (Motion picture)	PN1997.N5215
Nightmare on Elm Street (Motion picture)	PN1997.N5224
Nightmare on Elm Street II, Freddy's revenge (Motion picture)	none
Nightmare on Elm Street III (Motion picture)	none
Nosferatu (Motion picture)	PN1997.N563
On Her Majesty's secret service (Motion picture)	PN1997.O423
Outland (Motion picture)	PN1997.O9
Play it again, Sam (Motion picture)	PN1997.P5243
You only live twice (Motion picture)	PN1997.Y53

V
TELEVISION PROGRAM MAIN ENTRIES AND CLASSIFICATION NUMBERS

INTRODUCTION

Books about specific television programs are classed in PN1992.77. Each program receives a unique subject cutter derived from the first letter of the show's title; a second cutter for main entry completes the classification for particular books. The subject heading for each show is its name plus the appellation (Television program).

Alfred Hitchcock presents (Television program)	PN1992.77.A479
Avengers (Television program)	PN1992.77.A923
Dark shadows (Television program)	PN1992.77.D343
Get Smart (Television program)	PN1992.77.G4773
Girl from U.N.C.L.E. (Television program)	PN1992.77.G553
Hardy boys (Television program)	PN1992.77.H346
Man from U.N.C.L.E. (Television program)	PN1992.77.M2653
Prisoner (Television program)	PN1992.77.P7
Return of the man from U.N.C.L.E. (Television program)	PN1992.77.R483
Spider-Man (Television program)	PN1992.77.S643

VI
COMIC STRIP MAIN ENTRIES AND CLASSIFICATION NUMBERS

INTRODUCTION

Comic books, strips, etc., are classified into PN6728, cuttered by the first letter of the title, and cuttered again by main entry of the book. The subject heading is the name of the comic plus the appellation (Comic strip). As this is a fairly new development, relatively few comics have received numbers thus far.

Avengers (Comic strip)	PN6728.A9
Batman (Comic strip)	PN6728.B36
Captain America (Comic strip)	PN6728.C35
Fantastic Four (Comic strip)	PN6728.F33
Hulk (Comic strip)	PN6728.H8
Spider-Man (Comic strip)	PN6728.S6
Superman (Comic strip)	PN6728.S9
X-Men (Comic strip)	PN6728.X2

www.ingramcontent.com/pod-product-compliance
Lightning Source LLC
LaVergne TN
LVHW041620070426
835507LV00008B/364